A Bilingual Introduction to
Valuation

対訳 英語で学ぶ

バリュエーション
入門

本合暁詩
Akashi Hongo

中央経済社

Preface

Welcome to Valuation. The person who grabs this book must be interested in learning valuation, particularly someone who wants or needs to learn valuation in ENGLISH.

Mergers and acquisitions (M&A) based on company valuation are frequently attempted on a cross-border basis and require understanding terminologies and participating in English negotiation, even if you are in Japan. This book will assist you in learning valuation in English and Japanese simultaneously. Similar to the sister textbook named "A Bilingual Introduction to Corporate Finance", **this book deploys English on the left page and Japanese on the right page, offering a reader an English textbook and a Japanese textbook at the same time.**

This book is organized in five parts including 12 chapters. Following part 1 which overviews the significance and the process of valuation and strategic analysis, part 2 introduces financial measures to evaluate a company's performance and analyze historical financial data. A detailed discussion about cost of capital is also covered. Future performance forecast is introduced in part 3, and part 4 discusses how to estimate a company's value and share price based on those forecasts. Part 5 considers how a company uses the outcome of valuation in its management initiatives. The appendix introduces an Excel-based spreadsheet named "financial analysis and valuation file" which is demonstrated throughout part 2 to 4. Since the excel file is available on a website prepared by Chuo-keizai, you can feel free to download and use it as you read this book and thereafter.

Despite packing in two-books-worth of content, this book covers sufficient topics and will adequately work as an introduction textbook for undergraduate/ graduate students but also as a robust reference for business professionals who need knowledge of valuation.

Well, we do not have a lot of space, so let's begin the lecture now.

は じ め に

　企業価値評価へようこそ。本書を手にしている方は，企業価値評価を学びたい，特に英語でValuationを学びたいと考えている，あるいは学ぶ必要があると感じている方でしょう。

　企業価値評価の代表的な活用場面であるM&A（企業の合併買収）は，国をまたいで行われることが多く，日本にいても必然的に英語での用語理解や交渉が必要となります。そのため企業価値評価を日本語・英語両方一度に学びたいというニーズは高く，それに応えるのが本書です。姉妹書ともいえる『英語で学ぶコーポレートファイナンス入門』と同様に，見開きの左ページを英語，右ページを日本語とした本書により，**読者の皆さんは，この1冊で日本語と英語の教科書を同時に手に入れることができます。**

　本書は12章からなる5部構成となっています。企業価値評価の意味とプロセス，および戦略分析を概観する第1部に続き，第2部では企業の業績を分析するための財務指標を紹介し，過去の財務分析を行います。資本コストの推定に関する詳細な議論もここでカバーします。第3部では将来業績の予測を行い，第4部ではそれらの予想に基づいてどのように企業価値や株価が推定されるのか議論します。そして，第5部では，企業価値評価の結果をどのように経営において活用していくべきなのかを考えます。本書巻末の付録には，第2－4部において解説のために使用するエクセルファイル（財務分析・企業価値評価ファイル）を紹介しています。必要な数値を入力することで企業価値と株価が推定できるこのファイルは中央経済社のホームページにてダウンロードが可能となっていますので，本書を読みながら，あるいは，その後実際の実務や演習において活用いただければと思います。

　本書では2冊分の内容をコンパクトに詰め込んでいるわけですが，大学生・大学院生の入門テキストとしてだけではなく，Valuationの知識が必要な社会人の方にもお使いいただける十分な内容になっていると思います。

　さて，スペースに余裕はありませんので，さっそく講義を始めましょう。

Table of Contents

Preface / 2

Part 1 — Fundamental Knowledge of Valuation

Chapter 1 — What Is Valuation? ———— 18

Purposes of Valuation / 18
Knowledge Required for Valuation / 20
What Is the Value of a Company? / 22
Process for Valuation / 24

Chapter 2 — Analyzing Business Environment and Strategy — 30

Strategy Frameworks / 30
PEST / 32
Five Forces / 36
3Cs / 40
Value Chain / 42
SWOT / 44

Part 2 — Financial Analysis

Chapter 3 — Analyzing Financial Performance 1: Income Statement and Balance Sheet ———— 50

Obtaining an Income Statement and Balance Sheet / 50

目　　次

はじめに／3

第1部　企業価値評価の基礎と前提

第1章　企業価値評価とは何か ——————— 19

企業価値評価の目的／19
企業価値評価に求められる知識／21
企業価値とは／23
企業価値評価のプロセス／25

第2章　事業環境と戦略の分析 ——————— 31

戦略フレームワーク／31
PEST 分析／33
5 フォース分析／37
3C 分析／41
バリューチェーン分析／43
SWOT 分析／45

第2部　財務分析

第3章　財務業績の分析1：損益計算書と貸借対照表 —— 51

損益計算書，貸借対照表の入手／51

The Income Statement / 50

The Balance Sheet / 52

Analysis with the Common-size Financial Statements / 54

The Common-size Income Statement / 56

The Common-size Balance Sheet / 58

Combination of Income Statement and Balance Sheet / 62

Chapter 4

Analyzing Financial Performance 2: Various Financial Measures ———————— 64

Basic Financial Measures / 64

Measures Regarding Growth and Efficiency / 66

Measures Regarding Debt Usage and Financial Health / 68

Financial Analysis Example for Nike ① / 72

Measures for Valuation / 76

Other Variables Influencing Value / 82

Supplementary Note: EBITDA / 84

Chapter 5

Estimating Cost of Capital ———————————— 86

Weighted Average Cost of Capital / 86

Cost of Debt / 88

Cost of Equity / 96

Capital Structure / 108

Weighted Average Cost of Capital for Nike / 110

Reference 5.1: Excel-based File to Estimate Beta / 112

Reference 5.2: Website List for Necessary Data / 116

損益計算書／ 51

貸借対照表／ 53

標準化財務諸表による分析／ 55

標準化損益計算書／ 57

標準化貸借対照表／ 59

損益計算書と貸借対照表の組み合わせ／ 63

第4章　財務業績の分析2：数々の財務数値 —————— 65

基本的な財務数値／ 65

成長と効率を表わす財務数値／ 67

負債の活用と安全性を表わす財務数値／ 69

財務分析例：ナイキ①／ 73

企業価値評価のための財務数値／ 77

企業価値に影響を与える変数／ 83

補足：EBITDA ／ 85

第5章　資本コストの推定 ————————————— 87

加重平均資本コスト／ 87

負債コスト／ 89

株主資本コスト／ 97

資本構成／ 109

資本コストの推定例：ナイキ／ 111

参考5.1：ベータ推定のためのエクセルファイル／ 113

参考5.2：データソースサイト／ 117

Chapter 6

Analyzing Financial Performance 3: EVA and Strategy ————————— 118

EVA Definition and Its Essence ╱ 118
EVA Calculation ╱ 120
EVA and ROC ╱ 122
Analysis of Efficiency and Size ╱ 122
Analysis Based on Margin and Velocity ╱ 126
Financial Analysis Example for Nike ② ╱ 130

Part 3

Future Forecasting

Chapter 7

Forecasting Future Performance ————————— 136

Items to Be Forecasted ╱ 136
Forecast Sales ╱ 138
Forecast NOPAT and Capital Using Drivers ╱ 138
Performance Forecast of Nike ① ╱ 138
Forecast FCF and EVA ╱ 142
Performance Forecast of Nike ② ╱ 142

Chapter 8

Forecasting Terminal Value ————————— 144

Terminal Value ╱ 144
Calculating Terminal Value ╱ 144
Perpetuity Formula ╱ 146
Perpetuity with Growth Formula ╱ 146
Common Mistakes in Terminal Value ╱ 148
Terminal Value in Growth Deceleration ╱ 150
Value Driver Model ╱ 152
Growth Rate for Terminal Value ╱ 154

| 第6章 | 財務業績の分析3：EVA と戦略 —————— 119 |

EVA の定義と本質／119

EVA の計算／121

EVA と ROC／123

事業効率と規模の分解による分析／123

収益性と資本効率に基づく分析／127

財務分析例：ナイキ②／131

第3部　将来の予測

| 第7章 | 将来業績の予測 —————————————— 137 |

予測すべき項目／137

売上高の予測／139

ドライバーを活用した NOPAT，投下資本の予測／139

ナイキの業績予測①／139

FCF，EVA の予測／143

ナイキの業績予測②／143

| 第8章 | ターミナル・バリューの予測 ——————— 145 |

ターミナル・バリュー／145

ターミナル・バリューの計算／145

永久年金式／147

定率成長の永久年金式／147

ターミナル・バリューの陥りがちな間違い／149

成長鈍化の場合のターミナル・バリュー／151

価値ドライバーモデル／153

ターミナル・バリューの成長率／155

Supplementary Note for Value Driver Model / 156

Part 4 — Value Estimate

Chapter 9 — Valuing Company, Equity and Shares ——— 162

Value of Operation / 162

Sensitivity Analysis and Scenario Analysis / 162

Evaluating Non-operating Assets / 164

Value of Equity / 166

Price per Share / 168

EVA and Valuation / 168

MVA Connecting EVA to Value / 172

Estimated Share Price of Nike / 174

Chapter 10 — Valuing with Multiples ——— 178

Basic of Multiples / 178

Selection of Comparable Companies / 180

PER and PBR / 180

Mathematical Breakdown of PER and PBR / 182

EBITDA Multiple / 184

Company Valuation for Conglomerate / 186

Pros and Cons of Discounting Approach / 190

Pros and Cons of Multiple Approach / 190

Combination Use in Practice / 192

価値ドライバーモデルの補足／157

第4部　価値の推定

第9章　企業価値，株主価値，および株価 ———— 163

事業の価値／163

感応度分析とシナリオ分析／163

非事業資産の加味／165

株主価値の推定／167

株価の推定／169

EVA と価値評価／169

EVA と企業価値を結びつける MVA ／173

ナイキの株価の推定／175

第10章　価値倍率法 ———————————— 179

価値倍率法の基本／179

比較類似企業の選定／181

PER と PBR ／181

PER，PBR の数式展開／183

EBITDA 倍率／185

多事業展開をする企業の評価／187

割引現在価値法のメリット・デメリット／191

価値倍率法のメリット・デメリット／191

実務においては併用／193

Part 5	**Valuation in Management**

Chapter 11	**Merger and Acquisition** ——————————— 196

Valuation for Management ╱ 196

Conditions for a Successful M&A ╱ 196

The Reason for Value Difference ╱ 200

Classification and Formation of M&A ╱ 200

Distribution of Value Created by M&A ╱ 202

Merger in Cash ╱ 204

Merger with Stock ╱ 206

Leveraged Buyout and Management Buyout ╱ 210

Chapter 12	**Fulfilling Value** ——————————————— 212

Absorbing the Value of Company ╱ 212

Analyzing Expectation Gap ╱ 212

Integrating into Mid-term Plan ╱ 214

Delegation of Authority to Activate Plan ╱ 216

Incentive Compensation for Value Creation ╱ 218

Equity Compensation ╱ 220

Profit-based Compensation ╱ 222

Driver-based Compensation ╱ 222

Separation of Ownership and Management ╱ 224

Elements of Corporate Governance ╱ 224

Governance from Inside Stem from Valuation ╱ 226

第5部　企業価値評価に基づく経営

第11章　合併と買収 ——————— 197

経営に不可欠な企業価値評価／ 197

成功するM&Aの条件／ 197

価値の差の理由／ 201

M&Aの分類と形式／ 201

合併・買収の価値の分配／ 203

現金支払いによる合併／ 205

株式による合併／ 207

レバレッジ・バイアウトとマネジメント・バイアウト／ 211

第12章　価値の具現化 ——————— 213

企業価値の理解／ 213

期待のギャップ分析／ 213

中期計画への統合／ 215

権限移譲による計画の実行／ 217

企業価値を高めるインセンティブ報酬設計／ 219

株式報酬／ 221

利益連動報酬／ 223

ドライバー連動報酬／ 223

所有と経営の分離／ 225

コーポレート・ガバナンスの要素／ 225

企業価値評価による内からのガバナンス／ 227

Appendix: Financial Analysis and Valuation File ——————— 230

Historical Data Input ╱ 232

Drivers & Forecast ╱ 238

Figures ╱ 248

WACC ╱ 250

DCF ╱ 252

DCF Figure ╱ 256

Multiples ╱ 258

Summary ╱ 260

Postface and Acknowledgement ╱ 262

Index ╱ 264

付録：財務分析・企業価値評価ファイルの紹介 ———————— 231

Historical Data Input／233

Drivers & Forecast／239

Figures／249

WACC／251

DCF／253

DCF Figure／257

Multiples／259

Summary／261

あとがきと謝辞／263

索　引／264

Part 1
Fundamental Knowledge of Valuation

- This part serves as an introduction. In the first chapter we will get an overview of what valuation is, including a discussion about its purpose, knowledge utilized, and the common valuation process.

- The next chapter introduces representative strategic frameworks for business and company analysis with examples, as valuation requires them before you deal with financial data of a company.

Chapter 1   What Is Valuation?

Chapter 2   Analyzing Business Environment and Strategy

第 1 部
企業価値評価の基礎と前提

- 導入章となる第 1 章では，企業価値評価とは何かについて，目的や必要となる基礎知識，そしてそのプロセスについて概観する。

- 企業価値評価のためには，企業の財務数値の分析に取りかかる前に，事業環境や戦略を定性的に分析することが重要である。第 2 章ではそれらに有効な代表的な戦略フレームワークを事例とともに紹介する。

第 1 章　企業価値評価とは何か

第 2 章　事業環境と戦略の分析

Chapter 1 What Is Valuation?

Points!

- ✓ Valuation is an indispensable initiative for managing a company as well as for judging an investment
- ✓ The value of a company is determined by the present value of future cash flows
- ✓ Valuation requires broad-ranging knowledge of finance, accounting, and strategy

● Purposes of Valuation

Valuation is referred to as the procedure to estimate the value of an asset such as a company, business, stock, bond, or real estate. Estimating the total value of a company or a price of its share is called company valuation.

Valuation analysis is conducted for various purposes. It is commonly used when individual and institutional investors judge the appropriate price of securities. An investor buys and sells stocks based on the result of valuation and a security analyst writes a report recommending to "buy" or "sell" after valuation.

A company executes valuation when it attempts to purchase another company. When an attractive takeover target emerges, a company will examine the target company, taking into account possible synergy or other complementary effects and make a decision for an acquisition and its purchase price.

Valuation is important for a company's long term strategic business planning. A company is supposed to meet or exceed investors' expectations reflected in the stock price. Therefore, the share price which can be attained when its plan has been achieved successfully should be equal to or higher than the current price. The current price available in the market can be and should be used as a guideline for strategic planning. If there is a considerable gap between the current price and the price

第1章 企業価値評価とは何か

ポイント！

✔ 企業価値評価は投資判断だけではなく企業経営においても不可欠な取り組みである

✔ 企業の価値は将来のフリー・キャッシュフローの現在価値によって決まる

✔ 企業の価値を評価するためにはファイナンス，会計，戦略といった広範な知識が必要となる

● 企業価値評価の目的

　バリュエーションとは企業，事業，株式，債券，不動産等の資産の価値を推定するプロセスのことである。企業価値評価においては企業全体の価値あるいは株式の価格である株価を推定することになる。

　企業価値評価の目的はさまざまである。一般的なのは個人あるいは機関投資家が株式投資を行う際の価格判断であろう。投資家は価値評価の結果に基づいて株式を売買する。また，証券アナリストは価値評価に基づき，株式の「買い」あるいは「売り」を推奨するレポートを発行する。

　企業が他の会社を買収する際の分析にも企業価値評価は必要である。企業は買収対象として魅力的な会社を見つけると，自社の事業とのシナジー効果やその他の関係する影響を加味しながら価値評価を行い，買収の可否と適切な買収額を決定する。

　さらに，中長期的な戦略や事業計画立案のためにも企業価値評価は必要である。企業は株価に織り込まれた投資家の期待に応える，あるいはその期待を超えていく必要がある。そのため，事業計画が実行された場合に実現できるであろう株価は，その時点での株価以上であることが望ましい。すなわち，市場における株価は事業計画の指針となりうるし，またそうすべきであるということである。また，もし投資家の期待が反映されているその時点での株価と，事業

第1章　企業価値評価とは何か　　19

according to the strategic plan formulated, a company needs to study the reason and communicate it with investors.

Figure 1.1 | Purposes of Valuation

Investment evaluation by investors
M&A analysis by companies
Guideline for strategic business planning
Communication with investors

● Knowledge Required for Valuation

In order to analyze and estimate the value of a company, you must understand basic corporate finance theory explaining what and how value is determined.

Fundamental accounting knowledge of financial statements such as the income statement, the balance sheet and the cash flow statement, and an understanding of accounting items are necessary because you are to assess the historical and the current financial performance of a company using financial data.

Moreover, the business environment outside of a company and internal factors such as strengths and weaknesses are factors to include in valuation. Multi-level analysis from many sides and utilizing various strategic frameworks will be necessary.

計画が実行された場合に実現できるであろう株価に乖離がある場合には，その理由を分析し投資家との適切なコミュニケーションをとることが必要となるだろう。

図表 1.1 ┃ 企業価値評価の目的

投資家による株式投資の判断
企業による M&A 分析
中長期的な戦略と事業計画立案のための指針
投資家との対話の材料

❶ 企業価値評価に求められる知識

　企業価値を分析し評価するためには，企業の価値がどのように決まるのかといったコーポレートファイナンスの基本的な理論を理解しておかなければならない。

　また，企業価値評価においては企業が公開する財務データに基づいて過去および現在の業績を分析することが必要となるため，損益計算書，貸借対照表，キャッシュフロー計算書等の財務諸表の読み取り方，および各会計項目の意味合いの理解といった基礎的な会計知識が必要となる。

　さらに，企業の価値を評価するためには，企業を取り巻く外部環境の分析や，強み・弱みといった内部分析を行う必要がある。このためには，企業・事業戦略全体を多面的に分析するさまざまな戦略フレームワークが活用される。

第 1 章　企業価値評価とは何か　　21

Figure 1.2 | Knowledges Required for Valuation

In addition to a broad-ranging knowledge required, everything transcending business management such as a literacy in operating activities like marketing and supply chain, human resource management, organizational design, and perception of trends in technology will be utilized for company valuation.

What Is the Value of a Company?

Let us simply define the value of a company. We will define the value of a firm as **the present value of the cash flows the company will generate in the future**.

The cash flow generated by operations is, in effect, the result of various corporate activities. Customer satisfaction and loyalty, branding, product development capability, efficient manufacturing and supply chain, the leadership of top management, capable employees, and organizational structure to make decisions swiftly all contribute to the company's future cash flows and therefore have an impact on the value of a company. This is consistent with the argument that valuation requires a vast range of knowledge.

図表 1.2 ｜ 企業価値評価に必要な知識

　このような広範な知識理解に加えて，マーケティングやサプライチェーンなどのより事業活動レベルの経営知識や，人的資源管理，組織設計などの経営管理上の知識，さらにはテクノロジーの動向なども含めた事業経営におけるほぼすべての領域をまたがる知識を総動員して行うのが企業価値評価である。

● 企業価値とは

　企業価値とは何か簡単におさえておこう。企業価値は以下のように定義される。

「企業が将来にわたって生み出すキャッシュフローの現在価値」

　企業が生み出す現金（キャッシュフロー）は，さまざまな企業活動の最終的な結果である。顧客満足度やロイヤリティー，ブランド，商品開発力，効率的な製造工程やサプライチェーン，経営者のリーダーシップ，従業員の能力，迅速な意思決定ができる経営体制などはすべて企業が生み出すキャッシュフローに大きく関係しており，したがって企業価値に影響を及ぼす。このことは企業価値評価には広範な知識が必要だということとも整合している。

Figure 1.3 | **Value of Company**

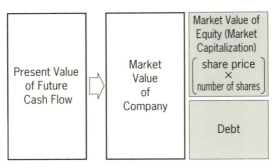

The value of a company can be thought of as comprising two components: the value of debt and the value of equity. As we mentioned earlier, the value of a company is determined by cash flows generated by the company in the future. The stream of cash flow can be divided into those attributed to debt holders and those attributed to equity shareholders. Cash flow attributed to debt holders come in the form of interest and principal payments. This cash outflow to the creditors is considered relatively stable as they are paid at predetermined rates. It follows that the value of corporate debt is usually stable unless there is financial distress. On the other hand, cash outflow attributed to equity shareholders is the residual cash flow after subtracting the cash outflow to the creditors from the total cash flow of the company. Therefore, cash flows attributed to equity shareholders are often more volatile, and thus we can expect to see larger movements in equity values due to changes in the expectations of a company's cash flows.

Process for Valuation

A company valuation starts from business environment analyses. This includes an assessment for the entire economic condition, market trends, and competitors' movements, on which an internal strategy is based.

Next, the financial performances of a company and its competitors are analyzed.

図表 1.3　企業価値

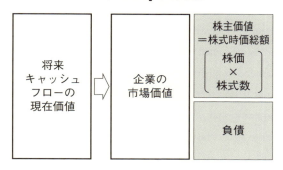

　企業価値は大きく負債の価値と，株式つまり株主資本の価値に分けられる。企業価値は企業が将来にわたって生み出すキャッシュフローによって決まるが，そのキャッシュフローが債権者や銀行に帰属するものと，株主に帰属するものとに分けられるということである。債権者・銀行に帰属するキャッシュフローは企業にとってみると利息の支払いと元本の返済である。このキャッシュフローは契約によって前もって決まっているから安定しており，負債の価値というのはよほどでない限り（企業が倒産の危機に瀕しない限り）変動しないと考えられる。一方，株主に帰属するキャッシュフローは，企業が生み出したキャッシュフローから，負債に帰属するキャッシュフローを差し引いた残りである。そのため，株主に帰属するキャッシュフローは安定せず，株主資本の価値は企業の将来のキャッシュフローの見通しにより大きく変動する。

● 企業価値評価のプロセス

　企業価値評価は事業を取り巻く環境分析からスタートする。環境分析にはマクロ経済の動向や市場・競合の動向の分析が含まれ，これを踏まえて自社戦略の分析を行う。
　次に自社や競合他社の財務業績を分析し，この財務業績の分析と戦略面など

The results of financial analysis and qualitative analysis regarding an environment and strategy are combined and constitute the foundation of a performance forecast. Meanwhile, the weighted average cost of capital(WACC), which is the expected return by investors is estimated and incorporated in the financial analysis. Combined results shows whether a company has created value or not in the past.

The most difficult part is forecasting future performance. Sales growth, changes in cost structure, and additional investments going forward are projected. All projected figures are reflected in forecasted future free cash flows. Although it is extremely difficult to forecast the future, the value associated with cash flows in the distant future is captured as a terminal value.

The future cash flows and a terminal value are discounted with WACC, and converted into the value at present. The value produced by operation is calculated tentatively at this stage, but it is not final. Impacts with respect to multiple possible scenarios are commonly considered.

The total value of a company consists of the value generated by its operation and the value of non-operating assets. Subtracting the value of debt from the value of a company leaves the value of equity. The value per share will be calculated as the value of equity divided by the number of shares.

While discounting relying on future performance forecasts is the main approach for valuation, there are multiple approaches that provide simple estimates using the share price data of comparable companies. There exists both advantages and disadvantages of both discounting and multiple approaches. Therefore in practice, they are frequently used in combination.

It is interesting to know how far the estimated share price is from the actual price, or if they are the equivalent level. In either case, the estimated value will not be realized with only valuation. It requires an actual transaction to purchase a target company for valuation, or detailed arrangements to activate a grand forecast. Needless to say, it is one of the most important roles for top executives to consider how the organization acts to increase the value of a company.

This book will discuss valuation according to the process described above and as

26 | Chapter 1   What Is Valuation?

の定性的な事業環境分析は統合され，企業の将来の業績予測の土台となる。あわせて，投資家が求める期待リターンである加重平均資本コスト（WACC）を推定し，統合した財務分析を行うと，企業のこれまでの価値の創造状況を把握することができる。

　これに続くのが企業価値評価において最も難しいプロセスである，事業の将来の業績予測である。今後の売上の伸びやコスト構造の変化，追加的な投資などを予測していく。これらの予測は最終的に事業が生み出すフリー・キャッシュフローの予測に反映される。将来を正確に予想することは不可能だが，さらに遠い将来における価値はターミナル・バリューとして予測する。

　将来のキャッシュフローとターミナル・バリューは，WACC によって割り引かれ，現時点の価値に変換される。これにより，事業がもたらす価値は一次的には計算できるが，価値評価はここでは終わりではない。将来の状況に関して複数のシナリオを考慮しその影響を把握することはよく行われる。

　企業全体の価値は，事業活動が生み出す価値だけではなく，事業活動とは関係のない資産がもたらす価値を加えたものである。また，企業全体の価値から負債の価値を差し引くと株主価値となる。1株あたりの価値を算出するためには，株主価値を株式数で割ることになる。

　将来の業績予測に基づいた割引現在価値法は，企業価値評価での王道の手法だが，競合の株価に基づく簡便的な価値評価の方法が価値倍率法と言われるものである。割引現在価値法と価値倍率法には長所と短所が存在し，実務においては両方の手法が併用されることが多い。

　推定された株価が実際の株価とどれだけ乖離しているのか，あるいは同水準なのかというのは興味深いが，推定された価値は評価しただけでは実現されない。評価した企業を実際に買収したり，大きな戦略を実行に移すための細かい組み立てをすることも必要となってくる。いうまでもなく，企業価値を高めるために組織をどのように動かすのかを考えることは企業経営者の最も重要な役割の1つである。

　本書は，図表1.4でも示している以上のような企業価値評価のプロセスに沿っ

shown in Figure 1.4.

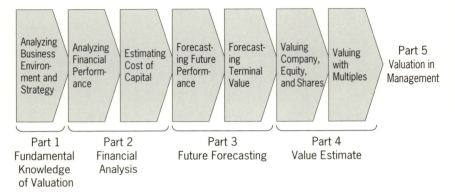

Figure 1.4 | Process for Valuation

て展開していく。

図表 1.4 企業価値評価のプロセス

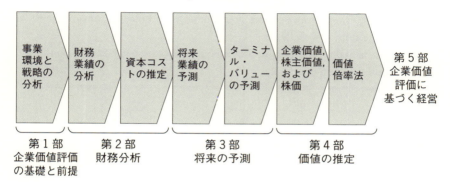

Chapter 2 Analyzing Business Environment and Strategy

Points!

✔ Strategy frameworks enable you to analyze a business environment and strategy efficiently
✔ Understanding the unique features of each framework helps you to use them more effectively

● Strategy Frameworks

Although this book does not dwell on a detailed discussion about strategy, valuation requires analyses of a business environment and strategy. This chapter introduces representative strategy frameworks that are commonly used.

A strategy framework is an effective thinking tool to examine and analyze the current condition and the future directionality of a business and helps you to study various factors comprehensively and consistently. You can spend less time sorting out vast amounts of information and more time interpreting and analyzing them.

Each strategic framework has a unique feature and a difference in its purpose. Major frameworks include: PEST marshals macro level factors associated with a business environment, Five Forces analyzes the structure of an industry and a market, 3Cs overviews internal as well as external elements, Value chain reveals the internal process to create value, and SWOT integrates all information inside and outside of the business and provides the foundation of strategic planning.

第2章 事業環境と戦略の分析

ポイント！

✔ 戦略フレームワークを活用することにより，効率的に事業環境や戦略を分析することができる
✔ フレームワークにはさまざまなものがあるが，それぞれの特徴を理解することにより有効な活用が可能となる

● 戦略フレームワーク

　本書では戦略論の深い議論には立ち入らないが，企業価値評価においては事業環境や戦略の分析が必要である。そのため本章ではそれらの分析に活用される代表的な戦略フレームワークを紹介する。

　戦略フレームワークは現状の事業環境や将来の事業の方向性について検討，分析する際に有効な思考ツールであり，さまざまな要素を包括的にかつ整合的に考えることを手助けしてくれる。フレームワークを活用することにより，情報を取りまとめる時間を削減し，その時間を，情報を解釈し分析することにあてられるようになる。

　それぞれの戦略フレームワークには特徴があり，使用する目的にも違いがある。マクロ経済レベルで外部環境を整理する PEST 分析，産業の全体構造や市場を分析する 5 フォース分析，外部環境とともに社内の状況までを概観する 3C 分析，社内の価値創造プロセスを明らかにするバリューチェーン分析，社内外の状況を統合して戦略立案のベースを示す SWOT 分析などがある。

第 2 章　事業環境と戦略の分析　31

Figure 2.1 | **Major Strategy Frameworks**

Purpose	Framework
Sort out macro level factors about business environment	PEST
Analyze the structure of an industry and a market	Five Forces
Overview internal as well as external situation	3Cs
Reveal the internal process to create value	Value Chain
Integrate all information inside and outside of the business and provide the foundation of strategic planning	SWOT

The frameworks shown in Figure 2.1 are reviewed as follows. PEST, Five Forces and SWOT, which are frequently utilized in practice among them are introduced coupled with a simple example of the outcome.

○ PEST

PEST identifies the Political, Economic, Socio-Cultural, and Technological factors that can potentially affect a business. This gives a broad overview about a business environment and the outcome of the analysis is effective to study possible changes in the future of a business environment. PEST will be used for opportunities and threats in SWOT analysis. Unfortunately, many materials listed in PEST are uncontrollable, therefore, you should think about how to deal with them rather than how to change them.

図表 2.1 ┃ 代表的な戦略フレームワーク

目的	フレームワーク
マクロ経済レベルで外部環境を整理する	PEST
産業の全体構造や市場を分析する	5フォース
外部環境と社内状況まで概観する	3C
社内の価値創造プロセスを明らかにする	バリューチェーン
社内外の状況を統合して戦略立案のベースを示す	SWOT

　以下では図表2.1に示されたフレームワークについてレビューする。中でも，特に使用される頻度が高いPEST分析，5フォース分析，SWOT分析については簡単な分析例を合わせて紹介する。

● PEST 分析

　PEST分析は事業に影響を及ぼしうる政治・政策，経済，社会・文化，技術の各要素を明確にする枠組みである。PEST分析では事業を取り巻く環境を概観し，その分析結果は今後の事業環境の変化の可能性を探索するために有効である。また後述するSWOT分析における機会と脅威に入力する情報となる。ただし，PEST分析でリストアップされた内容はえてして自らはコントロールができないものが多いため，それらの状況・現象を変えるというよりもどのように対処するのかを考える枠組みといえる。

第2章　事業環境と戦略の分析　　33

Figure 2.2 | **PEST**

	Factors
Political	Regulations/ Tax, Subsidy/ Legal precedent/ Political body
Economic	Economic condition, Growth/ Price (inflation, deflation)/ Interest/ Foreign exchange/ Stock price/ Unemployment/ Export, Import
Socio-Cultural	Population/ Public sentiment/ Trend/ Education/ Security/ Religion, Language/ Natural resources/ Environment/ Disaster
Technological	Innovation/ New technologies/ Patents

Figure 2.3 shows the example of PEST analysis for the sportswear industry where Nike and Adidas compete.

Figure 2.3 | **PEST Example for the Sportswear Industry**

Political	• Enhancement of regulation and further requirement for working condition in factories • Increased tariff and the possibility of trade war between the U.S. and China • Corporate tax reduction
Economic	• Change in disposable income in the biggest market, the U.S. • Foreign exchange rate
Socio-Cultural	• Increasing health awareness (especially for Millennials and Generation Z) • Popularity of outdoor recreation such as jogging and hiking • Reputation and performance of sponsored athletes • Casualization of dress codes
Technological	• Growing E-commerce • Development of new functional materials and fabrics • Integration of technology into smart sportswear (internet of things) • Promoting with social media (Facebook, Instagram, Twitter)

Derived based on the works of Temple University students, Jonnathan H. Kwon and Tiana M. Ranjo

34 | Chapter 2 Analyzing Business Environment and Strategy

図表 2.2 ┃ PEST 分析

	要素
政治・政策	規制，税制・補助金，裁判制度，政党・政治団体
経済	景況感・成長率，物価（インフレ・デフレ），金利，為替，株価，失業率，輸出入
社会・文化	人口動態，世論，トレンド，教育水準，治安・安全保障，宗教・言語，天然資源，環境，自然災害
技術	技術革新，新技術，特許

　図表 2.3 では，ナイキやアディダスといったスポーツウェア業界における PEST 分析の例を示している。

図表 2.3 ┃ スポーツウェア業界における PEST 分析の例

政治・政策	・ 労働規制の強化や製造現場での環境改善要請 ・ 関税の引き上げや米国・中国の貿易戦争の可能性 ・ 法人減税
経済	・ 特に大きな市場である米国の可処分所得の増減 ・ 為替レート
社会・文化	・ 健康志向の高まり（特にミレニアル世代とZ世代） ・ ジョギングやハイキングなどのアウトドア活動の増加 ・ スポンサー契約アスリートの評判と成績 ・ ドレスコードのカジュアル化
技術	・ E コマースの高まり ・ 高機能素材の開発 ・ IoT のスポーツウェアへの適用（スマート・スポーツウェア） ・ ソーシャルメディアの活用（フェイスブック，インスタグラム，ツイッター）

テンプル大学生，ジョナサン クウォン，ティアナ ランジョの分析を参考に著者作成

第 2 章　事業環境と戦略の分析

Five Forces

Developed by Professor Michael E. Porter, Five Forces is a framework to analyze the attractiveness and the degree of competitiveness of an industry from five dimensions. Five Forces consists of the bargaining power of suppliers, the bargaining power of buyers, the industry rivalry, the threat of substitutes, and the threat of new entrants.

Figure 2.4 outlines the elements to be concerned in each force.

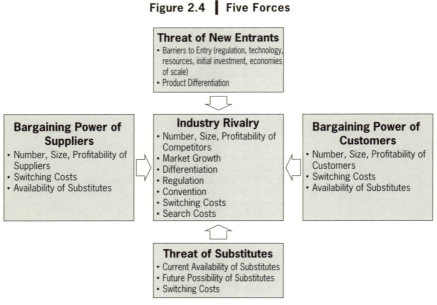

Figure 2.4 | Five Forces

Derived from "Porter, Michael. The Five Competitive Forces That Shape Strategy. *Harvard Business Review*, January 2008"

Five Forces enables you to understand an industry with a wider field of view, not limited to direct competitors. However, you need further analysis in order to formulate a future strategy because five forces is a static model exhibiting the current or past condition of an industry.

● 5フォース分析

マイケル・E・ポーター教授が提唱した5フォース分析は，産業の魅力度，競争状況の激しさを5つの観点から評価するフレームワークである。5つの観点は，供給業者つまりその業界から見た売り手の交渉力の強さ，顧客つまり買い手の交渉力の強さ，現在の業界内の競合度合い，代替品の脅威，および新規参入の脅威からなる。

各観点で考慮すべき要素は図表 2.4 に示されている。

図表 2.4 ｜ 5フォース分析

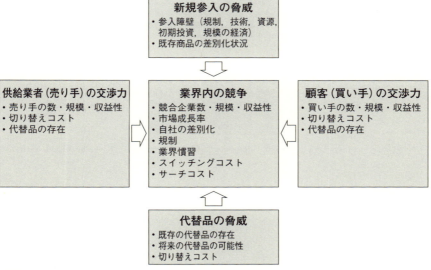

Porter, Michael. The Five Competitive Forces That Shape Strategy. *Harvard Business Review*, January 2008 を参考に著者加工

5フォース分析では5つの観点を合わせて考えることにより，直接的な競合だけではなくより広い視界で事業環境を把握することができる。一方で，この分析は現時点あるいは過去の業界の状況を把握するいわば静的なモデルであり，将来的な戦略を検討する際にはさらなる分析が必要となる。

Figure 2.5 shows an example of Five Forces analysis for the sportswear industry.

Figure 2.5 | Five Forces Example for the Sportswear Industry

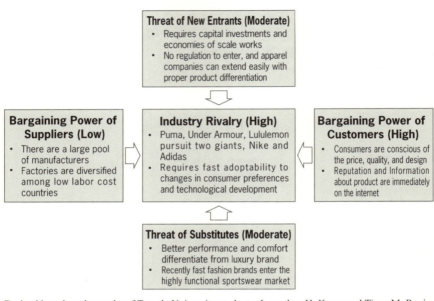

Derived based on the works of Temple University students, Jonnathan H. Kwon and Tiana M. Ranjo

図表2.5は，スポーツウェア業界における5フォース分析の例を示している。

図表2.5 スポーツウェア業界における5フォース分析の例

新規参入の脅威（中）
- 一定の初期投資が必要であり，規模の経済も有効
- 新規参入規制はなく，差別化された商品があればアパレル業界からの展開は容易

供給業者（売り手）の交渉力（弱）
- 多くの製造業者が存在
- 製造拠点は低賃金の国に分散

業界内の競争（強）
- ナイキ，アディダスの2強に加えて，プーマ、アンダーアーマー、ルルレモンなどが追撃中
- 顧客の嗜好の変化や技術革新へのスピーディーな適応が必要

顧客（買い手）の交渉力（強）
- 顧客は常にトレンドを追いかけ，価格，品質，デザインに敏感
- 顧客の評判は即座にインターネットなどで拡散

代替品の脅威（中）
- 高機能と着心地のよさにより高級ブランドとの代替性は限定的
- ファストファッションブランドの高機能化商品には注意が必要

テンプル大学生，ジョナサン クウォン，ティアナ ランジョの分析を参考に著者作成

第2章　事業環境と戦略の分析　　39

3Cs

3Cs is a framework to analyze a company focusing on three elements: the customers, the competitors and the company. By analyzing market trends and competitors movements, you will be able to find your competitive advantages and success factors.

Figure 2.6 | 3Cs

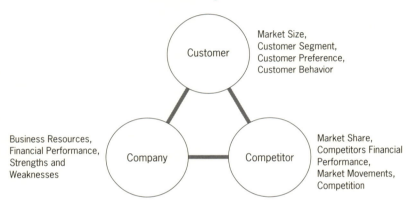

3Cs is a simple and therefore useful tool to summarize the current status about a company and its products. However, 3Cs sometimes misses items that should be examined thoroughly because three elements are very broad and vague.

3C 分析

3C 分析は企業の状況を顧客，競合，そして自社の 3 点から分析するフレームワークである。顧客のトレンドと競合の状況を分析することにより，自社の競争優位性を抽出し，成功要因を発見するために行われる。

図表 2.6 ｜ 3C 分析

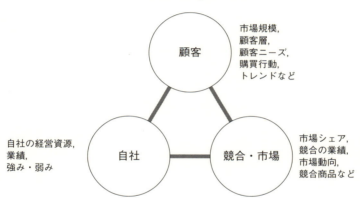

3C 分析は非常にシンプルであるため，自社の状況や自社製品の現状を概観するために有効である。一方で，3 つの要素は非常に幅広く，あいまいであるため，本来詳細に分析すべき項目が見逃されてしまう傾向があることには注意が必要である。

Value Chain

Value chain, developed by Professor Michael E. Porter, is a model to show internal business activities and articulates how a company creates value. Value chain analysis helps to spot where and what is a source for value creation and which activity should be improved to enhance the competitive advantage of a company among all internal business processes. Outcomes of value chain analysis will be input for strengths and weaknesses in SWOT analysis. However, please note that actual business activities are not simple enough to be easily illustrated.

Figure 2.7 | Value Chain

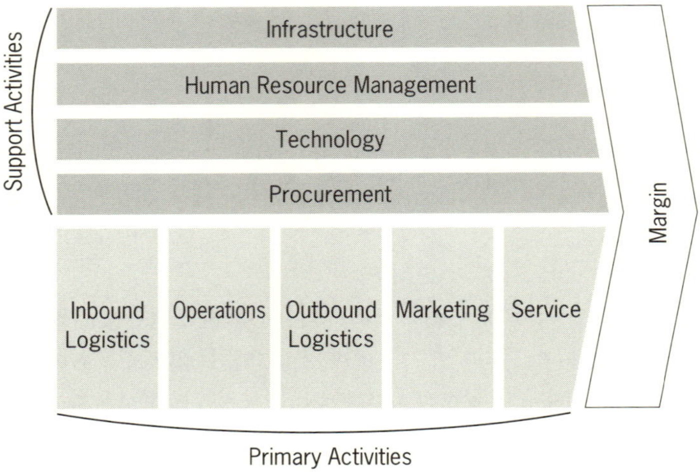

Derived from "Porter, Michael. *Competitive Advantage: Creating and Sustaining Superior Performance*. The Free Press, 1998"

● バリューチェーン分析

バリューチェーン分析はマイケル・E・ポーター教授が提唱した企業の内部の活動を表わすモデルであり，企業がどのように価値を創造していくのかを明らかにする。企業の内部プロセスの中でどこに，そして何が価値の源泉であり，どの活動を改善することにより競争優位性をさらに強化できるのか，といったことを探索するために行われる。この分析の結果は SWOT 分析における強みと弱みに入力する情報ともなる。ただし，現実の事業活動の流れは簡単に図示できるほど単純ではないことには留意が必要である。

図表 2.7 ┃ バリューチェーン分析

支援活動
- インフラストラクチャー
- 人事・労務管理
- 技術開発
- 調達

主活動
- 購買物流
- 生産
- 出荷物流
- マーケティング販売
- サービス

利益（マージン）

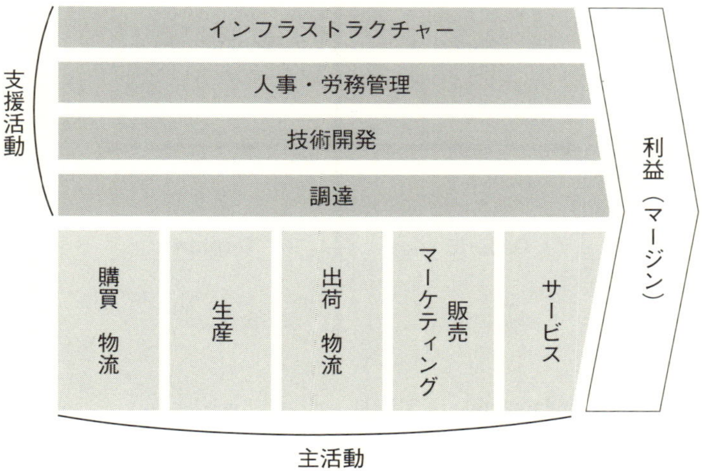

Porter, Michael. *Competitive Advantage: Creating and Sustaining Superior Performance*. The Free Press, 1998 を参考に著者加工

⊙ SWOT

SWOT helps to understand the strengths and the weaknesses of a business and the opportunities and threats being faced. It reveals how a company utilizes its strength to leverage upcoming opportunities, and how it improves on its weaknesses to eliminate confronting threats. It integrates all outcomes of analyses via strategy frameworks as introduced above.

Figure 2.8 | SWOT

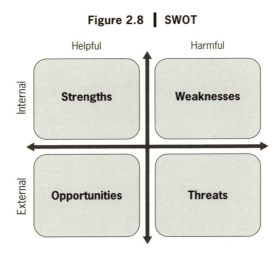

Figure 2.9 shows the example of SWOT analysis for Nike Inc.

● SWOT 分析

　SWOT 分析は，企業の強み・弱みと，企業が直面する機会と脅威を理解する分析である。企業が事業機会に対してどのように強みを活用するのか，脅威を取り除くためにどのように弱みを改善するのかなどを明らかにするために行われる。ここまで紹介した戦略フレームワークでの分析結果を統合するものといえる。

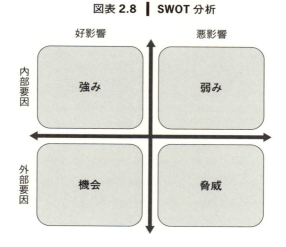

図表 2.8　SWOT 分析

　図表 2.9 では，ナイキの SWOT 分析の例を示している。

Figure 2.9 | SWOT Example for Nike

Strengths
- Established brand image
- Excellent marketing capability
- Innovative product development
- Consistently sponsoring legendary athletes
- Highly profitable

Weaknesses
- Heavily dependent on footwear sales
- Reliance on low cost production in developing countries
- Relatively high price
- Stagnating sales growth

Opportunities
- More customization via online shop
- E-commerce expansion (more products, improved interface)
- Decrease in corporate tax rate

Threats
- Criticism of bold marketing approach
- Rising demand of laborers and wages
- Improved working conditions in factories
- Strong competition with Adidas and others

Derived based on the works of Temple University students, Jonnathan H. Kwon

The analysis combining the strengths and weaknesses with the opportunities and threats is called "Cross SWOT". It facilitates figuring out more concrete strategic initiatives as introduced in Figure 2.10. Note that the strengths can be the weaknesses and the opportunities can be threats, and vice versa. Therefore, it is often difficult to define each item clearly.

Figure 2.10 | Cross SWOT

External

		Opportunities	Threats
Internal	Strengths	**Offense: S × O** • How can you make the most of your advantages with your strengths? • What businesses offer the most opportunities?	**Confrontation: S × T** • How can the strengths overcome the threats? • Can you change the threat to an opportunity with your strengths?
	Weaknesses	**Reinforcement: W × O** • Can you improve on your weaknesses so that you can leverage opportunities?	**Defense: W × T** • How can you minimize losses and negative impacts caused of weaknesses and threats?

46   Chapter 2   Analyzing Business Environment and Strategy

図表 2.9 ┃ ナイキの SWOT 分析の例

強み	弱み
・ 確立されたブランドイメージ ・ 卓越したプロモーション能力 ・ 革新的な商品開発力 ・ 伝説的なアスリートとの継続的なスポンサー契約 ・ 高い利益率	・ シューズへの大きな依存 ・ 途上国における低コスト生産への依存 ・ 比較的高価格 ・ 売上成長の鈍化
機会	脅威
・ オンライン店舗によるカスタマイズの増加 ・ E コマースの拡張（商品数, インターフェイス改善） ・ 法人税率の削減	・ 大胆なプロモーションへの批判 ・ 労働力の不足と賃金上昇 ・ 製造現場の環境改善 ・ アディダス他との競争激化

テンプル大学生, ジョナサン クウォンの分析を参考に著者作成

　また, クロス SWOT 分析と呼ばれる, 強み・弱みと機会・脅威を組み合わせた分析をすることにより, 具体的な戦略施策を考えることもできる（図表2.10）。ただし, しばしば強みは弱みにもなり, また機会は脅威にもなりうることから明確にそれぞれを表わすことは難しい場合も多い。

図表 2.10 ┃ クロス SWOT 分析

外部要因

		機会	脅威
内部要因	強み	攻勢：強み×機会 ・機会の中でどのように強みを活用するか ・どの事業が機会を生かせるか	対抗：強み×脅威 ・強みによってどのように脅威に立ち向かうか ・強みによって脅威を機会に変えられないか
	弱み	強化：弱み×機会 ・機会を有効に活用するために弱みをどのように強化するか	防衛：弱み×脅威 ・弱みと脅威から生じる損失や負の影響をどのように最小化するか

第 2 章　事業環境と戦略の分析　　47

Part 2
Financial Analysis

- Following business environment and strategy analysis, we then turn to the financial analysis. The past and current financial performance and condition of a company should be captured in order to forecast future financial performance for valuation.

- This part begins with basic financial statements such as the income statement and the balance sheet, and then provides you with a broad introduction to many financial measures for analysis.

- Next, we take a detailed look at cost of capital which is an indispensable factor for valuation.

- Finally, the approach for analysis taking advantage of important financial measures for valuation is covered.

Chapter 3 Analyzing Financial Performance 1:
　　　　　 Income Statement and Balance Sheet

Chapter 4 Analyzing Financial Performance 2:
　　　　　 Various Financial Measures

Chapter 5 Estimating Cost of Capital

Chapter 6 Analyzing Financial Performance 3: EVA and Strategy

第2部
財務分析

★★

- 事業環境，戦略分析に続くのは，財務数値の分析である。企業価値評価において将来の財務業績を適切に予測するためには，その事前情報として現在，過去の業績，財務状態を把握しておかなければならない。

- 第2部では損益計算書と貸借対照表といった基本的な財務諸表に続き，財務業績を分析するためさまざまな財務数値を紹介する。

- また，企業価値を把握するために不可欠な要因である資本コストを詳細に議論する。

- 最後の第6章では，企業価値評価に重要な財務指標を活用した分析手法を紹介する。

第3章　財務業績の分析1：損益計算書と貸借対照表

第4章　財務業績の分析2：数々の財務数値

第5章　資本コストの推定

第6章　財務業績の分析3：EVA と戦略

Chapter 3 Analyzing Financial Performance 1: Income Statement and Balance Sheet

Points!

✓ Common-size financial statements express all items in an income statement and a balance sheet as a percentage

✓ Analyses on common-size financial statements helps to reveal the business model and the earning structure of a company

● Obtaining an Income Statement and Balance Sheet

Accounting information shows the results of various business activities. The income statement shows how much profit or loss is generated during a specific period, and the balance sheet summarizes the assets and capital.

All listed companies usually disclose this data on the company's website, and it is also available on a website called "EDGAR", prepared by the U.S. Securities and Exchange Commission:

https://www.sec.gov/edgar/searchedgar/companysearch.html

Accounting files for Japanese companies are also available on the Financial Services Agency website of called "EDINET":

http://disclosure.edinet-fsa.go.jp/

Various websites including Yahoo!Finance and Bloomberg also provide accounting data with a standard format, so you can typically get access to information quite easily.

● The Income Statement

The income statement (profit and loss statement, or P/L) is a financial statement that shows revenues, expenses and income of a company over a period of time and reveals whether a company will record a profit or a loss. Thus, an income statement

50 | Chapter 3 Analyzing Financial Performance 1: Income Statement and Balance Sheet

第3章 財務業績の分析1： 損益計算書と貸借対照表

ポイント！

✔ 基本的な財務諸表である損益計算書，貸借対照表の各項目を比率で表わしたものが標準化財務諸表である

✔ 標準化財務諸表を分析することにより，企業のビジネスモデルや利益の上げ方を把握することができる

● 損益計算書，貸借対照表の入手

　会計情報は企業のさまざまな活動の結果を数値で表わすものである。このうち，損益計算書は一定期間にどれだけの利益・損失が生み出されたのかを示し，貸借対照表は一時点における資産と資本の状態を示す財務諸表である。

　これらの情報は上場企業であれば通常は企業のホームページに開示されており，加えて証券取引委員会のホームページ「EDGAR」，

https://www.sec.gov/edgar/searchedgar/companysearch.html

日本企業であれば金融庁のホームページ「EDINET」，

http://disclosure.edinet-fsa.go.jp/

には上場企業すべての財務決算書類がまとめられている。また，Yahoo!Financeやブルームバーグなどのホームページでも，統一フォーマットで会計情報が提供されており，必要な情報は容易に入手可能である。

● 損益計算書

　損益計算書（P/L）は一期間における売上高，費用，利益を示し，企業が利益を生んだのか，損失を出したのかを明らかにする財務諸表である。四半期や年度における財務的な業績を表わす。損益計算書は事業活動によって生み出さ

provides a financial picture of the company over a specific period of time, such as one quarter or a fiscal year. We begin with the sales revenue generated from business operations. Sales less the cost of sales or cost of goods sold (COGS) and selling, general and administrative expenses (SG&A) result in an operating profit. Another profit measure is net income, which is calculated by taking operating profits and adding or subtracting non-operating profits such as interest income (non-operating losses such as interest expense), adding or subtracting unusual gains (losses), and subtracting corporate tax payments.

Figure 3.1 | Income Statement

	Sales
−	COGS
−	SG&A
=	Operating Profit
±	Non-operating Profit
±	Unusual Profit/Loss
−	Tax
=	Net Income

● The Balance Sheet

The balance sheet (B/S) provides us with a snapshot of the company's financial health at a point in time. The cash raised from creditors and shareholders is recorded to the right (or credit side) of the balance sheet. The portion attributed to creditors, including banks, is categorized as a liability. The portion attributed to shareholders is categorized under shareholders' equity or net worth. The profits retained from business operations are also recorded under shareholders' equity. The shares bought back by the company (share repurchase), are recorded as a negative account of shareholders' equity as a treasury stock.

れた売上高からスタートし，そこから（売上）原価と販売費・一般管理費（販管費）といった営業活動に伴う費用を差し引いたものが営業利益である。営業利益に利息の受け取りといった営業外利益を加え，利息の支払いといった営業外費用を差し引き，一時的に発生する非経常的な特別利益および特別損失を加味し，税金を差し引くと当期純利益が計算される。

図表 3.1 ┃ 損益計算書

	売上高
−	（売上）原価
−	販管費
=	営業利益
±	営業外損益
±	特別損益
−	法人税等
=	当期純利益

◉ 貸借対照表

貸借対照表（B/S）は，ある一時点における企業の財政状態を表わす。企業が債権者と株主から調達した金額が B/S の右側（貸方）に記録される。銀行のような債権者に帰属する分は負債と分類され，その残りの株主に帰属する部分は純資産（株主資本）に分類される。企業が上げた利益が内部留保されたものも株主資本となる。なお，企業が一度売り出した株式を買い戻した場合は（自社株買い），株主資本のマイナスとして記録される。

第3章　財務業績の分析1：損益計算書と貸借対照表

The cash (capital) raised and recorded on the right side is used to purchase assets to run its business operations. These assets are recorded to the left (or debit side) of the balance sheet. Assets include current assets (such as accounts receivable and inventories), tangible assets (such as property or equipment), intangible assets and long-term financial investments. Those assets that can be converted to cash within a short period of time (less than one year) are classified as current assets. Fixed assets are longer-term assets.

The balance sheet reflects the book value (BV) or recorded value of an asset, which is often different from its market value. The market value (MV) of a company is determined by the expected cash flow to be generated in the future, but the figure recorded on the balance sheet is based on the historical purchase price or original value of the asset.

Figure 3.2 | Balance Sheet

Total Assets	Current Assets	Cash & Securities	Payables	Current Liabilities
		Receivables	Short-term Debt	
		Inventories	Long-term Debt	Fixed Liabilities
	Fixed Assets	Tangible Assets		
		Intangible Assets/ Financial Investments	Shareholders' Equity	Net Worth

○ Analysis with the Common-size Financial Statements

The common-size financial statements express all items in the income statement as a percentage of sales and all items in the balance sheet as a percentage of total assets. Eliminating the magnitude, they reveal a company's cost structure, use of capital to produce profits, and what kind of assets are owned.

調達した資金は事業活動を行うための資産購入にあてられるが、どれだけの資産をどのように所有しているのかがB/Sの左側（借方）に記録される。企業の資産には売掛金や在庫（棚卸資産）に代表される流動資産や、土地・設備などの有形固定資産、無形固定資産や長期の金融投資が含まれる。流動・固定の分類は資産が現金に換わるまでの期間の長さによって決まる（1年以内が流動、それ以外が固定）。

B/Sは、取得した資産の帳簿上の価値を表わすものであり、多くの場合時価とは異なる。企業の価値は将来生み出されると期待されるキャッシュフローによって決まるが、そうした時価とは異なり、B/Sには取得した価格、もともとの価格で記録される。なお、取得した資産の帳簿上の価値のことを簿価と呼ぶ。

図表 3.2 ▎ 貸借対照表

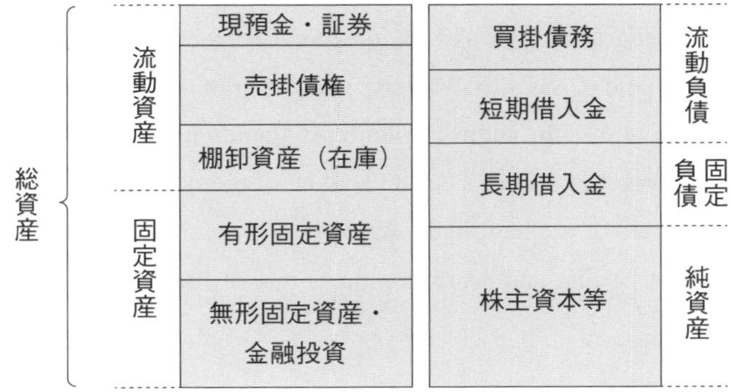

◉ 標準化財務諸表による分析

標準化財務諸表とは損益計算書の項目を売上を100%として比率で表わし、貸借対照表の項目を総資産を100%として比率で表わしたものである。規模の影響を排除することにより、企業がどのようにコストをかけて利益を上げているのか、またその利益を上げるためにどのように資本を活用しているのか、どのような資産を有しているのかを把握することができる。

The common-size financial statements of three companies will help to understand the effectiveness of analysis using them. We will see financial data of a Pfizer; pharmaceutical company, Boeing; an aircraft manufacturer and Walmart; a discount retailer.

● The Common-size Income Statement

Comparison of common-size income statements demonstrates that Pfizer is highly profitable and that the profitability of a retail store Walmart is relatively low. The higher profitability of Pfizer can be achieved by extremely low COGS of 21.4%. On the other hand, SG&A including research and development costs for a new drug exceeds 50% of sales. This reflects that a pharmaceutical company bears significant amount of time and costs before the launch of new products (getting new approval from government and so on), but manufacturing costs after launch tend to be low.

COGS of Boeing is as high as 80% of sales because it assembles a lot of parts to make an airplane. COGS of Walmart which purchases and sells goods is also relatively high, 74.6%. In addition, Walmart spends more than 20% of sales on SG&A because it seems to need a decent amount of promotion and advertisement.

Although the rate of profitability of Walmart is low, sales of Walmart is more than five times that of Boeing and nearly ten times that of Pfizer, resulting in the largest operating profits.

Figure 3.3 | Common-size Income Statement

	Pfizer		The Boeing Company		Walmart Stores	
Sales	100.0%	52,546	100.0%	93,392	100.0%	500,343
COGS	21.4%	11,240	81.4%	76,066	74.6%	373,396
SG&A	52.7%	27,686	7.5%	7,048	21.3%	106,510
Operating profit	25.9%	13,620	11.0%	10,278	4.1%	20,437
Income before taxes	23.4%	12,305	10.8%	10,047	3.0%	15,123
Net income	40.6%	21,353	8.8%	8,197	2.0%	9,862

Fiscal year ended in Dec 2017 for Pfizer and Boeing, Jan 2018 for Walmart. In million dollars.

この分析の有効性を理解するために3社の標準化財務諸表を見比べてみよう。取り上げるのは医薬品メーカーのファイザー，飛行機を製造するボーイング，そしてディスカウントストアを経営するウォルマートである。

● 標準化損益計算書

損益計算書に注目するとファイザーが高い利益を上げていることがわかる。小売業のウォルマートの利益率は比較的低い。ファイザーの高い利益率に大きく貢献しているのが21.4%と極めて低い原価である。一方で，販管費の割合は売上の50%を超えており，ここには新たな医薬品の研究開発コストが含まれている。新たな商品を市場に出すまでにさまざまな承認プロセスがあり長い期間がかかる医薬品メーカーにおいては，研究開発コストが膨大にかかる一方で，一度商品開発が進めば，その製造コストは低いことが表われている。

さまざまな部品を仕入れ飛行機を組み立てるボーイングの原価は高く，売上高の80%を超える水準となっている。商品を仕入れて販売するウォルマートの原価率も74.6%と他の業界に比べて高い。また小売業であるウォルマートは販促費も一定程度かかると考えられ販管費が20%を超えている。

比率だけ見るとウォルマートの利益率は低いが，ウォルマートの売上高はボーイングの5倍以上，ファイザーの10倍弱であるため，営業利益の絶対額はウォルマートのほうが高い。

図表 3.3 ┃ 標準化損益計算書

	ファイザー		ボーイング		ウォルマート	
売上高	100.0%	52,546	100.0%	93,392	100.0%	500,343
原価	21.4%	11,240	81.4%	76,066	74.6%	373,396
販管費	52.7%	27,686	7.5%	7,048	21.3%	106,510
営業利益	25.9%	13,620	11.0%	10,278	4.1%	20,437
税引前利益	23.4%	12,305	10.8%	10,047	3.0%	15,123
当期純利益	40.6%	21,353	8.8%	8,197	2.0%	9,862

決算期：ファイザーとボーイングは2017年12月，ウォルマート2018年1月，単位：百万ドル

● The Common-size Balance Sheet

Comparison of common-size balance sheets demonstrates that Boeing which trades with companies tends to keep relatively high accounts receivables. In general, sales in retail stores are executed with cash or credit cards with a shorter period before settlements. That characteristic corresponds to low accounts receivables of Walmart.

Because a retail store needs to stock some goods to sell, inventories of Walmart dominates more than 20% of its total assets. However, Boeing keeps a higher inventory level of 48%, about half of total assets. It can be explained by the huge amount of work-in-process inventories, because it takes quite a long time and needs a massive amount of parts to make an aircraft.

When you focus on fixed assets, the ratio of property, plant, and equipment (PPE) of Walmart is more than half of the total assets. Among the two makers, Pfizer which does not have an extensive fabrication process, has a lower PPE ratio than Boeing. On the other hand, Pfizer's other assets are considerably high, which is contributed by goodwill recorded when it acquired many start-up firms and indicates its aggressive business expansion.

Figure 3.4 | Common-size Balance Sheet (Debit)

	Pfizer		The Boeing Company		Walmart Stores	
Cash and cash equivalents	0.8%	1,342	9.5%	8,813	3.3%	6,756
Receivables	6.6%	11,271	11.7%	10,825	2.7%	5,614
Short term investments	10.9%	18,650	1.3%	1,179	0.0%	0
Inventories	4.4%	7,578	48.0%	44,344	21.4%	43,783
Other current assets	1.3%	2,300	0.0%	0	1.7%	3,511
Total current assets	23.9%	41,141	70.6%	65,161	29.2%	59,664
Property, plant, and equipment(net)	8.1%	13,865	13.7%	12,672	56.1%	114,818
Other assets	63.9%	109,776	11.4%	10,500	14.7%	30,040
Long term investments	4.1%	7,015	4.3%	4,000	0.0%	0
Total Asset	100.0%	171,797	100.0%	92,333	100.0%	204,522

Fiscal year ended in Dec 2017 for Pfizer and Boeing, Jan 2018 for Walmart. In million dollars.

● 標準化貸借対照表

　次に貸借対照表に注目してみよう。企業相手に取引を行うボーイングは売掛金の比率が他の2社よりも大きくなっている。一般的に小売業の売上は現金取引か，または支払いまでの期間が短いサイトで取引を行うため，ウォルマートの売掛金は低い。

　また，小売業ではある程度の在庫を抱えることが必要となるため，ウォルマートの棚卸資産の総資産に占める比率は20%を超えている。しかし，棚卸資産だけで見るとボーイングの比率は48%と総資産の約半分を占めている。これは飛行機の製造過程が極めて長く，多くの部品を組み立てていく過程での仕掛品の在庫が大きいためと考えられる。

　固定資産に目を向けると，多くの店舗を有しているウォルマートの有形固定資産が総資産の半分以上となっている。同じ製造業であっても大規模な製造工程を有しないファイザーの有形固定資産比率はボーイングよりも低い。一方で，ファイザーのその他の資産は極めて高くなっており，これは多くのベンチャー企業を買収した際ののれんが計上されており，積極的な事業拡大の結果が表われている。

図表 3.4 ┃ 標準化貸借対照表（借方）

	ファイザー		ボーイング		ウォルマート	
現金および現金同等物	0.8%	1,342	9.5%	8,813	3.3%	6,756
売掛金	6.6%	11,271	11.7%	10,825	2.7%	5,614
短期投資	10.9%	18,650	1.3%	1,179	0.0%	0
棚卸資産	4.4%	7,578	48.0%	44,344	21.4%	43,783
その他流動資産	1.3%	2,300	0.0%	0	1.7%	3,511
流動資産	23.9%	41,141	70.6%	65,161	29.2%	59,664
有形固定資産	8.1%	13,865	13.7%	12,672	56.1%	114,818
その他資産	63.9%	109,776	11.4%	10,500	14.7%	30,040
長期投資	4.1%	7,015	4.3%	4,000	0.0%	0
総資産	100.0%	171,797	100.0%	92,333	100.0%	204,522

決算期：ファイザーとボーイングは2017年12月，ウォルマート2018年1月，単位：百万ドル

第3章　財務業績の分析1：損益計算書と貸借対照表　　59

It is interesting to see the liabilities and shareholders' equity of Boeing. Current non-interest bearing liabilities including accounts payable stands at about 60% of totals, indicating that it finances free capital through operating activities for its business. Its shareholders' equity is only 0.4%, associated with total liabilities which exceeds 99%. Yet, Boeing does not rely much on (interest bearing) debts. Instead it utilizes funds generated by the operation wisely to run the business consistently. Since only minimal shareholders' equity is necessary, Boeing seems to return its excess cash to investors generously, resulting in large amounts of treasury stocks (a negative figure in shareholders' equity).

Pfizer is also actively paying out cash to shareholders by repurchasing its own shares, recognizing more than (negative) 50% treasury stock. However, it still has more than 40% shareholders' equity because of sufficient retained earnings backed by its extremely high profitability.

Figure 3.5 | Common-size Balance Sheet (Credit)

	Pfizer		The Boeing Company		Walmart Stores	
Short-term borrowing	5.8%	9,953	1.4%	1,335	4.7%	9,662
Others (non interest bearing liabilities)	11.9%	20,474	59.5%	54,934	33.7%	68,859
Total current liabilities	17.7%	30,427	60.9%	56,269	38.4%	78,521
Long-term debt	30.4%	52,235	10.6%	9,782	18.0%	36,825
Others	10.4%	17,827	28.1%	25,927	5.5%	11,307
Total long-term liabilities	40.8%	70,062	38.7%	35,709	23.5%	48,132
Common stock, capital surplus, retained earnings	99.0%	170,054	61.9%	57,185	43.1%	88,050
Treasury stock	-52.1%	-89,425	-47.1%	-43,454	0.0%	0
Other stockholder equity	-5.4%	-9,321	-14.5%	-13,376	-5.0%	-10,181
Shareholders' equity	41.5%	71,308	0.4%	355	38.1%	77,869
Total	100.0%	171,797	100.0%	92,333	100.0%	204,522

Fiscal year ended in Dec 2017 for Pfizer and Boeing, Jan 2018 for Walmart. In million dollars.

ボーイングの負債・純資産の情報は興味深い。買掛金等を含む短期の無利子負債の比率が約 60% となっており，営業活動を通じて利子の発生しない資金調達によって事業を行っていることがわかる。負債の合計比率は 99% を超えており株主資本は 0.4% しかない。かといって有利子負債をそれほど活用しているわけではなく，あくまで営業活動の中での資金をうまくまわしつつ事業を継続させているのである。そのため株主資本がそれほど必要とはならず，多額の自己株式の（マイナスの）比率からもわかるように，不要な資金は積極的に株主に還元しているようである。

ファイザーの自己株式もマイナス 50% を超えており多くの自己株式取得により株主還元を行っていることが表われている。しかしながら，極めて高い利益率を背景に多くの剰余金が積み上がっているため，株主資本は 40% を超えている。

図表 3.5 ┃ 標準化貸借対照表（貸方）

	ファイザー		ボーイング		ウォルマート	
短期借入金	5.8%	9,953	1.4%	1,335	4.7%	9,662
その他無利子負債	11.9%	20,474	59.5%	54,934	33.7%	68,859
流動負債	17.7%	30,427	60.9%	56,269	38.4%	78,521
長期借入金	30.4%	52,235	10.6%	9,782	18.0%	36,825
その他負債	10.4%	17,827	28.1%	25,927	5.5%	11,307
固定負債	40.8%	70,062	38.7%	35,709	23.5%	48,132
資本金，資本準備金，剰余金	99.0%	170,054	61.9%	57,185	43.1%	88,050
自己株式	-52.1%	-89,425	-47.1%	-43,454	0.0%	0
その他株主資本	-5.4%	-9,321	-14.5%	-13,376	-5.0%	-10,181
株主資本	41.5%	71,308	0.4%	355	38.1%	77,869
株主資本および負債合計	100.0%	171,797	100.0%	92,333	100.0%	204,522

決算期：ファイザーとボーイングは 2017 年 12 月，ウォルマート 2018 年 1 月，単位：百万ドル

Combination of Income Statement and Balance Sheet

So far, we have seen the income statements and balance sheet separately. Finally, we will see them at the same time. Asset turnover of Pfizer, Boeing and Walmart are calculated as sales divided by total assets, and turned out to be, 0.31, 1.01, and 2.45, respectively. Those numbers show how efficiently companies use assets to generate sales. While sales of Pfizer represent only one third of total assets, sales and total assets of Boeing are similar. Sales of Walmart are about 2.5 times their total assets. Even if the profitability is less-attractive, Walmart seems to use the assets efficiently to produce sales and profits.

Figure 3.6 | Asset Turnover

	Pfizer	The Boeing Company	Walmart Stores
Sales/Total Assets	0.31	1.01	2.45

Expressing the income statement and balance sheet via ratios as well as absolute values provide insights with regard to the characteristics and the earning structure of a business. Business models vary by industry, and the differences are reflected in financial statements.

◉ 損益計算書と貸借対照表の組み合わせ

これまで貸借対照表と損益計算書を別々に見てきたが，最後にこの2つの表を同時に見てみよう。売上高を総資産で割って総資産回転率を計算すると，ファイザーは0.31，ボーイングが1.01，ウォルマートは2.45である。この数値は売上を生み出すために資産をどれだけ効率的に活用しているのかを示している。ファイザーの売上は資産の3分の1でしかないのに対して，ボーイングは総資産と売上の額がほぼ同じ水準である。また，ウォルマートの売上は資産の約2.5倍になっており，利益率は他社に比べて低いものの，使っている資産を効率的に売上，利益に変えていることが示されている。

図表 3.6 ┃ 総資産回転率

	ファイザー	ボーイング	ウォルマート
総資産回転率	0.31	1.01	2.45

このように，損益計算書と貸借対照表を絶対額だけではなく比率で表わすことにより，事業の特徴や儲け方に関する洞察を得ることができる。産業によってビジネスモデルは異なり，それらは財務諸表に反映されるのである。

Chapter 4
Analyzing Financial Performance 2: Various Financial Measures

> **Points!**
> ✓ There are a number of measures to show the financial performance of a company with respect to growth, efficiency and stability
> ✓ The measures used for valuation; NOPAT, capital and FCF are converted from accounting figures

● Basic Financial Measures

This chapter covers various representative measures. Let us review some figures in financial statements. **Sales** shows the size of business run by a company. **Total assets** expresses how much assets a company owns. **Net income** is the bottom line accounting profit generated by a company.

There are also important figures in cash flow statement. **Cash flow from operating activities or operating cash flow** shows how much cash is generated by its operation. **Cash flow from investing activities or investing cash flow** shows how much cash is spent on tangible and intangible assets such as properties and equipment as well as financial assets. **Cash flow from financing activities or financing cash flow** shows how much cash is raised from capital providers and how much cash is paid out to capital providers, and contains the amount due to share issuance, borrowing, dividend payments and share repurchase. All cash inflows are entered with positive figures and all cash outflows are entered with negative figures in cash flow statements. For example, a capital investment and dividend payments are recorded negatively, while sales proceed of assets and additional borrowing are recorded positively.

_第4_章 財務業績の分析2：数々の財務数値

ポイント！

✔ 企業の業績を示す財務数値には，成長，効率，安全性などを表わすさまざまな指標がある
✔ 企業価値評価のためには，会計上の数値に修正を加えた NOPAT や投下資本，および FCF といった数値を用いる

● 基本的な財務数値

本章では，注目すべき数値を1つひとつ取り上げていく。まずは単純な財務諸表上の数字の復習から始めよう。**売上高**は企業の商売の規模を示す数値である。**総資産**は企業が保有している資産の額を表わす。そして**当期純利益**は企業が生み出した最終的な会計上の利益を表わしている。

次にキャッシュフロー計算書上の数値を取り上げよう。**営業活動からのキャッシュフロー（営業 CF）**は事業を行うことによって生み出された現金の額を表わす数値である。**投資活動からのキャッシュフロー（投資 CF）**は設備，備品などの有形・無形の資産や金融資産等に投じられた資金の額を表わしている。**財務活動からのキャッシュフロー（財務 CF）**は企業が資金をどれだけ調達し，還元したのかを表わす数値であり，増資額，借入額，および配当の支払い額や自社株買いの購入額が含まれる。キャッシュフロー計算書上では企業にキャッシュが入ってくる場合はすべてプラスで，キャッシュが出ていく場合にはすべてマイナスで記入を行う。そのため設備投資額や配当の支払いはマイナス，資産の売却額や追加的な借り入れはプラスで記録される。

第4章　財務業績の分析2：数々の財務数値　　65

Figure 4.1 | Basic Financial Measures

Measure	Means
Sales	Size of business
Total Assets	Size of assets owned
Net Income	Bottom line accounting profit
Operating Cash Flow	Cash generated by operation
Investing Cash Flow	Cash invested in assets
Financing Cash Flow	Cash raised from and paid out to capital providers

● Measures Regarding Growth and Efficiency

Financial measures to show growth and efficiency are likely expressed as a percentage. **Sales growth** (rate) explains how much a business expands over a period.

Sales growth is a crucial figure because it will be one of the first items to be projected when you forecast the future performance of a business.

ROA (Return on Assets) and **ROE (Return on Equity)** combines the income statement and balance sheet. ROA is calculated as profits divided by total assets, and ROE is calculated as profits divided by shareholders' equity.

ROA uses total assets as the denominator and thus measures how efficiently the total amount of assets are used to generate returns for the company. On the other hand, ROE tells us how much return is created from the capital provided by shareholders. They are profitability ratios that reveal the efficiency of business operations in generating profits relative to the amount of capital employed in the business. Note, if ROA is the same, a company utilizing more debt and less equity can increase ROE because assets consist of debt and equity.

66   Chapter 4   Analyzing Financial Performance 2: Various Financial Measures

図表 4.1 ▎基本的な財務数値

指標	意味
売上高	商売の規模
総資産	保有する資産規模
当期純利益	最終的な会計上の利益
営業 CF	事業活動から生み出された現金
投資 CF	資金の投資額
財務 CF	資金の調達，または還元額

● 成長と効率を表わす財務数値

　成長や効率を表わす財務数値は通常％の形で表わされることが多い。**売上成長率**は事業が一定期間においてどれだけ拡大・伸張したのかを示すものである。

　売上成長率は将来の業績を予測する際に通常最初に検討する項目であり，非常に重要な数値となる。

　ROA（総資産利益率・総資本利益率）や，ROE（株主資本利益率）は P/L と B/S を統合した数値である。ROA は利益を総資産で割ることで求められ，ROE は利益を株主資本で割ることによって求められる。

　ROA は分母に総資産をとるため，企業の使用しているすべての資産がどれだけのリターンを生み出しているのかを示し，一方で ROE は，株主から調達した資本がどれだけのリターンを生み出しているのかを示す。これらの指標はどれだけの資本（お金）を使って，どれだけの利益を上げているのかという事業活動の効率性を表わす利益率指標である。なお，総資産は負債と株主資本とによって構成されるから，同じ ROA であれば，少ない株主資本でより多くの負債を活用する企業ほど ROE は高まることになる。

第 4 章　財務業績の分析 2：数々の財務数値　　**67**

Figure 4.2 | **Measures Regarding Growth and Efficiency**

Measure	Formula	Means
Sales Growth	$\dfrac{\text{Current Sales} - \text{Previous Sales}}{\text{Previous Sales}}$ $= \dfrac{\text{Current Sales}}{\text{Previous Sales}} - 1$	How much a business expand over the period
ROA	$\dfrac{\text{Profit}}{\text{Assets}}$	Profitability of all assets
ROE	$\dfrac{\text{Profit}}{\text{Equity}}$	Profitability of shareholder's equity

The profit measure used in the ROA calculation often varies depending on the objective. Commonly used profit measures include operating profit and net income. Net income is most commonly used for ROE calculations. The total assets or shareholders' equity should be fundamentally based on a beginning balance, but the average of beginning and ending balance or simply ending balances are frequently used to calculate ROA and ROE in practice.

● Measures Regarding Debt Usage and Financial Health

There are dozens of measures to assess the financial stability of a company focusing on how much it relies on debt or liabilities. However, classic measures introduced in a traditional financial textbook such as current ratio, quick ratio, and accounting-based equity ratio are not commonly used in the valuation context.

We will now discuss the limited number of financial measures to overview financial stability of a company. **The total liabilities to total assets ratio** simply shows how much liabilities are utilized among total assets. The high ratio might indicate the potential solvency problem of a company in the future.

The total amount of interest bearing debt (short-term and long-term debt)

図表 4.2 ┃ 成長と効率を表わす財務数値

指標	計算式	意味
売上成長率	$\dfrac{当期売上高 - 前期売上高}{前期売上高}$ $= \dfrac{当期売上高}{前期売上高} - 1$	企業・事業がどれだけ拡大・伸張したのか
ROA	$\dfrac{利益}{総資産}$	企業が使用するすべての資産の利益率
ROE	$\dfrac{利益}{株主資本}$	株主から調達した資本の利益率

　ROA の分子にどの利益を使用するのかは，その目的によって異なり，画一的ではない。場合に応じて，営業利益，当期純利益，あるいはその他の指標が使われる。ROE の分子には当期純利益が使用されることがほとんどである。また，分母の総資産あるいは株主資本は，本来的にはその期の初め（期首）の数値を使うべきであるが，実務においては期首と期末の平均値（期中平均）や期末の値が使用されることが多い。

◉ 負債の活用と安全性を表わす財務数値

　企業がどれだけ負債を使っているのかを目安にして企業の財務上の安全性を評価する財務数値には数多くのものがある。しかしながら，流動比率，当座比率，あるいは自己資本比率などといった伝統的な財務分析の教科書などで紹介されている指標は，企業価値評価の際にはあまり使用されることがない。

　ここでは企業の安全性を概観するに十分な指標のみを紹介する。1つ目が**負債総資産比率**である。負債総資産比率は企業が総資産のうちどれだけ負債を活用しているのかを表わす健全性指標である。この数値が高すぎると潜在的な支払い能力に関する危険性が示唆されることになる。

　次に，短期と長期の**有利子負債**の合計額は企業の全体的な財務状況を示して

第 4 章　財務業績の分析 2 : 数々の財務数値　　69

provides information about overall financial position of a company. The figure subtracting cash and cash equivalent, and financial investments from debt is called **net debt**. Net debt demonstrates solvency of a company if all debt it owes mature simultaneously. A company with a large debt but having huge cash in hand in the meantime can generally be considered a favorable financial condition even if it faces a downturn in business.

It is difficult to judge whether long term financial assets are incorporated in the calculation of net debt (subtracting from debt) or not. If you can apply long term financial assets for debt service, then you should subtract it from debt to get net debt. Though, it is usually impossible to know from outside a company.

Figure 4.3 | Measures Regarding Debt Usage and Financial Health

Measure	Formula	Means
Total Liabilities to Total Assets Ratio	$\dfrac{\text{Total Liabilities}}{\text{Total Assets}}$	How much liabilities are utilized among total assets
Debt	Short-term Interest Bearing Debt + Long-term Interest Bearing Debt	Amount of debt capital
Net Debt	Debt − Cash and Financial Assets	Debt taking into account financial assets in hand

70   Chapter 4   Analyzing Financial Performance 2: Various Financial Measures

いる。この額から現金および現金同等物さらに短期長期の金融資産を差し引いた数値を**純有利子負債**と呼ぶ。この数値は，有利子負債の支払期限がすべて同時に来た際の，それに対する企業の支払い能力を示すものである。仮に企業が多くの有利子負債を抱えているとしても，一方で多くの現金を所有していれば，業績が悪化した場合でも良好な財務状態を保つことができると一般的には考えられる。

　なお，固定資産に分類される金融資産を純有利子負債の計算に含めるのか（負債額から控除するのか）どうかは微妙な判断となる。長期的な金融資産への投資が負債の返済に充当できるのかどうかが判断の分かれ目となるが，外部からそれを正確に判断することは難しいからである。

図表 4.3 ▎負債の活用と安全性を表わす財務数値

指標	計算式	意味
負債総資産比率	$$\dfrac{負債}{総資産}$$	資産のうちどれだけを負債でまかなっているか
有利子負債	短期有利子負債＋長期有利子負債	負債の額
純有利子負債	有利子負債－金融資産	金融資産を考慮した後の正味の負債の額

第4章　財務業績の分析2：数々の財務数値　　71

● Financial Analysis Example for Nike ①

Let us take a brief look at Nike's performance using financial measures discussed above. Figure 4.4 is the summarized income statement of Nike. Nike has been steadily increasing sales in recent years, but the increase of expenses was faster than sales in 2018, resulting in the decline of operating profit. Moreover, the net income in 2018 fell significantly due to a one-time tax burden on foreign earnings.

Figure 4.4 | Income Statement of Nike

	2014	2015	2016	2017	2018
Sales	**27,799**	**30,601**	**32,376**	**34,350**	**36,397**
− Cost of Sales	15,353	16,534	17,405	19,038	20,441
− Selling, General, Admin. Expenses	8,766	9,892	10,469	10,563	11,511
= **Operating Profit**	**3,680**	**4,175**	**4,502**	**4,749**	**4,445**
Income Before Tax	**3,544**	**4,205**	**4,623**	**4,886**	**4,325**
− Tax	805	932	863	646	2,392
= **Net Income**	**2,739**	**3,273**	**3,760**	**4,240**	**1,933**

Fiscal year ending in May. In million dollars.

Figure 4.5 shows operating cash flow increased in 2018 despite the decreased operating profit. Meanwhile, financing cash flow was significantly negative, because Nike returned a lot of its cash to investors via increased dividend payments and share repurchases. Focusing on financial position, total liabilities to total assets ratio has had an uptrend for the past years, yet Nike's net debt is still negative, indicating a strong financial position to distribute a lot of cash to investors in the period when profit declines.

● 財務分析例：ナイキ①

　ここまで紹介してきた財務数値を使用してナイキの業績を概観してみよう。図表4.4はナイキの損益計算書の概要である。ここ数年売上は順調に増加して来ているが，2018年度は売上の増加よりもコストの増加のほうが多く，営業利益は減益となった。加えて，海外での利益に課された税金の影響で，一時的に税金負担が増えたことにより当期純利益は大きく減少した。

図表4.4 ┃ ナイキの損益計算書

	2014	2015	2016	2017	2018
売上高	**27,799**	**30,601**	**32,376**	**34,350**	**36,397**
− 原価	15,353	16,534	17,405	19,038	20,441
− 販管費	8,766	9,892	10,469	10,563	11,511
＝ 営業利益	**3,680**	**4,175**	**4,502**	**4,749**	**4,445**
税引前利益	**3,544**	**4,205**	**4,623**	**4,886**	**4,325**
− 税金	**805**	**932**	**863**	**646**	**2,392**
＝ 当期純利益	**2,739**	**3,273**	**3,760**	**4,240**	**1,933**

各年5月末に終了する年度の実績。単位：百万ドル

　図表4.5でキャッシュフローの状況を確認すると，2018年は，当期純利益が減少する一方で営業キャッシュフローは増加していることがわかる。また，財務キャッシュフローは大きなマイナスとなっており，これは配当と自社株買いによって多くの資金を投資家に還元した結果である。財務の健全性を見てみるとこの数年にわたり負債総資産比率は上昇傾向にあるが，依然として純有利子負債はマイナスであり，減益時に多くの株主還元を行ったとしても，財務の健全性は問題がないと考えられる。

第4章　財務業績の分析2：数々の財務数値　　73

Figure 4.5 | **Cash Flow and Financial Health of Nike**

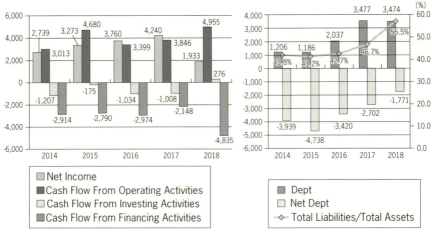

Fiscal year ending in May. In million dollars.

Figure 4.6 presents that although Nike increased sales, it's growth rate has declined from over 10% to 6%. ROE was increasing at a stable rate up until 2017 despite slowed sales growth, but drastically fell to lower than 20% in 2018 due to the reduction in income.

Figure 4.6 | **Sales Growth and ROE (right axis) of Nike**

Fiscal year ending in May.

74 | Chapter 4 Analyzing Financial Performance 2: Various Financial Measures

図表 4.5 ｜ ナイキのキャッシュフローと財務健全性

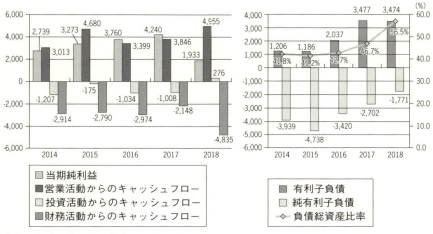

各年5月末に終了する年度の実績。単位：百万ドル

　次に，売上成長率と利益率を確認すると，図表4.6にあるように，売上成長はしているもののその率は10%台から6%まで低下していることがわかる。ROEは売上成長が鈍化するなかでも，近年まで高い水準で上昇させてきたが，2018年度は減益を反映して20%以下まで低下した。

図表 4.6 ｜ ナイキの売上成長率とROE（右軸）

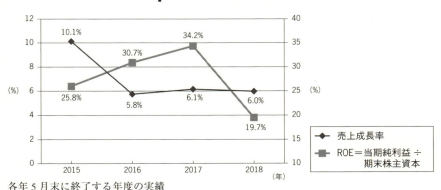

各年5月末に終了する年度の実績

第4章　財務業績の分析2：数々の財務数値　　75

Measures for Valuation

The measures used for valuation are commonly obtained from accounting figures with some adjustments. The **net operating profit after tax, or NOPAT** is calculated by multipling operating profit by (1 − effective tax rate).

Capital represents the amount of capital invested for operating activities among total assets or the total of liabilities and shareholders' equity. The accounting balance sheet includes accounts payables as a non-interest bearing liability, but accounts payable is accrued through daily operating activities, not capital invested in operation. Therefore, accounts payable does not constitute a part of capital and is deducted from capital.

There are two ways of calculating capital. Capital consists of short-term and long-term interest bearing debt and shareholders' equity when you focus on the right side of a balance sheet, and working capital net of accounts payables and fixed assets when you focus on the left side of a balance sheet. The working capital is constantly changing its components, unlike fixed assets. Accounts receivable and inventories, less accounts payables comprises working capital, which is also referred to as net working capital because accounts payable is netted out.

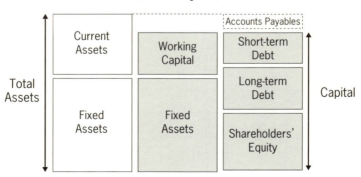

Figure 4.7 | **Capital**

● 企業価値評価のための財務数値

　企業価値評価のための数値は会計上の数値に若干の修正を加えるのが一般的である。NOPAT は営業利益から税金を差し引いた税引後の営業利益のことであり，営業利益に（1－実効税率）を掛けて計算する。

　投下資本は総資産，負債・株主資本のうち，営業・事業活動に行うにあたり企業が投下している資本である。会計上の貸借対照表には無利子負債である買掛金が含まれるが，買掛金は企業が営業活動を行うにあたって投下した資金ではなく，営業活動を行っている中で日常的に発生してくるものである。そのため，事業活動に投下されている資本とはいえず，投下資本の計算上取り除かれる。

　投下資本は貸借対照表の右側（負債・資本サイド）からみると短期・長期の有利子負債と株主資本となり，左側（資産サイド）からみると無利子負債を差し引いた運転資本と固定資産で構成される。運転資本は，設備などの固定資産と異なり，常に中身が入れ替わっている資本である。運転資本は売掛金などの売掛債権と棚卸資産（在庫）の合計と，買掛金に代表される買掛債務の差として表わされ，買掛債務を差し引いていることから正味運転資本とも呼ばれる。

図表 4.7　┃　投下資本

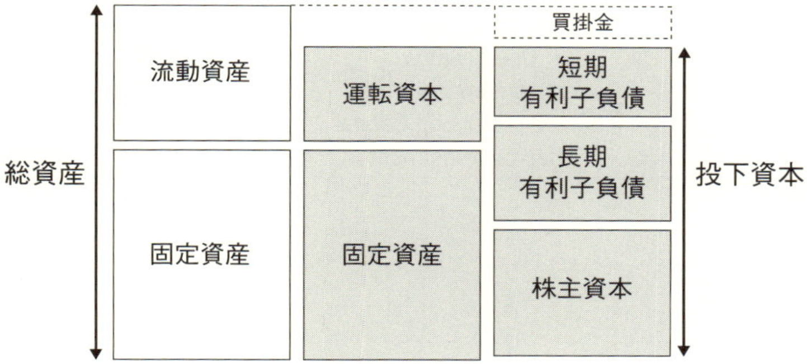

第 4 章　財務業績の分析 2：数々の財務数値　　77

The reserve accounts such as retirement benefit obligations can be regarded as a part of interest bearing debts. However, you should handle the estimate of capital consistently with NOPAT calculation. If reserves are deducted as expenses to calculate NOPAT, the reserves are considered outflowed from a company and does not constitute capital. If they are not deducted from NOPAT, then the reserves stay in a company and are considered invested for the operation. It will be simplest to recognize reserves as expenses for NOPAT calculation (same as accounting treatment) and subtract them from capital. This treatment allows only interest bearing debts and shareholders' equity to comprise capital.

The change in capital from the beginning to the end of the period expresses **net investment**. As a company invests more, capital increases, and as it reduces an investment, capital decreases.

Figure 4.8 | Measures for Valuation

Measure	Formula	Means
NOPAT	Operating Profit × (1 − Effective tax rate)	After tax operating profit
Capital	Debt + Shareholders' Equity = Net Working Capital + Fixed Assets	Capital invested for operating activities
Net Investment	Ending Capital − Beginning Capital	Increase in investment
FCF	NOPAT − Net Investment = NOPAT + Depreciation − Capital Investment − Increase in Working Capital = OCF − Capital Investment	Cash generated by operation and remained after the necessary investments

なお，退職給付債務などの固定負債の一部である引当金は有利子負債とみなされる場合もある。気を付けるべきことは，投下資本の計算は NOPAT の計算と整合していなければならないということである。NOPAT の計算の際に費用として計上されているのであれば，その費用はすでに流出しているものであり，企業の使用している投下資本を構成しない。もし NOPAT の計算上費用として計上されていないのであれば，その分は企業の中にとどまっており，後の事業活動を行うための資本として投下されていることになる。最もシンプルな取扱いは，NOPAT の計算上は引当金をコストとして認識し（会計上の取扱いと同じ），投下資本からは除くことである。これにより投下資本は有利子負債と株主資本のみとなる。

　期首（前期末）から期末にかけた投下資本の変化額が**純投資額**である。多くの投資を行えば投下資本は増加し，投資を減らしたら投下資本は減少する。

図表 4.8 ┃ 企業価値評価のための財務数値

指標	計算式	意味
NOPAT	営業利益×（1 − 実効税率）	税引後の営業利益
投下資本	有利子負債＋株主資本 ＝ 正味運転資本 ＋ 固定資産	営業・事業活動に行うにあたり企業が投下している資本
純投資額	期末の投下資本－期首の投下資本	どれだけ投資を行ったのか，投資額の増加分
FCF	NOPAT － 純投資額 ＝ NOPAT ＋ 減価償却費 　　－ 設備投資額 　　－ 運転資本増額 ＝ 営業 CF － 設備投資額	営業・事業活動を通じて企業が生み出し，必要な投資を行った後の残ったキャッシュ

第 4 章　財務業績の分析 2：数々の財務数値　　79

When you estimate the value of a company, **free cash flow (FCF)** is often used to gauge the cash flow generated by a company. FCF is the cash flow that remains in the company after taking into account the cash required for investment over a period of time, and is calculated by subtracting net investment from NOPAT. This can be disintegrated as follows:

FCF = NOPAT + Depreciation − Capital Investment − Increase in Working Capital

Depreciation expense is a fraction of the cost of fixed assets, such as property or plant, distributed over the life of the asset. Although depreciation expense is allocated across the life of the asset, cash outflows do not actually occur at each point in time; rather, a lump sum cash payment is assumed when the asset is purchased. Depreciation expense is deducted to derive operating profit, therefore, it will be added back to profit to obtain cash flow.

An increase in working capital means more capital tied up in business operations, thus requiring additional cash. In short, the increase in working capital has a negative impact on cash flow, and the decrease in working capital has a positive impact on cash flow.

Profit after tax and depreciation less the increase in working capital is classified as cash flow from operating activities, or operating cash flow (OCF). FCF can be calculated as subtracting capital investment from operating cash flow.

The present value of future FCF determines the value of an investment or of a company.

企業価値を評価する際には，企業が生み出すキャッシュフローとしてフリー・キャッシュフロー（FCF）が用いられる。FCF は一期間において生み出された，企業が必要な投資を行った後の残余的なキャッシュであり，NOPAT から純投資額を差し引いて計算される。これをもう少し細かくすると以下のように表わせる。

$$FCF = NOPAT + 減価償却費 - 設備投資額 - 運転資本増額$$

　減価償却費は，工場や設備などの有形固定資産に関する費用を，それが使用できる各期間に配分したものである。減価償却費は会計上の費用であるが，その期において現金の支出があるわけではない。現金支出はすでに設備の購入時点（設備投資時点）で発生しているからである。営業利益算出の際には，減価償却費は費用の一部として差し引かれているため，キャッシュフローを計算する際には，利益に減価償却費を足し戻す必要がある。

　また，キャッシュフローを計算するためには，運転資本の増加額も差し引く必要がある。運転資本は営業活動に必要な資金であり，運転資本の増加は追加的な資金の投入を意味する。したがって，運転資本の増加はキャッシュフローにマイナスの影響を，減少はキャッシュフローにプラスの影響を与える。

　運転資本の増減と減価償却費は税引後利益とあわせ，営業活動からのキャッシュフロー（営業 CF）とも整理されることから，FCF は営業 CF から設備投資額を差し引いても計算できる。

　将来の FCF の現時点における価値が，投資や企業の価値を決定する。

第 4 章　財務業績の分析 2：数々の財務数値　　81

Other Variables Influencing Value

There are some important variables that influence the value of a company to be covered.

Return on Capital or ROC, (or return on invested capital or ROIC) is calculated by dividing NOPAT by capital, showing the pure profitability of operating activities. The beginning capital is commonly used to calculate ROC.

Investment rate (I%) expresses how much NOPAT is utilized for the investment in operation once again. Investment rate is calculated by dividing net investment by NOPAT.

The Weighted Average Cost of Capital, or WACC is the rate of return expected by investors on the capital provided to the company, and the weighted average of a cost of debt and equity according to the capital structure. WACC is the appropriate discount rate to calculate the present value of future value or FCF. WACC will be discussed in detail in the next chapter.

Figure 4.9 | Other Variables Influencing Value

Measure	Formula	Mean
ROC	$\dfrac{\text{NOPAT}}{\text{(Beginning) Capital}}$	Profitability of operation
Investment rate(I%)	$\dfrac{\text{Net Investment}}{\text{NOPAT}}$	How much profit is reinvested
WACC	$\dfrac{\text{Debt}}{\text{Company Value}} \times (1 - \text{Tax Rate}) \times \text{Cost of Debt}$ $+ \dfrac{\text{Equity}}{\text{Company Value}} \times \text{Cost of Equity}$	Expected return on company, discount rate to get present value
(Sustainable) Growth rate	$\dfrac{\text{Current NOPAT (FCF)} - \text{Previous NOPAT (FCF)}}{\text{Previous NOPAT (FCF)}}$ $= \dfrac{\text{Current NOPAT (FCF)}}{\text{Previous NOPAT (FCF)}} - 1$ $\text{I\% } \times \text{ROC}$	Increases of NOPAT and FCF

82   Chapter 4   Analyzing Financial Performance 2: Various Financial Measures

● 企業価値に影響を与える変数

企業の価値に影響を与える重要な変数があるため，それらの数値もカバーしておこう。

投下資本利益率（ROC または ROIC）は NOPAT を投下資本で割った数値であり，営業・事業活動の純粋な利益率を表わす指標である。投下資本は通常は期首の値が使用される。

再投資率（I%）とは生み出された利益である NOPAT のうち，どれだけが事業に再度投資されているのかを表わしている。再投資率は純投資額を NOPAT で割ることにより計算される。

加重平均資本コスト（WACC）は投資家が企業に投資を行う際に期待するリターンの率であり，負債コストと株主資本コストを資本構成によって加重平均した数値である。WACC は将来の価値・FCF などを割り引く適切な割引率である。これについては次章でさらに詳しく議論する。

図表 4.9 ┃ 企業価値に影響を与える変数

指標	計算式	意味
ROC	$$\dfrac{\text{NOPAT}}{\text{（期首）投下資本}}$$	営業・事業活動の利益率
再投資率 (I%)	$$\dfrac{\text{純投資額}}{\text{NOPAT}}$$	NOPAT がどれだけ事業に再投資されるか
WACC	$$\dfrac{\text{負債}}{\text{企業価値}} \times (1-\text{税率}) \times \text{負債コスト}$$ $$+ \dfrac{\text{株主資本}}{\text{企業価値}} \times \text{株主資本コスト}$$	投資家の期待リターン，現在価値を計算するための割引率
（サステイナブル）成長率	$$\dfrac{\text{当期 NOPAT (FCF)} - \text{前期 NOPAT (FCF)}}{\text{前期 NOPAT (FCF)}}$$ $$= \dfrac{\text{当期 NOPAT (FCF)}}{\text{前期 NOPAT (FCF)}} - 1$$ $$\text{I\% } \times \text{ROC}$$	NOPAT，FCF がどれだけ増加するか

第 4 章 財務業績の分析 2：数々の財務数値

Growth rate (g) is the percentage increases of NOPAT and FCF. Note that if investment rate is constant in the future, the growth rate of NOPAT must be always equal to the growth rate of FCF. A growth rate can be calculated by multiplying an investment rate by ROC (g = I%×ROC). This relationship indicates the portion of additional investments out of the profit and the return of the investments determine the profit growth of a company. This rate is also called "sustainable growth rate" because it relies solely on internally produced and retained earnings and does not rely on an additional funds from outside.

⬤ Supplementary Note: EBITDA

EBITDA, or Earnings Before Interest Taxes Depreciation and Amortization is calculated as adding interest expenses, depreciations and amortizations to profit before tax. EBITDA can be explained as the figure adding depreciations to operating profit. Therefore, it is a simplified proxy for operating cash flow, neglecting the effect of the change in working capital.

EBITDA compares companies in different regions because it eliminates the effects of interest rates and tax rates which vary by country. The effect of different treatment of depreciation expenses based on accounting regulations is also eliminated. More recently there has been a big discussion about depreciation for goodwill which emerges as a balance amount between the price paid to acquire another company and its book value, but EBITDA is insulated from that type of debate.

Figure 4.10 ▎ EBITDA

Measure	Formula	Mean
EBITDA	Profit Before Tax + Interest Expenses + Depreciations and Amortizations	Simplified OCF neglecting the change in working capital

成長率（g）は企業の生み出す NOPAT や FCF が増える率である。もし再投資率が将来において一定であるならば，NOPAT の成長率 は常に FCF の成長率と一致することになる。また，成長率は再投資率と ROC を掛け合わせることでも計算できる（g = I% × ROC）。この関係は企業が利益のうち追加的に投資をする割合と，その投資額が生み出すリターンが企業の利益成長を決めることを表わしている。なお，この成長率は，外部からの資金調達に頼っておらず，内部で創出する利益によって可能な成長であるため，「サステイナブル成長率」とも呼ばれる。

◉ 補足：EBITDA

EBITDA（利払前・税引前・減価償却前・その他償却前利益）は，税引前利益に支払利息，固定資産の減価償却費を加えて求める。営業利益に減価償却費を加えた数値ともいえ，運転資本増減の影響を加味せず，簡易的に営業キャッシュフローを求めた指標と言うこともできる。

EBITDA は，異なる地域の企業を比較する際に，国ごとに異なる金利水準や税率の違いを取り除いた評価が可能になる。また，会計基準によって計上額が変わってくる減価償却費の影響も取り除かれている。特に最近では，会計上の取扱いとして，企業を買収した際に買収額と買収される会社の帳簿価格との差額として発生する「のれん」を償却すべきかどうかが常に大きな議論となっているが，EBITDA ではこの影響が排除できる。

図表 4.10 ┃ EBITDA

指標	計算式	意味
EBITDA	税引前利益＋支払利息＋減価償却費	運転資本増減の影響を加味しない簡易的な営業 CF

第 4 章　財務業績の分析 2：数々の財務数値　　85

Chapter 5 Estimating Cost of Capital

Points !

- ✓ WACC used as the discount rate in present value calculation consists of a cost of debt and a cost of equity
- ✓ A risk-free rate and the corresponding risk premium constitute both a cost of debt and equity, and they should be estimated appropriately

● Weighted Average Cost of Capital

The Weighted Average Cost of Capital, or WACC is the overall expected return on capital employed in the company and is used as the discount rate in present value calculation. WACC is determined by the cost of debt, the cost of equity, and the company's capital structure or the mix of debt and equity financing. Note that non-interest bearing liabilities such as accounts payables and reserves are not considered part of debt capital in a similar fashion to the definition of a capital.

$$\text{WACC} = \frac{D}{V} \times (1-T) r_d + \frac{E}{V} \times r_e$$

D: market value of debt
V: market value of company = D + E
r_d: cost of debt

E: market value of equity, market capitalization
T: effective corporate tax rate
r_e: cost of equity

Figure 5.1 | **Weighted Average Cost of Capital**

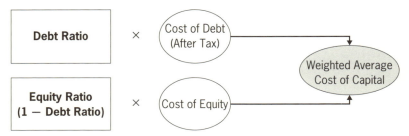

86 | Chapter 5 Estimating Cost of Capital

第5章 資本コストの推定

> **ポイント！**
> - 企業価値を算出する際に使用される加重平均資本コストは，負債コストと株主資本コストからなる
> - 負債コスト，株主資本コストともにリスクフリー・レートとリスク・プレミアムによって構成され，それぞれ適切な値を推定する必要がある

● 加重平均資本コスト

　加重平均資本コスト（WACC）は企業の資本全体にとっての利率であり期待リターンである。現在価値を算出する際の割引率として使用される。WACCは，負債コスト，株主資本コストと企業の資本構成によって決まる。資本構成とは企業の資本全体における負債，株主資本それぞれの割合のことである。なお，ここでの負債には投下資本の定義と同様に買掛金や引当金のような無利子の負債は含まない。

$$\text{WACC} = \frac{D}{V} \times (1-T)r_d + \frac{E}{V} \times r_e$$

D：負債の時価　　　　　　E：株式時価総額
V：企業の市場価値 = D + E　　T：法人実効税率
r_d：負債コスト　　　　　　r_e：株主資本コスト

図表 5.1 ｜ 加重平均資本コスト

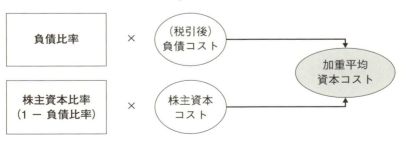

The capital structure for the WACC calculation should be based on the market value rather than the book value (the value on the balance sheet) because investors expect a return on the current value of their investment. The market value of equity is equal to the market capitalization, which is generally calculated as the share price multiplied by the number of outstanding shares. The market value of debt can be considered the same as the book value unless the company faces financial difficulty.

⊙ Cost of Debt

The cost of debt is the cost of interest-bearing liabilities such as bank borrowing and bonds. This corresponds to bank interest whenever a company borrows money from a bank. The more credit worthy a company is, the lower the interest rate, and vice versa. The cost of debt consists of the risk-free rate and a "credit risk premium" that is the extra return required according to the risk of default, or credit risk.

$$\text{Cost of Debt} = \text{Risk-free Rate} + \text{Credit Risk Premium}$$

The cost of debt is sometimes set based on the interest rate of existing debt. However, the marginal interest rate or the marginal cost of debt financing at that point should be estimated fundamentally because you use the cost of capital for an investment decision going forward.

The Risk-free Rate

The expected return on a riskless investment is called the "risk-free rate." In practice, the yield on government bonds with high liquidity is used as a proxy for the risk-free rate. Information about government bond yields is available in newspapers or websites like Bloomberg. Figure 5.2 summarizes 10-year government bond yields for major countries.

WACC の算出においては，資本構成は簿価（B/S 上の価格）ではなく時価を使用する。投資家が期待するリターンは現時点における価値に対するリターンだからである。株主資本の時価は，一般的に株価と流通株式数を掛け合わせた時価総額である。負債の時価は企業が倒産の危機に瀕しない限り簿価と同じと考えてよい。

● 負債コスト

負債コストは借入金・社債などの有利子負債にかかるコストである。通常お金を借りれば銀行金利のように利子が発生するが，それに相当するものである。負債コストは企業の信用力が高いほど低く，信用力が低いほど高くなる。負債コストはリスクフリー・レートと，信用リスクに応じたリターンの上乗せ分である「信用リスク・プレミアム」からなる。

負債コスト＝リスクフリー・レート＋信用リスク・プレミアム

負債コストの推定にあたっては，既存の負債の利子率を使用することも一般的には行われるが，投資の意思決定は今後に向けた意思決定であるため，本来的には，その時点で借り入れたら負債コストはいくらになるのかという「限界的な」利子率を使用すべきである。

リスクフリー・レート

リスクがない資産に期待されるリターンのことを「リスクフリー・レート」という。実務においてはリスクフリー・レートとして流動性の高い長期国債の利回りが使用される。利回りの情報は新聞やブルームバーグなどのホームページでも入手可能である。図表 5.2 は主要国の満期までの期間が 10 年の国債利回りをまとめている。

第 5 章　資本コストの推定　89

Figure 5.2 | **Yields on 10-year Government Bonds**

Americas		Europe		Asia Pacific	
United States	3.15%	United Kingdom	1.63%	Japan	0.13%
Canada	2.49%	Germany	0.49%	Australia	2.69%
Brazil	10.81%	France	0.85%	New Zealand	2.62%
Mexico	8.10%	Italy	3.55%	Hong Kong	2.38%
		Spain	1.66%	Singapore	2.54%
		Netherlands	0.60%	South Korea	2.40%
		Portugal	2.02%	India	7.97%
		Greece	4.36%	China	3.61%
		Switzerland	0.03%		

As of October 2018. Derived from:
https://www.bloomberg.com/markets/rates-bonds
https://tradingeconomics.com/china/government-bond-yield

For example, 10-year government bonds in the U.S. offer a return of 3.15% in October 2018, which is applied for the risk-free rate in the U.S. dollar. 0.13% which is the yield of 10-year Japanese government bonds, is used for the risk-free rate in Japanese yen.

The risk-free rate to calculate a cost of capital must be in the currency used to forecast future cash flows. That is, when you project future cash flows in U.S. dollars, the risk-free rate should be based in U.S. dollars, and when you project cash flows in Euros, the risk-free rate should be based in Euros.

Euro denominated government bonds are issued by each country using Euros in European regions with different yields. Figure 5.2 shows, for example, that the German 10-year government bonds offer a rate of 0.49%, while the Italian government bonds offer 3.55%. Since they are all in the same currency, the difference is attributed to the creditworthiness of a country or default risk of it. Considering a risk-free rate as the return on a riskless asset, the lowest rate on the German Euro bond is the most appropriate estimate of the risk-free rate in Euros.

図表 5.2 ┃ 各国の 10 年国債の利回り

アメリカ		ヨーロッパ		アジア・パシフィック	
米国	3.15%	英国	1.63%	日本	0.13%
カナダ	2.49%	ドイツ	0.49%	オーストラリア	2.69%
ブラジル	10.81%	フランス	0.85%	ニュージーランド	2.62%
メキシコ	8.10%	イタリア	3.55%	香港	2.38%
		スペイン	1.66%	シンガポール	2.54%
		オランダ	0.60%	韓国	2.40%
		ポルトガル	2.02%	インド	7.97%
		ギリシア	4.36%	中国	3.61%
		スイス	0.03%		

2018 年 10 月時点，ブルームバーグなどの以下のホームページのデータを著者加工
　https://www.bloomberg.com/markets/rates-bonds
　https://tradingeconomics.com/china/government-bond-yield

　たとえば 2018 年 10 月の米国の 10 年国債の利回りは 3.15% であり，これが米国ドル建てのリスクフリー・レートとして使われる。また，日本国債の利回りは 0.13% であり，日本円のリスクフリー・レートとして使用される。

　資本コストの推定に使用されるリスクフリー・レートは，キャッシュフローの予測に使用される通貨と一致していなければならない。つまりキャッシュフローの予測が米国ドル建てであるならばリスクフリー・レートは米国ドル建てであり，キャッシュフローの予測がユーロ建てであるならばリスクフリー・レートもユーロ建てである。
　ところでユーロ建ての国債はヨーロッパのユーロを使用する各国で発行されており，その利回りは国によって異なっている。たとえば，図表 5.2 では，ドイツ国債の利回りが 0.49% なのに対し，イタリア国債の利回りは 3.55% である。通貨が同一の国債の利回りの違いは，各国の信用力の違いを原因としている。リスクフリー・レートはリスクがない資産のリターンであるから，最も低いユーロ建ての国債を発行するドイツの国債の利回りがユーロ建てのリスクフリー・レートとしては最も適切な値であるといえる。

第 5 章　資本コストの推定　　91

Credit Risk Premium

The expected return or yield on corporate bonds depends on the creditworthiness of the company (issuer). The required yield on bonds issued by a reliable company is low, and by a less reliable company, high. It is less probable that a credit-worthy company will have difficulties in paying interest and principal. Lending money to such a company carries a low risk. Therefore, the expected return would be low. Providing money to less credit-worthy companies carries a higher risk and the expected return would be higher.

As rational investor requires a higher return on risky investments as compensation for taking more risk, the extra rate of return on a bond in addition to the risk-free rate is called a "credit risk premium".

Credit Rating

Debt ratings issued by credit rating agencies reflect the credit risk of a company. Credit ratings are measurements of the creditworthiness of a specific bond and its issuer and the certainty of interest and principal payments are depicted as letter grades.

Figure 5.3 summarizes the grades issued by the major credit rating agencies, Standard&Poors (S&P) and Moody's. The most credit-worthy companies would be rated AAA (triple-A, Aaa in Moody's). The second from the safest is AA (double-A), followed by A (single-A)

Figure 5.3 | **Credit Rating Agencies and Grades**

S&P	Moody's
AAA	Aaa
AA+	Aa1
AA	Aa2
AA−	Aa3
A+	A1
A	A2
A−	A3
BBB+	Baa1
BBB	Baa2
BBB−	Baa3
BB+	Ba1
BB	Ba2
BB−	Ba3
B+	B1
B	B2
B−	B3
CCC+	Caa1
CCC	Caa2
CCC−	Caa3
CC	Ca

信用リスク・プレミアム

　企業が発行する社債の利回りは，その企業の信用力によって変わる。信用力の高い企業に求められる利回りは低く，信用力の低い企業に求められる利回りは高い。信用力が高いということは，借りたお金の利子を払ったり，返済することに問題が生じる可能性が低いので，貸し手から見た場合リスクが低く，期待リターンが低くなるためである。一方で信用力が低いということはリスクが高いので，期待リターンは高くなる。

　リスクの高い資産に対しては，その代償としてより高いリターンを求めるということであり，債券に求められる上乗せ分のリターンは「信用リスク・プレミアム」と呼ばれる。

債券格付

　企業の信用リスクを表わしているのが国内外の格付機関によって付与された格付である。格付は債券，あるいはその債券の発行体である企業の信用力に対する評価の指標であり，債券の元本と利息支払いの確実性がアルファベットで表示されている。

　図表5.3では代表的な格付機関であるスタンダードアンドプアーズ（S&P）とムーディーズの格付の符号を表わしている。最も信用力が高く，債券が投資資産として安全だという企業の符号がAAA（トリプルA，Moody'sではAaa）である。その次に安全なのがAA（ダブルA）で，

図表 5.3 ┃ 格付機関と格付

スタンダード アンドプアーズ	ムーディーズ
AAA	Aaa
AA+	Aa1
AA	Aa2
AA−	Aa3
A+	A1
A	A2
A−	A3
BBB+	Baa1
BBB	Baa2
BBB−	Baa3
BB+	Ba1
BB	Ba2
BB−	Ba3
B+	B1
B	B2
B−	B3
CCC+	Caa1
CCC	Caa2
CCC−	Caa3
CC	Ca

第5章　資本コストの推定　93

and then BBB (triple-B). The credit risk premiums of higher grades are relatively low, with a AAA company's being the lowest. The companies with higher grades can be regarded as less risky, resulting in a lower expected return; consequently, they are able to finance debt at low interest rates.

A credit risk premium for each grade can be calculated as deducting the risk-free rate from the yield of bonds corresponding to the grade.

The Risk-free Rate for a Developing Country

Although a risk-free asset does not assume the possibility of default, not all nations are viewed as default-free. The yield of government bonds issued by countries with default risk is not regarded a risk-free rate and requires an adjustment. For example, in October 2018, the yield of the Indian government rupee bond was 7.97% (Figure 5.2). And Moody's rated Baa3 on the Indian government bond denominated in the local currency. Supposing that the credit risk premium of a 10-year bond with Baa3 rating was 2.5%, the risk-free rate in Indian rupee would be estimated as subtracting a presumed risk premium of 2.5% from a risky government bond yield of 7.97% to be 5.47%.

Tax Savings Effect of Debt

In order to estimate the WACC, one more adjustment to the cost of debt is required. Debt has a tax benefit because the associated interest expense is tax deductible, which lowers taxable income and results in reducing the tax payment.

The after tax cost of debt is estimated by incorporating a tax saving effect calculated as the before tax cost of debt consisting of a risk-free rate and a credit risk premium multiplied by (1 − tax rate). Here, it is advisable that you apply the tax rate a company will bear going forward. WACC is used to discount future value, and the cost of debt is a component of WACC. Therefore, the future tax rate rather than the rate in the past should be applied.

94 | Chapter 5 Estimating Cost of Capital

A（シングル A），BBB（トリプル B）と続く。上位の格付となる企業の信用リスク・プレミアムは低く，AAA 格の企業の信用リスク・プレミアムは最も小さいということになる。このような企業はリスクが小さいため，期待されるリターンが低くて済み，結果として低金利の資金調達が可能になる。

　各格付の信用リスク・プレミアムは各債券の利回りと，リスクフリー・レートの差として算出することができる。

発展途上国のリスクフリー・レート

　リスクフリーの資産は債務不履行を前提としていないが，すべての国の政府が債務不履行を起こさないとみなされているわけではない。そのような国が発行する国債の利回りはリスクフリー・レートとはいえず，そのため調整が必要となる。たとえば，2018 年 10 月末におけるインド政府が発行するルピー建ての 10 年物の国債の利回りは 7.97％であった（図表 5.2）。そして，ムーディーズはインドの自国通貨建ての国債に Baa3 の格付を付与している。仮に Baa3 格付をもつ 10 年物の債券の信用リスク・プレミアムが 2.5% であれば，インドルピー建てのリスクフリー・レートは，7.97% − 2.5% = 5.47% と計算して推定するのがより望ましい。

負債の節税効果

　企業の加重平均資本コストを算出する際には，負債コストにもう一段の調整が必要である。負債コストに該当する支払利息が，税金の計算上差し引かれ，課税対象となる税引前利益を小さくするため，支払う税金の額が少なくなるという「節税効果」があるためである。

　リスクフリー・レートに信用リスク・プレミアムを足し合わせて計算した税前の負債コストに（1 − 税率）を掛け合わせ，節税効果も反映させた税引後の負債コストとする。ここでの税率は今後法人が負担する税率を用いるのが望ましい。加重平均資本コストは将来価値を割り引くために使用され，負債コストはその構成要素となるため，過去の税率ではなく，将来に向けた税率を使用するのである。

第 5 章　資本コストの推定　　95

Cost of Equity

The cost of equity is most commonly estimated based on Capital Asset Pricing Model, or CAPM in practice. The theory founding CAPM and its detail are discussed in corporate finance textbooks (such as "A Bilingual Introduction to Corporate Finance"). We overview CAPM and examine composing elements of it in this book.

CAPM states that the risk premium on any security equals its beta times the market risk premium. The expected return on the security, namely the cost of equity, would be the risk premium plus the risk-free rate.

$$\text{Cost of Equity} = \text{Risk-free Rate (rf)} + \text{Risk Premium}$$
$$= \text{rf} + \text{Beta} \times \text{Market Risk Premium}$$

Market Risk Premium

The market risk premium is the average risk premium that investors demand for investing in the overall market. It depends on the degree of risk aversion of investors at that time (more risk averse investors require higher premium). The demographic change as well as change in attitudes toward risk (as right after financial crisis) can influence it. Therefore, it is not easy to estimate the market risk premium in practice.

The market risk premium is commonly estimated based on past data, measuring the historical difference between the return on the stock market index and the yield of government bonds. This approach assumes the extra return in the past will be expected in the future, but can have wide fluctuations depending on the time period when the data is analyzed. While the yield of government bond as a proxy for the risk-free rate is relatively stable over time, the stock market return is very volatile and can even be negative. Sometimes the results of your estimate are found to be unreasonable. For example, you might calculate a negative risk premium (meaning your compensation for taking risk is negative) which obviously makes no sense.

96　　Chapter 5　Estimating Cost of Capital

● 株主資本コスト

　株主資本コストは，通常 CAPM（Capital Asset Pricing Model，キャップエム）に基づき推定されるのが，実務において最も一般的である。CAPM の理論的な説明はファイナンスの専門書に譲り（たとえば『英語で学ぶコーポレートファイナンス入門』），ここでは CAPM の概要とその構成要素について議論する。

　CAPM は，証券のリスク・プレミアムは，ベータと市場リスク・プレミアムを掛け合わせたものだとする理論である。そして，証券の期待リターン，すなわち株主資本コストはこのリスク・プレミアムにリスクフリー・レートを加えたものとなる。

　　　株主資本コスト ＝リスクフリー・レート＋リスク・プレミアム
　　　　　　　　　　　＝リスクフリー・レート＋ベータ×市場リスク・プレミアム

市場リスク・プレミアム

　市場リスク・プレミアムは市場全体に投資した場合の平均的なリスク・プレミアムである。市場リスク・プレミアムは，その時点における投資家のリスク回避度合い（リスクを嫌う投資家はより高いプレミアムを求める）に依存する。そのため，投資家そのもの（人口構成など）が変化したり，金融危機が発生して投資家がリスクに対して敏感になったりする場合に変化するものと考えられる。そのため，市場リスク・プレミアムの推定は簡単ではないのが現実である。

　市場リスク・プレミアムを推定するアプローチで一般的なものは，過去のデータに基づくものである。過去の国債のリターンと株式市場インデックスのリターンの差を計算し，その実績値を使用するのである。このアプローチは過去の実際の超過リターンが今後も期待されるという前提に立っているが，過去データの期間によって大きく値が変動するという欠点がある。国債のリターンつまりリスクフリー・レートは時系列的にも比較的安定している一方で，株式市場全体のリターンは大きく変動し，しばしばマイナスになりうる。そのため，市場リスク・プレミアムの推定値は安定せず，またリスクを取った見返りがマイナスのプレミアムというナンセンスな分析結果となる場合もある。

第 5 章　資本コストの推定　　97

Other possible approaches include calculating the risk premium based on the current share price and forecasted future performance, or simply distributing a questionnaire asking investors opinion. Many analyses for the market risk premium have been conducted by academic researchers and practitioners, but none of them are conclusive. Having said that, we share the common view of the appropriate range of the market risk premium, which is between 4% and 6% in general.

Beta

Beta reflects the sensitivity of the return of an individual stock to the return of the overall market. In comparison to the overall market, the relative volatility, or the relative degree of risk for the individual stock, is depicted as beta.

The average beta of all stocks is 1.0 by definition. Some stocks are less affected than others by market fluctuations; such stocks would have a beta of less than 1.0. On the other hand, beta for companies that are significantly influenced by market movements would be greater than 1.0. Beta varies by industry.

Market Beta

The beta based on actual share price movements is called a market beta. A market beta is usually estimated with a statistical analysis called regression utilizing the stock return data of a company and the return of a stock market index. It is common to use 5 years of monthly return data (60months); however, sometimes weekly returns or a period of 36 months of returns are used. You can visit Yahoo!Finance or other websites where a beta is measured and presented, and a beta can also be calculated by taking advantage of spreadsheet software. The reference at the end of this chapter introduces a simple Excel-based file to calculate a beta.

A market beta has inherent faults. Firstly, beta can vary considerably depending on the time period analyzed. Secondly, an unlisted company and a business unit run by a company do not have available stock price data to calculate the beta. Thirdly, a market beta corresponds to the average risk of a company. Therefore, it is an irrelevant input to estimate the cost of capital when a company advances into

98   Chapter 5   Estimating Cost of Capital

現在の株価と将来の業績予想の推移から，リスク・プレミアムを逆算するというアプローチや，単純に投資家にアンケートを配布して回収するというアプローチもありうる。学者，実務家ともに多くの実証分析が行われているが，いずれも決定的な手法はない。しかし，一般的に市場リスク・プレミアムの水準としては 4 ～ 6% 程度というのが共通の認識となっている。

ベータ

　ベータは，市場全体のリターンに対する個別株式のリターンの感応度を表わす。市場全体と比較して，個別の株式リターンの相対的な変動性の大きさ，すなわち相対的なリスク量を示す数値である。

　すべての株式のベータの平均値は定義上 1.0 になる。市場の変動を受けにくい企業の株式のベータは 1 以下となる。一方で，市場の変動を大きく受ける企業のベータは 1 以上となる。ベータは産業によっても異なる。

市場ベータ

　実際の株価データから算出されるベータを市場ベータと呼ぶ。市場ベータは通常特定の企業の株式リターンと株式市場インデックスのリターンを統計分析の一手法である回帰分析を行うことによって求める。60 カ月の月次リターンが使用されることが多いが，場合によっては週次リターンが使用されたり，あるいは期間を 36 カ月にしたりということも行われる。Yahoo!Finance（英語サイト）などもベータを算出し提供しているのでそれらを確認してもいいが，表計算ソフトを活用すればベータは算出できる。本章末に株価データから市場ベータを算出する簡単なエクセルファイルを紹介している。

　市場ベータにはいくつかの問題がある。まずは，算出されるベータは使用するデータの期間によって大きく異なることも多いことである。また，そもそも企業が上場していない未公開企業や企業内における事業には株価データがないため，ベータは計算できない。さらに，市場ベータはその企業の平均的なリスクを表わすものと考えられるため，企業が既存のビジネスとは異なる事業に進

第 5 章　資本コストの推定　　99

a new field of business. Some devices are essential to deal with those problems. The approach referring to market beta for comparable companies (peer companies) to construct a beta, called bottom-up beta approach, will be introduced in the next paragraph.

Bottom-up Beta Based on Other Company's Beta

The analysis starts with estimates of peer companies' betas. You pick up several listed companies in the same industry sector, or running a similar business assuming equivalent level of risk, and calculate a beta for each.

A market beta contains not only a business risk but also a financial risk that emerge when a company utilizes debt. Debt amplifies profits, losses and shareholder return (positive as well as negative), resembling the effect of a lever, and so is referred to as leverage, financial leverage or debt leverage.

Excessive leverage is frequently the cause of crisis for companies. Leverage works well to generate more profits when a company achieves solid results but it can also wreak considerable damage when performance is poor. Leverage increases the volatility of a company's performance and increases the risk as well. The additional risk corresponds to financial risk.

Debt usage depends on companies. The component associated with business risk will be extracted from a market beta when financial risk is removed. This process is called "unlever", and the beta corresponding to only business risk is called "unlevered beta". Unlevered beta is the beta assuming the company has no debt (the beta of an all-equity company), and is considered to contain no financial risk.

Extracting Unlevered Beta

The departure point of unlevered beta calculation is an assumption that the total value of a company consists of the value of a company without debt and the value of the tax saving effects produced by debt usage, namely;

100 | Chapter 5   Estimating Cost of Capital

出する際の資本コストの推定には適切ではない。これらの問題を解決するためには工夫が必要であり，以下では，他社（比較類似企業）の市場ベータを活用してベータを構成する方法，ボトムアップ・ベータによるアプローチを紹介する。

他社のベータを使用したボトムアップ・ベータの推定

分析は比較類似企業のベータを推定することから始まる。同じ事業を営む会社や，ビジネスモデルが似ており，リスクが同等と考えられる上場企業をできれば複数社ピックアップし，市場ベータを求める。

市場ベータには事業としてのリスクだけではなく，各社が負債を活用することにより発生する財務リスクも含まれている。負債は企業があげる利益，損失また株主リターンを増幅させる効果があり，この効果はテコの原理に似ているためレバレッジ，財務レバレッジ，負債レバレッジ等と呼ばれる。

過度なレバレッジは企業の財務危機を引き起こすことがしばしばある。レバレッジは企業の業績が良好な時は，より大きな利益を生み出す効果がある。しかし企業の業績が悪いときには企業に大きなダメージを与えることになる。レバレッジは企業の業績の変動性を高め企業の業績に関するリスクを高めるのである。この追加分のリスクが財務リスクである。

企業によって負債の活用度合いは異なっている。財務リスクの要素を取り除くと，市場ベータの中から事業リスクに対応する部分のみが抽出される。このプロセスをアンレバーと呼び，事業リスクのみに相当するベータをアンレバード・ベータ（無負債ベータ）と呼ぶ。アンレバード・ベータは企業が無負債であると仮定した場合のベータであり，財務リスクが含まれていないと考える。

アンレバード・ベータの抽出

アンレバード・ベータの計算は，企業全体の価値は無負債の場合の企業価値と，負債活用によって発生する節税効果による価値によって成り立っているという前提を出発点とする。つまり以下のように表わせる。

第5章　資本コストの推定　　101

$$V_c = V_u + V_{tax}$$

V_c : company value
V_u : value of unlevered company
V_{tax}: value of tax savings effect

In addition, the total value of a company comprises debt and equity, therefore;

$$V_c = V_u + V_{tax} = D + E$$

D: debt
E: equity

The total risk of a company should equal the weighted average of risks attributed to each components of the value of a company, thus;

$$\beta_c = \frac{V_u}{V_u + V_{tax}} \beta_u + \frac{V_{tax}}{V_u + V_{tax}} \beta_{tax} = \frac{D}{D + E} \beta_d + \frac{D}{D + E} \beta_e$$

β_c : beta of company
β_u : beta of unlevered company
β_{tax} : beta of tax saving effect
β_d : beta of debt
β_e : beta of equity

Starting from the equation above, there are two representative methods to derive unlevered beta being subject to certain assumptions.

One assumption is that a debt ratio out of total value of a company will be constant into the future, and that it is consistent with the WACC calculation. Based on this assumption, the amount of debt and the magnitude of the tax savings in the future are determined by the value of the company; therefore, it is natural to assume that the risk of the tax saving and the risk of the business are identical.

In addition, if we boldly view the risk of debt as zero(I understand treating corporate debt as risk-free is a bold assumption, but could be acceptable in the case that a company is regarded healthy enough to avoid default.), unlevered beta can be

$$V_c = V_u + V_{tax}$$

V_c：企業価値
V_u：無負債の場合の企業価値
V_{tax}：節税効果の価値

また，企業価値は負債と株主資本の合計であるから以下となる。

$$V_c = V_u + V_{tax} = D + E$$

D：負債
E：株主資本

企業全体のリスクは企業価値を構成するそれぞれの要素に帰属するリスクの加重平均になるはずであるから，以下の式が成り立つ。

$$\beta_c = \frac{V_u}{V_u + V_{tax}} \beta_u + \frac{V_{tax}}{V_u + V_{tax}} \beta_{tax} = \frac{D}{D + E} \beta_d + \frac{D}{D + E} \beta_e$$

β_c：企業全体のベータ
β_u：無負債の場合のベータ
β_{tax}：節税効果のベータ
β_d：負債のベータ
β_e：株主資本のベータ

この式をベースにした代表的な2つのアンレバード・ベータの計算方法とその前提を紹介しよう。

1つ目の前提は，企業価値に対する負債の比率が将来的にも一定であるとの仮定であり，WACCの算出式とも整合するものである。この前提に基づけば，将来的な負債の額とそれに伴う節税効果を決定するのは企業価値なので，事業そのもののリスクと節税効果のリスクは同一と考えることができる。

さらに，負債のリスクをゼロとすると（これは企業の負債をリスクフリー資産とみなすという大胆な前提ではあるが，企業が債務不履行を起こさない程度に健全であると考えるならばある程度妥当である），アンレバード・ベータは

第5章　資本コストの推定　103

expressed as follows;

$$\frac{V_u}{V_u + V_{tax}}\beta_u + \frac{V_{tax}}{V_u + V_{tax}}\beta_{tax} = \frac{D}{D + E}\beta_d + \frac{E}{D + E}\beta_e$$

Assuming $\beta_{tax} = \beta_u$ and $\beta_d = 0$, then,

$$\beta_u = \frac{E}{D + E}\beta_e$$

$$\beta_e = \frac{D + E}{E}\beta_u$$

$$\beta_e = \left(1 + \frac{D}{E}\right)\beta_u$$

The alternative assumption is that the amount of debt (not ratio) will be constant into the future. The tax savings effect is based on the magnitude of debt; therefore, it is natural to assume that the risk of the tax saving and the risk of debt are identical. With the same bold assumption that the risk of debt is zero, unlevered beta in this case can be expressed as follows;

$$\frac{V_u}{V_u + V_{tax}}\beta_u + \frac{V_{tax}}{V_u + V_{tax}}\beta_{tax} = \frac{D}{D + E}\beta_d + \frac{E}{D + E}\beta_e$$

Assuming $\beta_{tax} = \beta_d = 0$, then,

$$\frac{V_u}{V_u + V_{tax}}\beta_u + \frac{E}{D + E}\beta_e$$

Because $V_u + V_{tax} = D + E$, then,

$$V_u\beta_u = E\beta_e \text{ and,}$$

$$(D + E - V_{tax})\beta_u = E\beta_e$$

104 | Chapter 5   Estimating Cost of Capital

以下のように表わせる。

$$\frac{V_u}{V_u + V_{tax}} \beta_u + \frac{V_{tax}}{V_u + V_{tax}} \beta_{tax} = \frac{D}{D + E} \beta_d + \frac{E}{D + E} \beta_e$$

ここで $\beta_{tax} = \beta_u$ かつ $\beta_d = 0$ であるため，

$$\beta_u = \frac{E}{D + E} \beta_e$$

$$\beta_e = \frac{D + E}{E} \beta_u$$

$$\beta_e = \left(1 + \frac{D}{E}\right)\beta_u$$

もう 1 つの前提は，将来的な負債の額（比率ではなく）が一定であるとする仮定である。この前提では節税効果は負債の活用度合いによって発生するので，負債のリスクと節税効果のリスクが同等と考えることができる。負債のリスクがゼロという先ほどと同じ前提をおくと，アンレバード・ベータは以下のように表わせる。

$$\frac{V_u}{V_u + V_{tax}} \beta_u + \frac{V_{tax}}{V_u + V_{tax}} \beta_{tax} = \frac{D}{D + E} \beta_d + \frac{E}{D + E} \beta_e$$

ここで $\beta_{tax} = \beta_d = 0$ であるため，

$$\frac{V_u}{V_u + V_{tax}} \beta_u + \frac{E}{D + E} \beta_e$$

$V_u + V_{tax} = D + E$ なので，

$$V_u \beta_u = E \beta_e \; であり，$$

$$(D + E - V_{tax}) \, \beta_u = E \beta_e$$

第 5 章　資本コストの推定 | 105

$$\beta_e = \beta_u \left(\frac{D}{E} + 1 - \frac{V_{tax}}{E} \right)$$

Since the amount of debt is constant, the interest payments on debt will be constant, too. With the tax rate represented as T and using the perpetuity formula introduced in chapter 8, the value of tax saving is shown;

$$V_{tax} = \frac{D \times T \times r_d}{r_d} \text{ , then,}$$

$$\beta_e = \beta_u \left(\frac{D}{E} + 1 - \frac{DT}{E} \right)$$

$$\beta_e = \beta_u \left(1 + (1 - T) \frac{D}{E} \right)$$

Constructing Bottom-up Beta

Unlevered beta is thought to represent the risk of a business in its industry sector, and to be steady unless the risk profile of the industry changes drastically. However, unlevered beta based on the market beta of peer companies could be an extreme estimation and unstable over time, so it is advisable to calculate unlevered betas of multiple peer companies and take the average of them.

The bottom-up beta will be developed as adding the financial risk according to the capital structure of the company or business of interest to the average unlevered beta.

The process to estimate the bottom-up beta is summarized as following (Figure 5.4).

✓ Remove the financial risk incorporated in the market beta of a peer company to estimate the beta assuming no debt (unlevered beta).

✓ Average unlevered beta of multiple peer companies.

✓ Add the financial risk based on the capital structure of the company or business of interest to the average unlevered beta to develop bottom-up beta.

106   Chapter 5   Estimating Cost of Capital

$$\beta_e = \beta_u \left(\frac{D}{E} + 1 - \frac{V_{tax}}{E} \right)$$

負債の額が一定であれば，金利支払いは一定である。税率を T とすると，後の第 8 章で紹介する永久年金式を活用して，節税効果の価値は以下のように表わせる。

$$V_{tax} = \frac{D \times T \times r_d}{r_d} \text{，そのため，}$$

$$\beta_e = \beta_u \left(\frac{D}{E} + 1 - \frac{DT}{E} \right)$$

$$\beta_e = \beta_u \left(1 + (1 - T) \frac{D}{E} \right) \text{となる。}$$

ボトムアップ・ベータの組成

アンレバード・ベータは企業が属する産業の事業リスクを表わすものであり，その産業のリスクが大きく変化しない限り一定だと考えることができる。しかし，比較類似企業の市場ベータに基づいて計算されるアンレバード・ベータも，やはり異常値であったり，安定しない可能性があるため，複数の比較類似企業のアンレバード・ベータを計算し，その平均を用いるほうが望ましい。

平均したアンレバード・ベータは，分析対象企業もしくは事業の資本構成に基づき財務リスクを加味することでボトムアップ・ベータとなる。

ボトムアップ・ベータの推定プロセスは以下のようにまとめられる（図表5.4）。

✓ 比較類似企業の市場ベータに内在する財務リスクを取り除き，無負債であると仮定した場合のベータ（アンレバード・ベータ）を推計する。

✓ 複数の比較類似企業のアンレバード・ベータを平均する。

✓ 平均アンレバード・ベータに対象企業あるいは事業の資本構成に基づいて財務リスクを加え，ボトムアップ・ベータを算出する。

第 5 章　資本コストの推定　　107

Figure 5.4 | Process to Estimate the Bottom-up Beta

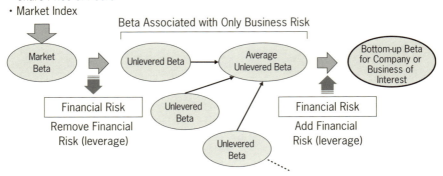

The reference at the end of this chapter introduces a simple Excel-based file to develop a bottom-up beta using market betas.

○ Capital Structure

The target capital structure should be applied to estimate WACC, rather than the capital structure at the time of analysis. The current capital structure reflects the temporary condition of a stock price movement, and is not necessarily appropriate. It is often considered no problem to use the current capital structure without change in practice because the current structure usually does not disperse significantly from the target. Yet, it is recommended that you check the traditional financial policy of the company or the capital structure of peer companies.

図表5.4 ┃ ボトムアップ・ベータの推定プロセス

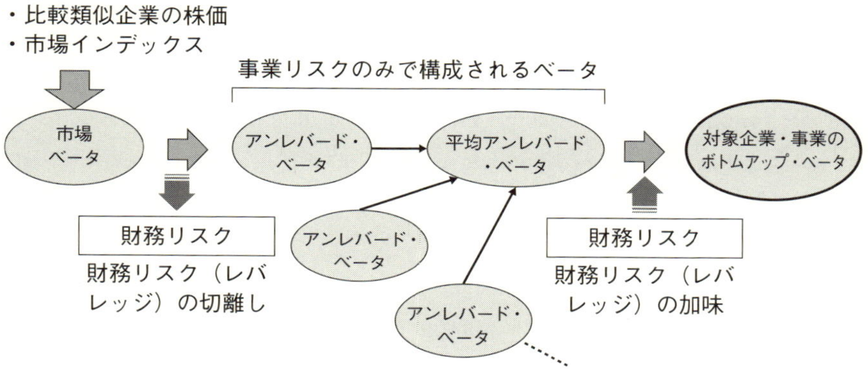

・比較類似企業の株価
・市場インデックス

事業リスクのみで構成されるベータ

市場ベータ ⇒ アンレバード・ベータ → 平均アンレバード・ベータ ⇒ 対象企業・事業のボトムアップ・ベータ

財務リスク

財務リスク（レバレッジ）の切離し

アンレバード・ベータ

アンレバード・ベータ

財務リスク

財務リスク（レバレッジ）の加味

　なお，本章末では市場ベータからボトムアップ・ベータを算出する簡単なエクセルファイルを紹介している。

◉ **資本構成**

　加重平均資本コストを算出する際の資本構成は現在の比率ではなく目標とする比率によるべきである。現在の資本構成は一時的な株価変動の状況が反映されており，適切ではない可能性もあるからである。実際には目標資本構成と現在の資本構成はそれほど乖離していないと考えられるため，現在の資本構成をそのまま使ってしまってもかまわない場合が多い。しかし，その企業の歴史的な財務政策に関する考え方や比較類似企業の資本構成などもレビューしておくとよい。

第5章　資本コストの推定　　109

◉ Weighted Average Cost of Capital for Nike

Figure 5.5 illustrates the calculation of the WACC for Nike. The risk-free rate is 3.15% as we have seen in Figure5.2. Nike has a credit rating of AA − from S&P and the corresponding credit risk premium is estimated to be 0.62%. Adding that to the risk-free rate brings the cost of debt to 3.77%. Considering the corporate tax rate in the U.S. of 25%, the after-tax cost of debt is calculated to be 2.83% (=3.77×(1 − 25%)).

The beta of Nike is estimated to be 0.8. Assuming a market risk premium of 5%, the equity risk premium is 0.8×5% = 4.00%. The cost of equity is 7.15% after adding the risk-free rate.

The capital structure is calculated based on the book value of interest-bearing debt at the end of the latest fiscal year (May 2018) and the current market capitalization. Taking into account the debt ratio and equity ratio of 2.82% and 97.18%, respectively, the WACC is estimated to be 7.03%.

Figure 5.5 | WACC for Nike

	Risk-free Rate	3.15%		
	Credit Rating	AA-		
+	Credit Risk Premium	0.62%		
=	Cost of Debt	3.77%		
	Tax Rate (T)	25.00%		
	After Tax Cost of Debt	2.83%		
	Beta	0.80		
×	Market Risk Premium	5.00%		
=	Equity Risk Premium	4.00%	Debt / (Debt + Equity)	2.82%
+	Risk-free Rate	3.15%	Equity / (Debt + Equity)	97.18%
=	Cost of Equity	7.15%	WACC	7.03%

◉ 資本コストの推定例：ナイキ

図表 5.5 はナイキの WACC を計算した例を示している。リスクフリー・レートは図表 5.2 の 3.15% を使用する。ナイキは S&P から AA−の格付を得ており，対応する信用リスク・プレミアムは 0.62% と推定した。これをリスクフリー・レートに上乗せし，負債コストは 3.77% となる。ここに米国の法人税率である 25% を加味すると税引後負債コストは 2.83%（=3.77 ×（1 − 25%））と算出される。

次に株主資本コストだが，ナイキのベータは 0.8 であった。市場リスク・プレミアムが 5% とすると，株式リスク・プレミアムは 0.8 × 5% = 4.00% となる。ここにリスクフリー・レートを加えると株主資本コストは 7.15% である。

資本構成は直前決算期末時点（2018 年 5 月末）の有利子負債の簿価と直近の株式時価総額に基づいて計算した。負債比率 2.82%，株主資本比率 97.18% をそれぞれ加味すると加重平均資本コストは 7.03% と推定される。

図表 5.5 ┃ ナイキの資本コスト推定例

	リスクフリー・レート	3.15%		
	信用格付	AA-		
+	信用リスク・プレミアム	0.62%		
=	負債コスト	3.77%		
	税率	25.00%		
	税引後負債コスト	2.83%		
	ベータ	0.80		
×	市場リスク・プレミアム	5.00%		
=	株式リスク・プレミアム	4.00%	負債比率	2.82%
+	リスクフリー・レート	3.15%	株主資本比率	97.18%
=	株主資本コスト	7.15%	加重平均資本コスト WACC	7.03%

Reference 5.1: Excel-based File to Estimate Beta

Two Excel-based files introduced in this chapter, Market Beta Calculation File and Bottom-up Beta Calculation File are downloadable at the following site:

(https://www.biz-book.jp/isbn/978-4-502-31671-5)

Market Beta Calculation File

Market Beta Calculation File answers the market beta of the company of interest based on share prices of the company and stock market index. The market beta is calculated using returns for 60 months, which is the most common duration for beta analysis in practice. A monthly return is measured as the price change from the beginning to the end of a month divided by the price at the beginning. Therefore, the data for 61 months is required to get 60 returns.

It is more precise to include dividend payments in the return of the share price, but this file neglects the contribution of dividends so that you can avoid a burdensome task.

As seen in Figure 5.6, gray cells request your input about the name of a company analyzed, share prices, the name of index and the prices of it for 61 months to respond to the beta. Share price information is available on websites including Yahoo!Finance and Google Finance.

Figure 5.6 | Image of Market Beta Calculation File

	Year.Month	MKT Index TOPIX		Company Seven&I			Sony		
Data		Price	Return	Price	Return	Beta	Price	Return	Beta
60	Mar - 12	854.35	0.021999	2,458	0.09	0.85	1,704	-0.02	1.64
59	Feb - 12	835.96	0.106836	2,246	0.05		1,737	0.25	
58	Jan - 12	755.27	0.03659	2,146	0.00		1,391	0.01	
57	Dec - 11	728.61	0.000206	2,145	0.01		1,382	0.01	
56	Nov - 11	728.46	-0.04659	2,127	0.01		1,372	-0.18	

112   Chapter 5   Estimating Cost of Capital

● 参考5.1：ベータ推定のためのエクセルファイル

本章で紹介した市場ベータとボトムアップ・ベータを計算するエクセルベースのファイルは以下のサイトからダウンロードできる。

(https://www.biz-book.jp/isbn/978-4-502-31671-5)

市場ベータ計算ファイル（Market Beta Calculation File）

市場ベータ計算ファイルは，企業の株価データと株式市場インデックスのデータを入力することで企業の市場ベータを算出する。このファイルでは実務において一般的な60カ月の月次リターンに基づいてベータを計算している。月次リターンは月初から月末までの値の変化を月初の値で割ることによって計算される。そのため60カ月のリターンのためには61カ月分のデータが必要になる。

なお，株式のリターンには厳密には配当も含めるべきだが，データ加工の手間が発生するため，配当の影響は無視している。

図表5.6に示すように，グレーに色つけされたセルに分析対象とする企業名と株価，使用する市場インデックス名とその値を61カ月分入力するとベータが計算される。株価データは Yahoo! ファイナンスや Google Finance などのホームページにおいて入手可能である。

図表5.6 ┃ 市場ベータ計算ファイルのイメージ

データ	日付		市場インデックス TOPIX 値	リターン	企業 セブン＆アイ 株価	リターン	ベータ	ソニー 株価	リターン	ベータ
60	2012年	3月	854.35	0.021999	2,458	0.09	0.85	1,704	-0.02	1.64
59	〃 年	2月	835.96	0.106836	2,246	0.05		1,737	0.25	
58	〃 年	1月	755.27	0.03659	2,146	0.00		1,391	0.01	
57	2011年	12月	728.61	0.000206	2,145	0.01		1,382	0.01	
56	〃 年	11月	728.46	-0.04659	2,127	0.01		1,372	-0.18	

日付を入力

市場インデックスを入力

分析対象とする企業名を入力

← ベータ

市場インデックスの値を入力

分析対象企業の株価を入力

第5章　資本コストの推定　　113

Bottom-up Beta Calculation File

Bottom-up Beta Calculation File develops the bottom-up beta of the company of interest based on betas of peer companies.

As seen in Figure 5.7, gray cells request your input of the market beta, debt to equity ratio, and tax rate of peer companies to measure the average unlevered beta. The bottom-up beta is calculated taking into account the debt to equity ratio of the company of interest. This file provides two bottom-up betas applying two different assumptions discussed in this chapter.

Figure 5.7 | Image of Bottom-up Beta Calculation File

Peer Data

Peer Company	Company1	Company2	Company3	Company4	Company5	Company6
Market Beta	1.2	0.91	0.83	1.03	0.95	1.15
D/E, Debt to Equity	0.1	0.6	0.8	0.66	0.2	0.3
Tax Rate	0.42	0.42	0.3	0.36	0.41	0.41

Assumption 1: Constant Debt Ratio

Unlevered Beta	1.13	0.68	0.53	0.72	0.85	0.98
Average Unlevered Beta	0.82					
Target Company D/E	0.6					
Bottom up Beta	1.10					

Assumption 2: Constant Amount of Debt

Unlevered Beta	1.09	0.57	0.46	0.62	0.79	0.88
Average Unlevered Beta	0.74					
Target Company D/E	0.6					
Bottom up Beta	1.18					

114   Chapter 5   Estimating Cost of Capital

ボトムアップ・ベータ計算ファイル（Bottom-up Beta Calculation File）

　ボトムアップ・ベータ計算ファイルは比較類似企業のベータからボトムアップ・ベータを計算するファイルである。

　図表5.7に示すように，グレーに色つけされたセルに比較類似企業の市場ベータ，負債株主資本比率（負債÷株主資本），税率を入力すると，平均アンレバード・ベータが計算される。また，分析対象企業の負債株主資本比率を考慮すればボトムアップ・ベータが計算される。このファイルでは本章で紹介した2つの異なる前提に基づいて2つのボトムアップ・ベータを算出している。

図表5.7 ▎ボトムアップ・ベータ計算ファイルのイメージ

比較類似会社データ

企業名	企業1	企業2	企業3	企業4	企業5	企業6
市場ベータ	1.2	0.91	0.83	1.03	0.95	1.15
負債株主資本比率，負債÷株主資本	0.1	0.6	0.8	0.66	0.2	0.3
税率	0.42	0.42	0.3	0.36	0.41	0.41

前提1：負債比率が一定

アンレバード・ベータ	1.13	0.68	0.53	0.72	0.85	0.98
平均アンレバード・ベータ	0.82					
分析対象企業の負債株主資本比率	0.6					
ボトムアップ・ベータ	1.10					

前提2：負債の額が一定

アンレバード・ベータ	1.09	0.57	0.46	0.62	0.79	0.88
平均アンレバード・ベータ	0.74					
分析対象企業の負債株主資本比率	0.6					
ボトムアップ・ベータ	1.18					

第5章　資本コストの推定　　115

Reference 5.2: Website List for Necessary Data

You have to gather various types of data in order to estimate WACC. Unfortunately, there is no convenient website that contains and organizes all relevant data, so you are required to search a number of websites to obtain the necessary information. Some useful and free-of-charge websites which can alleviate your painful work are listed below.

● **Current Government Bond Yields**

https://www.bloomberg.com/markets/rates-bonds

● **Historical Japanese Government Bond Yields**

https://www.mof.go.jp/jgbs/reference/interest_rate/index.htm

● **Sovereign Rating on Countries**

https://countryeconomy.com/ratings/moodys

● **Credit Rating on Japanese Companies**

https://www.r-i.co.jp/rating/data/rating.html

https://www.jcr.co.jp/en/ratinglist/corp

● **Yields on Corporate Bonds**

http://market.jsda.or.jp/html/saiken/kehai/downloadInput.php

● **Industry Beta, Credit Risk Premium, Market Risk Premium**

http://pages.stern.nyu.edu/~adamodar/New_Home_Page/datacurrent.html

(Professor Aswath Damodaran at the Stern School of Business at New York University

provides a vast amount of financial data on his website.)

● **Corporate Income Tax Rates**

http://stats.oecd.org/index.aspx?DataSetCode=TABLE_II1

● 参考 5.2：データソースサイト

　加重平均資本コストを推定する際には多くのデータを収集する必要がある。すべてのデータが整理されているような便利なホームページは残念ながら存在しないので，実際には多くのデータサイトを検索して必要な情報を集めなければならない。以下はそのような際に有益であり，かつ無料でアクセス可能なサイトのリストである。

● **各国の国債の利回り**

　https://www.bloomberg.com/markets/rates-bonds

● **日本の国債利回り推移**

　https://www.mof.go.jp/jgbs/reference/interest_rate/index.htm

● **各国の格付**

　https://countryeconomy.com/ratings/moodys

● **日本企業の債券格付**

　https://www.r-i.co.jp/rating/data/rating.html

　https://www.jcr.co.jp/en/ratinglist/corp

● **債券利回り**

　http://market.jsda.or.jp/html/saiken/kehai/downloadInput.php

● **産業別ベータ，信用リスク・プレミアム，市場リスク・プレミアム**

　http://pages.stern.nyu.edu/~adamodar/New_Home_Page/datacurrent.html

　（ニューヨーク大学のアズワス・ダモダラン教授はウェブサイトにおいて膨大なデータを提供してくれている。）

● **各国法人税率**

　http://stats.oecd.org/index.aspx?DataSetCode=TABLE_II1

第 5 章　資本コストの推定　　**117**

Chapter
6 Analyzing Financial Performance 3: EVA and Strategy

Points !

✔ EVA* is a profit measure taking into account WACC
✔ Analyses of financial performance from various aspects such as efficiency and size provides insightful information for performance forecasts and strategic planning

* EVA® is a registered trademark of Stern Stewart & Co. ® mark is omitted in this book.

● EVA Definition and Its Essence

The closing chapter for part 2 provides a detailed discussion about EVA, a true economic profit measure linked with the value of a company, and introduces analysis combining it with a strategy.

Economic Value Added or EVA is often referred to as economic profit because it takes into account the required return on the capital a company uses. EVA can be derived by subtracting a charge for capital usage from NOPAT.

$$EVA = NOPAT - Capital\ Charge$$

The capital charge is the product of capital and the weighted average cost of capital.

$$Capital\ Charge = Capital \times WACC$$

This is the essence of EVA. NOPAT is the profit a company generates through its operating activities. In order to generate such a profit, a company requires assets. Assets are owned by the company but are funded through cash (capital) provided by banks and investors. Those investors expect a certain level of return. The required return is also called the cost of capital for a company. Since utilizing capital is costly, this capital cost is deducted as absolute yen or dollar amounts from NOPAT

118 | Chapter 6 Analyzing Financial Performance 3: EVA and Strategy

第6章 財務業績の分析3：EVAと戦略

> **ポイント！**
> ✔ EVA* は加重平均資本コストを加味した利益指標である
> ✔ 企業の財務業績を，効率性や規模といった面から分析することは，企業の現状把握だけではなく，今後の業績予測や戦略立案にも有益な情報となる

* EVA® は，Stern Stewart & Co. の登録商標です。本書では®マークを省略しています。

● EVA の定義と本質

第2部を締めくくる本章では，企業価値とリンクしている経済的な利益指標であるEVAを詳細に議論し，戦略と結びつけた分析例を紹介する。

EVA（経済付加価値）は企業が使用する資本に求められるリターンを加味した経済的利益と定義される。EVA は税引後の営業利益である NOPAT から使用する資本の費用を差し引くことで計算される。

$$EVA = NOPAT - 資本費用$$

ここで，資本費用は投下資本に（加重平均）資本コストを掛け合わせたものである。

$$資本費用 = 投下資本 \times WACC$$

EVA の本質は以下のようになる。NOPAT は事業活動によって生み出された利益である。この利益を生み出すために企業は資産を使っている。資産は企業のものだが，銀行や株主から提供された資金（資本）によって成り立っている。そして銀行や株主などの資本提供者はただで資本を提供してくれるはずはなく，一定の見返りを求める。これが期待リターンであり企業にとっては資本コストだった。企業が資本を使用することにはコストが掛かっているため，この資本

to derive EVA. Note that the beginning capital is used to calculate the capital charge because a company conducts operating activities utilizing the capital that exists at the beginning of the period.

EVA is different from accounting profit. Accounting profit incorporates the costs associated with debt but ignores the costs associated with shareholder equity. Accounting income statements do not include the cost of equity as an explicit cost. In fact, it can be said that the accounting framework treats equity capital as if it is free. This is not consistent with finance theory. A shareholder requires higher return because equity investment is riskier, therefore the cost of equity is actually more expensive than the cost of debt. Accounting profit is not the appropriate measure to gauge the financial performance of a company or business because the cost of equity cannot be ignored. EVA includes all costs associated with capital and, therefore, is connected with company value.

O EVA Calculation

Figure 6.1 shows the EVA calculation process for companies A and B. Company A uses capital of 1,000 to generate NOPAT of 150. Assuming a 5% WACC, the capital charge is 50 (1,000×5%=50). EVA is then 100 (150–50=100). Company B generates the same amount of NOPAT as company A. However, company B uses 10 times more capital than company A, which results in a capital charge of 500 and a negative EVA of −350. If one were to focus only on NOPAT, then the financial performance of the two companies looks identical; however, there is a considerable difference in terms of capital efficiency between the two. EVA reflects not only a company's operating profit but also its capital efficiency; and therefore EVA represents a company's true profitability.

120   Chapter 6   Analyzing Financial Performance 3: EVA and Strategy

にかかわるコストを絶対額として，NOPAT から差し引いたものが EVA ということである。なお，資本費用の計算に使われる投下資本は期首の数値を使う。企業は期首にある資本を活用し，その期の事業活動を行うからである。

EVA は会計上の利益とは異なる。会計上の利益は負債に関するコストを加味してはいるが，株主資本に関するコストを無視している。損益計算書を思い浮かべれば，株主資本に関するコストが含まれていないことがわかるだろう。つまり会計は株主資本はただであると考えているということである。これはファイナンス理論とは整合しない。株式投資はリスクが高いため株主は高いリターンを求める。したがって株主資本コストはむしろ負債コストよりも高い。事業活動を行ううえで株主資本コストを無視してはならないため，会計上の利益は企業や事業の業績を把握するためには適切な指標とはいえない。EVA は資本にかかわるすべてのコストを加味しており，そのため企業価値ともつながっている。

◉ EVA の計算

図表 6.1 は単純な EVA の計算例を示している。企業 A は 1,000 の資本を活用して 150 の NOPAT を生み出している。資本コストを 5% とすれば，資本費用は 50（＝ 1,000 × 5%）である。EVA は 100（＝ 150 － 50）となる。企業 B も企業 A と同一の NOPAT を生み出している。しかしながら，企業 B は企業 A の 10 倍もの資本を使用しており，その結果資本費用は 500 となり，EVA はマイナス 350 となっている。もし NOPAT にだけ注目すると，2 つの企業の財務業績は同一に見える。しかし，企業 A と B では資本効率の点で大きな違いがある。EVA は企業の生み出す利益だけではなく資本の効率性も正しく反映し，真の利益率を表わすのである。

第 6 章　財務業績の分析 3：EVA と戦略　121

Figure 6.1 | EVA Calculation

	Company A	Company B
NOPAT	150	150
Capital	1,000	10,000
WACC	5%	5%
Capital Charge	50	500
EVA	**100**	**−350**

● EVA and ROC

The EVA formula can be rearranged as:

$$EVA = \left(\frac{NOPAT}{Capital} - WACC \right) \times Capital$$

The term NOPAT/Capital is ROC showing how much profit is gained from capital employed. The rearranged formula demonstrates how rate-of-return measures are incorporated into EVA. Since capital used in its operation is usually positive, ROC–WACC determines whether EVA is positive or negative. EVA is positive when the rate of return produced by the company exceeds the rate of return expected by investors; and EVA is negative when the rate of return produced by the company falls below the rate of return expected by investors. This relationship is consistent with the notion that when performance (rate of return) exceeds the expected return, it leads to value creation. The difference between ROC and WACC shown in parentheses is referred to as EVA spread.

● Analysis of Efficiency and Size

EVA spread indicates whether the return generated by a company exceeds the return expected by an investor or not. The figure expressed in a percentage shows

図表 6.1 ┃ EVA の計算

	企業 A	企業 B
NOPAT	150	150
投下資本	1,000	10,000
WACC	5%	5%
資本費用	50	500
EVA	100	−350

● EVA と ROC

EVA の定義式を変形すると以下のようになる。

$$EVA = \left(\frac{NOPAT}{投下資本} - 資本コスト \right) \times 投下資本$$

NOPAT÷投下資本は，投下資本からどの程度利益が上がっているのかを表わす投下資本利益率（ROC）である。この式からは，利益率を表わす指標もEVA には包含されていることがわかる。事業に使用されている投下資本はプラスなので，EVA のプラス，マイナスを決めるのが，ROC − WACC だということができる。企業があげるリターンが投資家から期待されるリターンを上回っていれば EVA はプラスであり，期待リターンを下回っていればマイナスなのである。この関係は，期待リターンを上回る成果（利益率）を上げることが価値創造に結びつくことと整合している。なお，ROC と WACC の差となる括弧でくくられた部分は，EVA スプレッドと呼ばれる。

● 事業効率と規模の分解による分析

EVA スプレッドは企業があげるリターンが投資家からの期待リターンを上回っているのか否かを表わす。"%"で表わされるこの数値は事業の効率を示

an operating efficiency. Meanwhile, capital invested in operations shows the size of operations. The rearranged formula separates EVA into "efficiency" and "size".

Figure 6.2 takes EVA spread on the vertical axis and capital on the horizontal axis. Moving upward means the improvement of efficiency and a rightward shift means the expansion of operation scale.

EVA will be calculated as EVA spread multiplied by capital. Hence, the product of a vertical and horizontal axes is EVA. Suppose that the original point of the figure is set to be a current EVA, the equivalent EVA can be achieved by various combinations of EVA spreads and capitals, which corresponds to the curve depicted from the top left to the bottom right. Traveling to the upper right region of the curve represents the increase in EVA and to the lower left of the curve represents the decrease in EVA.

Figure 6.2 | Analysis of Efficiency and Size

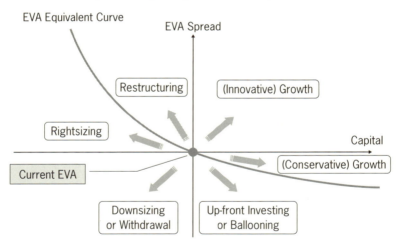

With this exhibition, you can diagnose the past performance as well as the future plan of a company from the two perspectives, the operating efficiency and the size.

Boosting EVA with the increase in invested capital and improving operating efficiency is described as "growth" without any doubt. If the additional investment is generating return higher than a cost of capital and contributes to value creation, that

すことになる。一方で，事業に投下された金額である投下資本は事業規模を示す。この式の変形により，EVA を事業効率と規模に分解することができる。

図表 6.2 は EVA スプレッドを縦軸に，投下資本を横軸にとっている。上方への移動は事業効率の改善を意味し，右への移動は事業規模の拡大を意味している。

EVA スプレッドと投下資本を掛け合わせると EVA になる。つまり，縦軸と横軸を掛け合わせると EVA になる。ここで，グラフの原点を現在の EVA とすると，現在と同額の EVA は，さまざまな EVA スプレッドと投下資本の組み合わせによって達成が可能であることがわかる。その組み合わせを左上から右下へ伸びる曲線で表わしている。この曲線よりも右上に移動すれば EVA は拡大，左下に移動する場合は EVA の減少ということである。

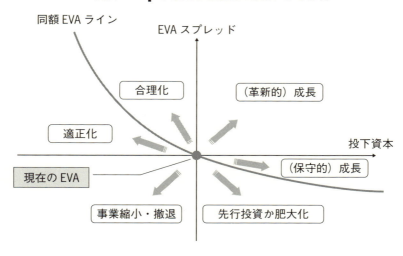

図表 6.2 事業効率と規模の分解による分析

EVA をこのように表わすことにより，業績や今後の計画がどのような意味をもつのかについて事業効率と規模の観点から検証することができる。

まず，事業効率を高めつつ投資規模を増やし，EVA を高めていればもちろん「成長」といえる。また，新たな事業への投資が資本コスト以上の利益を生むのであれば，現在より多少事業効率を悪化させたとしても価値創造に寄与す

can be defined as "growth" too, even if it lowers operating efficiency a bit. If you want to differentiate them, the shift to the upper right indicating the continuous value creation with the improvement of efficiency can be called "innovative" growth, and the shift to the (slightly) lower right indicating the continuous value creation with maintained or slight deterioration of efficiency can be called "conservative" growth.

A cost of capital divides the expansion of the scale of operation into "growth" and others. The new investment producing the higher return over a cost of capital deserves to be called growth. However, the downward movement to the right decreasing EVA is not categorized as "growth". A company sometimes tries to develop a new business and invests a significant amount of money into it, but unless the new business generates a sufficient return surpassing the cost of capital, the company is just "ballooning" or still in the "up-front investment" phase.

It is possible that a company withdraws capital while raising efficiency to gain more EVA, which is called "restructuring". It can be called "rightsizing" when a company increases efficiency while reducing the size of operation in the case of a downturn in the business environment.

You should be careful not to misunderstand ballooning as growth, or downsizing as restructuring. EVA can evaluate a company performance along multiple dimensions because it integrates the income statement and the balance sheet.

● Analysis Based on Margin and Velocity

We go one step further. ROC which is a component of EVA spread can be divided into two measures showing margin and velocity. Introducing sales in the denominator of NOPAT and in the numerator of capital, ROC can be expressed in two figures NOPAT margin and capital turnover.

$$ROC = \frac{NOPAT}{Capital} = \frac{NOPAT}{Sales} \times \frac{Sales}{Capital}$$

$$ROC = NOPAT\ Margin \times Capital\ Turnover$$

126　Chapter 6　Analyzing Financial Performance 3: EVA and Strategy

る「成長」と定義できる。これらの成長をあえてさらに分解して説明するのであれば，効率を高めながらさらに価値創造を継続する右上へのシフトを「革新的」な成長，効率を維持または若干落としながらも価値創造を継続する右下へのシフトは「保守的」な成長と呼ぶことができるかもしれない。

　規模の拡大は資本コストを分水嶺にして「成長」かそうでないかに分かれ，追加的な投資のリターンが資本コストを上回る限りにおいて，規模の拡大は「成長」と呼ぶに値する。しかし，EVA を減少させる右下への動きを「成長」と呼ぶことはできない。しばしば企業は新事業開発と多角化のために多額の投資を行うが，その事業が資本コスト以上の利益を生んでいないのであれば，成長ではなく単なる「肥大化」か，もしくは依然として「先行投資」の状態にとどまっていると考えるべきである。

　一方で，投下資本を縮小しながらも事業効率を引き上げた結果，EVA を増加させる「合理化」も考えられる。事業環境が悪化する中で事業規模を縮小させながらも効率をアップさせる動きは「適正化」と呼べるだろう。

　成長しているつもりが肥大化，あるいは合理化しているつもりが縮小均衡などといったケースには十分留意する必要がある。EVA は損益計算書と貸借対照表を統合した指標であるがゆえに，企業の業績に関して多面的な検証が可能になる。

● 収益性と資本効率に基づく分析

　もう一歩踏み込んでみよう。EVA スプレッドの構成要素である ROC は，収益性と資本効率を表わす 2 つの指標に分解することができる。売上高を導入し，NOPAT の分母と，投下資本の分子に売上高を入れると，ROC は NOPAT マージンと投下資本回転率という 2 つの指標に分解される。

$$ROC = \frac{NOPAT}{投下資本} = \frac{NOPAT}{売上高} \times \frac{売上高}{投下資本}$$

ROC ＝ NOPAT マージン × 投下資本回転率

NOPAT margin expresses how much profit is generated out of sales, and capital turnover expresses how efficiently and how fast capital is converted into sales. Of course, the product of the two figures is ROC, cancelling sales on the numerator and denominator.

Figure 6.3 puts NOPAT margin on the vertical axis and capital turnover on the horizontal axis. It indicates a company or business with a high margin is located in the upper area, and a company with higher capital efficiency or velocity is located in the right side area.

Since ROC will be calculated as margin multiplied by velocity, the intersection point of a vertical and horizontal axes explains the level of ROC. The curve from the top left to the bottom right shows there are countless combinations of margin and velocity to derive the same ROC.

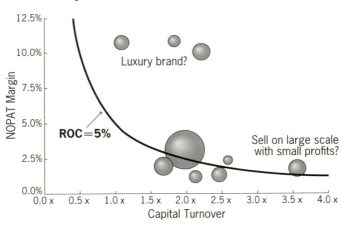

Figure 6.3 | Image of Analysis Based on Margin and Velocity

The size of bubble represents sales.

Holding a retail business up as an example, there exists a significant difference between a department store and a dollar shop. A department store dealing with luxury items that can generally enjoy high margin and low velocity, is considered to be situated in the upper left region. On the other hand, a dollar shop selling on a large

NOPATマージンは売上高のうち利益がどれだけであるのかという収益性を示す指標であり、投下資本回転率は投下資本がどれだけ速く効率的に売上高を生み出すのかという資本効率を示す指標である。もちろん2つの指標を掛け合わせると分子と分母の売上高が消え、ROCとなる。

　図表6.3は、収益性を表わすNOPATマージンを縦軸に、資本効率を表わす投下資本回転率を横軸にとった図である。上に位置する企業・事業ほど収益性が高く、右に位置する企業・事業ほど資本効率が高いということである。

　収益性と資本効率を掛け合わせるとROCとなるから、縦横の交点がROCである。同じROCだとしても収益性と資本効率の組み合わせはさまざまであり、無限の組み合わせがあることを左上から右下への曲線は示している。

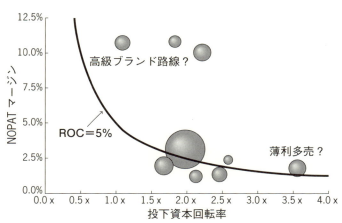

図表6.3 ｜ 収益性と資本効率に基づく分析イメージ

円の大きさは売上高のイメージ

　たとえば、同じ小売業であっても、百貨店と、100円ショップを展開する企業とでは大きな違いがある。一般に、高級品を取り扱う百貨店の収益性は高い一方で資本効率は比較的低く、左上のほうに位置すると考えられる。逆に薄利多売とも言える100円ショップでは、収益性は比較的低いものの資本効率が高

scale with small profit can achieve high velocity while the margin is limited, tends to take the lower right position. This type of analysis articulating the business model and financial figures will provide insightful information for strategic planning.

● Financial Analysis Example for Nike ②

Let us resume watching the financial performance of Nike. Figure 6.4 summarizes NOPAT, capital, EVA, and its components, ROC, NOPAT margin, and capital turnover of Nike for the past four years. (Note that the beginning capital is used for EVA and ROC calculation, resulting in only four years of data.) WACC of 7.0% (precisely, 7.03%) estimated in Figure 5.5 is used.

Figure 6.4 | EVA and Others of Nike

	2014	2015	2016	2017	2018
NOPAT		3,250	3,662	4,121	1,987
Capital (Beg.)		12,030	13,893	14,295	15,884
WACC		7.0%	7.0%	7.0%	7.0%
− Capital Charge		845	976	1,005	1,116
= **EVA**		**2,404**	**2,685**	**3,116**	**870**
ROC =NOPAT/Beg. Cap		27.0%	26.4%	28.8%	12.5%
− WACC		7.0%	7.0%	7.0%	7.0%
= EVA Spread		20.0%	19.3%	21.8%	5.5%
× Capital (Beg.)		12,030	13,893	14,295	15,884
= **EVA**		**2,404**	**2,685**	**3,116**	**870**
NOPAT Margin =NOPAT/Sales	10.2%	10.6%	11.3%	12.0%	5.5%
Capital Turnover =Sales/Beg. Cap		2.5	2.3	2.4	2.3

Derived from financial reports of Nike, fiscal year ending in May. In million dollars.

NOPAT and EVA in 2018 declined in accordance with the result of the income statement (Figure 4.4). However, FCF increased as seen in Figure 6.5.

130   Chapter 6   Analyzing Financial Performance 3: EVA and Strategy

く右下に位置すると考えられる。事業特性，ビジネスモデルと財務数値を結び
つけるこのような分析は，戦略立案の際に有用な情報となる。

● 財務分析例：ナイキ②

ナイキの業績をさらに分析してみよう。図表 6.4 はナイキの過去 4 年間の
NOPAT，投下資本，EVA や，その構成要素である ROC，NOPAT マージン，投
下資本利益率を示している。（EVA と ROC の計算には期首投下資本が使用さ
れるため 4 年間のデータとなっている。）WACC は図表 5.5 で推定した 7.0%（正
確には 7.03%）を使用した。

図表 6.4 ┃ ナイキの EVA 他

	2014	2015	2016	2017	2018
NOPAT		3,250	3,662	4,121	1,987
期首投下資本		12,030	13,893	14,295	15,884
WACC		7.0%	7.0%	7.0%	7.0%
－ 資本費用		845	976	1,005	1,116
＝ EVA		2,404	2,685	3,116	870
ROC ＝NOPAT ÷期首投下資本		27.0%	26.4%	28.8%	12.5%
－ WACC		7.0%	7.0%	7.0%	7.0%
＝ EVA スプレッド		20.0%	19.3%	21.8%	5.5%
× 期首投下資本		12,030	13,893	14,295	15,884
＝ EVA		2,404	2,685	3,116	870
NOPAT マージン ＝ NOPAT ÷ 売上高	10.2%	10.6%	11.3%	12.0%	5.5%
投下資本回転率 ＝ 売上高 ÷ 期首投下資本		2.5	2.3	2.4	2.3

ナイキ決算報告書類などから著者計算。各年 5 月末に終了する年度の実績。単位：百万ドル

損益計算書（図表 4.4）と整合するように，2018 年度は NOPAT，EVA も悪
化している。しかし，図表 6.5 が表わすように，FCF はむしろ増加している。

第 6 章　財務業績の分析 3：EVA と戦略　　131

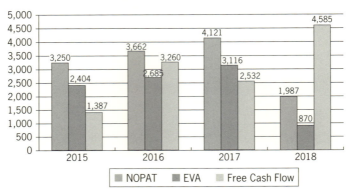

Figure 6.5 | NOPAT, EVA, and FCF of Nike

Derived from financial reports of Nike, fiscal year ending in May. In million dollars.

Analysis separating efficiency and size is conducted in Figure 6.6. Nike has increased capital in recent years, indicating it has been expanding its business operation. As in 2018, however, the investment has not contributed to its growth yet. It would be of key importance that Nike improves operating efficiency to let the investment create value.

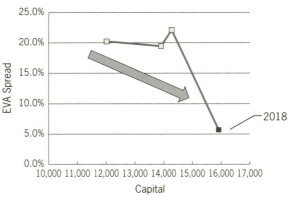

Figure 6.6 | Efficiency and Size of Nike

Derived from financial reports of Nike, fiscal year ending in May. Dark color represents the recent year. Capital: In million dollars.

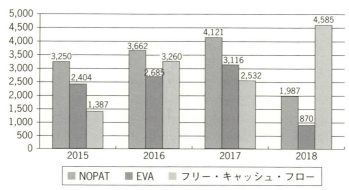

図表 6.5　ナイキの NOPAT，EVA，FCF

ナイキ決算報告書類などから著者計算。各年5月末に終了する年度の実績。単位：百万ドル

　事業効率と規模の分解による分析を行ったのが図表 6.6 である。ナイキは過去数年にわたり投下資本を増加させてきており，事業規模を拡大してきたことがわかる。しかし，2018年時点では，まだこれまでの投資を成長に結びつけられていない。今後投資が価値を生むかどうかは，事業効率を改善させることができるか否かにかかっていると考えられる。

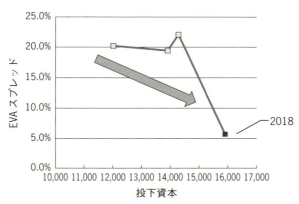

図表 6.6　ナイキの事業効率と規模

ナイキ決算報告書類などから著者計算。各年5月末に終了する年度の実績。最終年度が濃い点。投下資本の単位：百万ドル

第6章　財務業績の分析3：EVAと戦略　　133

Part 3
Future Forecasting

- After examining the business environment and competitive advantages as well as financial performance, it is time to forecast the future.

- No one can predict the future with perfect accuracy. However, you should make the best possible effort to project the financial performance going forward based on qualitative/quantitative analysis conducted.

- Next, we turn our attention to a terminal value which corresponds to the value in the far distant future and influences a company's valuation significantly. We will discuss how to calculate it and what to watch out for.

Chapter 7   Forecasting Future Performance

Chapter 8   Forecasting Terminal Value

第 3 部

将来の予測

★★★

● 事業を取り巻く環境分析や競争優位性に加えて財務業績の分析を終えたら，将来業績の予測にうつる。

● 正確に未来を見通すことは誰であっても不可能なことだが，これまで行ってきた定性的・定量的な分析を活用して，なるべく妥当な将来の財務業績を予測していく必要がある。

● 企業価値評価においては，予想期間終了後の遠い将来の価値を表わすターミナル・バリューが大きな影響をもつが，この算出方法と注意すべき点について議論する。

第 7 章　将来業績の予測

第 8 章　ターミナル・バリューの予測

Chapter 7 Forecasting Future Performance

> **Points!**
> ✓ It is necessary to forecast future FCF for valuation, but you do not have to forecast all accounting items
> ✓ You should start forecasting with sales, and other items will be forecasted based on the sales forecast

● Items to Be Forecasted

Having analyzed qualitative aspects including business environment and a strength or weakness of a company as well as financial aspects, it is time to forecast future performance.

It is not necessary to project all figures for accounting items in the income statement and the balance sheet.

You do not have to consider any future plan regarding a payout to investors such as dividends either. The current value of a company is determined by future cash flows generated and is independent of how it is distributed.

Similarly, the amount of cash and financial investments constituting future capital are not subject to forecasting except for some extraordinary reasons. The value of financial assets at the time of analysis is regarded to be maintained going forward and added as a part of non-operating assets later for valuation.

Moreover, unless a significant change in capital structure is assumed (such as leverage buy-out to be introduced in chapter 11), the prospect of fund-raising arrangement is also unnecessary. The information about future capital structure has been incorporated in the estimated WACC. After all, you are to predict future schedules of items associated with NOPAT and capital only.

第7章 将来業績の予測

> **ポイント!**
> ✓ 企業価値評価のためには将来の FCF を予測するが，すべての会計項目を予測する必要はない
> ✓ 業績予測は売上高からはじめ，そのほかの要素は売上高の予測に基づいて行う

● 予測すべき項目

　事業を取り巻く環境分析や強み・弱みを検討し，さらに財務業績を分析したら，いよいよ将来業績の予測を行う。

　将来業績の予測にあたっては，損益計算書，貸借対照表の項目すべてを予測する必要はない。

　また，配当といった投資家への資金の返還についても予測する必要がない。企業価値は企業が生み出すキャッシュフローによって決まるのであり，それが将来株主に返還されようがされまいが現時点の価値には影響を与えないからである。

　将来の投下資本を構成することになる現金および金融資産についても，よほどの事情がない限り予測する必要はない。現金および金融資産は分析時点での残高が維持されるとみなし，その時点の金融資産は非事業資産の価値の一部として後に加味すればよい。

　さらに，第11章で紹介するレバレッジ・バイアウトのように，よほど資本構成が変動するようなことを想定しない限り，負債と株主資本の調達額の予想も不要である。将来の資本構成はすでに WACC の推定において加味されているからである。結局のところ，予測すべき数値は NOPAT と投下資本の項目なのである。

Forecast Sales

It is advisable to start with sales revenue for a future forecast. Sales growth could relate to the growth of the entire economy and the market where a company operates. It is not an easy task to predict sales in the future. However, you cannot forecast financial performances going forward without a sales because almost all accounting items are coupled directly or indirectly with sales. Sales forecast will be a foundation to predict other factors.

Forecast NOPAT and Capital Using Drivers

You can avoid estimation errors when you use drivers as a percentage of sales to forecast NOPAT and capital. Projecting the figures of each item directly might make your input unreasonable. (For example, rises in expenses and investments are too fast relative to the increase in sales.) The change in each item will accommodate the change in sales if you use drivers based on sales. Of course, all forecasts should be consistent with the strategy and competitive advantages of a company.

Performance Forecast of Nike ①

Figure 7.1 demonstrates an example forecasting a 5-year NOPAT and capital of Nike (2019-2023). The average growth rate of sales for the past five years was 7%. Although the most recent fiscal year recorded only 6% sales growth, let us forecast as if it will recover going forward. The sales growth is assumed to increase gradually for the next five years up to 8.5%

Other items in the past are converted as ratios of sales and predicted based on the percentage. For example, cost to sales ratio in 2018 was 56.2%, and is expected to recover to the past average of 55% in two years. Other items are forecasted using drivers as a percentage of sales.

138   Chapter 7   Forecasting Future Performance

● 売上高の予測

　将来の業績の予測は売上高から始めるのが望ましい。売上高の成長はマクロ経済レベルの成長率や企業が事業を行う市場全体の成長率と関係していると考えられる。売上を予測することは簡単なことではないが，ほとんどその他のすべての会計項目は直接的あるいは間接的に売上高に結びついているため，売上高の予測なしには将来業績の予測は始められない。売上高はその他の項目の予測のベースとなるのである。

● ドライバーを活用した NOPAT，投下資本の予測

　NOPAT と投下資本の予測は，売上高の比率を予測の基準（ドライバー）として活用するほうが間違いが少ない。直接それぞれの項目の値を予測すると，しばしば現実的ではない予測をしてしまうことがある（たとえば，売上高の伸びに比して費用や投資の増加が過大など）。しかし，売上高の比率をドライバーにして各項目を予測すれば，売上高の変化と各項目の変化に一貫性を持たせることができる。むろん，それぞれの項目の予測値は企業の戦略や競争優位性と整合している必要がある。

● ナイキの業績予測①

　図表 7.1 は今後 5 年間（2019 年～ 2023 年）のナイキの NOPAT，投下資本を予測した例を示している。過去の売上高の平均成長率は 7% であった。直近年度の売上成長率は 6% だったが，今後回復していくと予想しよう。売上成長率は今後 5 年間において 8.5% まで徐々に高まると予想する。

　その他の過去の値はすべて売上高の比率を計算し，そのパーセントに基づいて予測する。たとえば，原価率は 2018 年度において 56.2% だったが，2 年後には過去の平均値である 55.5% に回復すると予想する。その他の項目も売上高の比率をドライバーにして予測を行った。

第 7 章　将来業績の予測　　139

Figure 7.1 | NOPAT and Capital Forecast of Nike (in million dollars)

NOPAT

	Actual					Estimate				
	2014	2015	2016	2017	2018	2019	2020	2021	2022	2023
Sales	27,799	30,601	32,376	34,350	36,397	38,763	41,476	44,587	48,154	52,247
− Cost of Sales	15,353	16,534	17,405	19,038	20,441	21,707	23,019	24,523	26,485	28,736
− Selling, General, Admin. Expenses	8,766	9,892	10,469	10,563	11,511	12,210	13,065	14,045	15,168	16,458
Depreciation	518	606	649	706	747	775	830	892	963	1,045
= **Operating Profit**	3,680	4,175	4,502	4,749	4,445	4,845	5,392	6,019	6,501	7,053
− Operating Tax	836	925	840	628	2,458	1,211	1,348	1,505	1,625	1,763
= **NOPAT**	2,844	3,250	3,662	4,121	1,987	3,634	4,044	4,514	4,876	5,290
NOPAT Growth		14.3%	12.7%	12.5%	-51.8%	82.9%	11.3%	11.6%	8.0%	8.5%

Capital

	Actual					Estimate				
	2014	2015	2016	2017	2018	2019	2020	2021	2022	2023
Cash and Equivalent	2,220	3,852	3,138	3,808	4,249	4,249	4,249	4,249	4,249	4,249
Short-term Investments	2,922	2,072	2,319	2,371	996	996	996	996	996	996
Long-term Investments	0	0	0	0	0	0	0	0	0	0
= **Cash and Investments**	5,142	5,924	5,457	6,179	5,245	5,245	5,245	5,245	5,245	5,245
Notes, Accounts Receivable	3,434	3,358	3,241	3,677	3,498	3,876	4,148	4,459	4,815	5,225
Inventories	3,947	4,337	4,838	5,055	5,261	5,582	5,931	6,331	6,790	7,315
Other Current Assets	1,173	2,357	1,489	1,150	1,130	1,551	1,659	1,783	1,926	2,090
− Others(Non interest bearing liab.)	5,020	6,227	5,314	5,468	6,034	6,435	6,885	7,401	7,994	8,673
= **Net Working Capital**	3,534	3,825	4,254	4,414	3,855	4,574	4,853	5,172	5,538	5,956
Property, Plant, Equipment	2,834	3,011	3,520	3,989	4,454	4,652	4,977	5,350	5,778	6,270
Other Assets	2,064	2,613	2,834	3,209	2,948	3,179	3,443	3,745	4,093	4,441
− Others(Non interest bearing liab.)	1,544	1,480	1,770	1,907	3,216	3,295	3,443	3,612	3,852	4,180
= **Fixed Operating Capital**	3,354	4,144	4,584	5,291	4,186	4,535	4,977	5,484	6,019	6,531
Capital (Operating Apporach)	12,030	13,893	14,295	15,884	13,286	14,354	15,075	15,901	16,802	17,732

図表 7.1 | ナイキの NOPAT，投下資本の予測（百万ドル）

NOPAT

	実績					予測				
	2014	2015	2016	2017	2018	2019	2020	2021	2022	2023
売上高	27,799	30,601	32,376	34,350	36,397	38,763	41,476	44,587	48,154	52,247
− 原価	15,353	16,534	17,405	19,038	20,441	21,707	23,019	24,523	26,485	28,736
− 販管費	8,766	9,892	10,469	10,563	11,511	12,210	13,065	14,045	15,168	16,458
減価償却費	518	606	649	706	747	775	830	892	963	1,045
= 営業利益	3,680	4,175	4,502	4,749	4,445	4,845	5,392	6,019	6,501	7,053
− 税金	836	925	840	628	2,458	1,211	1,348	1,505	1,625	1,763
= NOPAT	2,844	3,250	3,662	4,121	1,987	3,634	4,044	4,514	4,876	5,290
NOPAT 成長率		14.3%	12.7%	12.5%	-51.8%	82.9%	11.3%	11.6%	8.0%	8.5%

投下資本

	実績					予測				
	2014	2015	2016	2017	2018	2019	2020	2021	2022	2023
現金及び同等物	2,220	3,852	3,138	3,808	4,249	4,249	4,249	4,249	4,249	4,249
有価証券	2,922	2,072	2,319	2,371	996	996	996	996	996	996
投資有価証券	0	0	0	0	0	0	0	0	0	0
= 現金及び金融投資	5,142	5,924	5,457	6,179	5,245	5,245	5,245	5,245	5,245	5,245
売掛債権	3,434	3,358	3,241	3,677	3,498	3,876	4,148	4,459	4,815	5,225
棚卸資産	3,947	4,337	4,838	5,055	5,261	5,582	5,931	6,331	6,790	7,315
その他流動資産	1,173	2,357	1,489	1,150	1,130	1,551	1,659	1,783	1,926	2,090
− その他流動負債（無利子流動負債）	5,020	6,227	5,314	5,468	6,034	6,435	6,885	7,401	7,994	8,673
= 正味運転資本	3,534	3,825	4,254	4,414	3,855	4,574	4,853	5,172	5,538	5,956
有形固定資産	2,834	3,011	3,520	3,989	4,454	4,652	4,977	5,350	5,778	6,270
その他固定資産	2,064	2,613	2,834	3,209	2,948	3,179	3,443	3,745	4,093	4,441
− その他固定負債（無利子固定負債）	1,544	1,480	1,770	1,907	3,216	3,295	3,443	3,612	3,852	4,180
= 固定資本	3,354	4,144	4,584	5,291	4,186	4,535	4,977	5,484	6,019	6,531
投下資本	12,030	13,893	14,295	15,884	13,286	14,354	15,075	15,901	16,802	17,732

| | | | | | | **Forecast Drivers** | | | | | |
	2014	2015	2016	2017	2018	Avg	2019	2020	2021	2022	2023
Growth%		10.1%	5.8%	6.1%	6.0%	7.0%	6.5%	7.0%	7.5%	8.0%	8.5%
% of Sales	55.2%	54.0%	53.8%	55.4%	56.2%	54.9%	56.0%	55.5%	55.0%	55.0%	55.0%
% of Sales	31.5%	32.3%	32.3%	30.8%	31.6%	31.7%	31.5%	31.5%	31.5%	31.5%	31.5%
% of Sales	1.9%	2.0%	2.0%	2.1%	2.1%	2.0%	2.0%	2.0%	2.0%	2.0%	2.0%
% of Sales	13.2%	13.6%	13.9%	13.8%	12.2%	13.4%	12.5%	13.0%	13.5%	13.5%	13.5%
Tax Rate	22.7%	22.2%	18.7%	13.2%	55.3%	26.4%	25.0%	25.0%	25.0%	25.0%	25.0%
% of Sales	3.0%	3.0%	2.6%	1.8%	6.8%	3.4%	3.1%	3.3%	3.4%	3.4%	3.4%
% of Sales	10.2%	10.6%	11.3%	12.0%	5.5%	9.9%	9.4%	9.8%	10.1%	10.1%	10.1%
Validation	0.0%	0.0%	0.0%	0.0%	0.0%	0.0%	0.0%	0.0%	0.0%	0.0%	0.0%

| | | | | | | **Forecast Drivers** | | | | | |
	2014	2015	2016	2017	2018	Avg	2019	2020	2021	2022	2023
% of Sales	**18.5%**	**19.4%**	**16.9%**	**18.0%**	**14.4%**	**17.4%**	**13.5%**	**12.6%**	**11.8%**	**10.9%**	**10.0%**
% of Sales	12.4%	11.0%	10.0%	10.7%	9.6%	10.7%	10.0%	10.0%	10.0%	10.0%	10.0%
% of Sales	14.2%	14.2%	14.9%	14.7%	14.5%	14.5%	14.4%	14.3%	14.2%	14.1%	14.0%
% of Sales	4.2%	7.7%	4.6%	3.3%	3.1%	4.6%	4.0%	4.0%	4.0%	4.0%	4.0%
% of Sales	18.1%	20.3%	16.4%	15.9%	16.6%	17.5%	16.6%	16.6%	16.6%	16.6%	16.6%
% of Sales	**12.7%**	**12.5%**	**13.1%**	**12.9%**	**10.6%**	**12.4%**	**11.8%**	**11.7%**	**11.6%**	**11.5%**	**11.4%**
% of Sales	10.2%	9.8%	10.9%	11.6%	12.2%	11.0%	12.0%	12.0%	12.0%	12.0%	12.0%
% of Sales	7.4%	8.5%	8.8%	9.3%	8.1%	8.4%	8.2%	8.3%	8.4%	8.5%	8.5%
% of Sales	5.6%	4.8%	5.5%	5.6%	8.8%	6.0%	8.5%	8.3%	8.1%	8.0%	8.0%
% of Sales	**12.1%**	**13.5%**	**14.2%**	**15.4%**	**11.5%**	**13.3%**	**11.7%**	**12.0%**	**12.3%**	**12.5%**	**12.5%**
% of Sales	**43.3%**	**45.4%**	**44.2%**	**46.2%**	**36.5%**	**43.1%**	**37.0%**	**36.3%**	**35.7%**	**34.9%**	**33.9%**

| | | | | | | **予測ドライバー** | | | | | |
	2014	2015	2016	2017	2018	平均	2019	2020	2021	2022	2023
売上成長率		10.1%	5.8%	6.1%	6.0%	7.0%	6.5%	7.0%	7.5%	8.0%	8.5%
売上高比	55.2%	54.0%	53.8%	55.4%	56.2%	54.9%	56.0%	55.5%	55.0%	55.0%	55.0%
売上高比	31.5%	32.3%	32.3%	30.8%	31.6%	31.7%	31.5%	31.5%	31.5%	31.5%	31.5%
売上高比	1.9%	2.0%	2.0%	2.1%	2.1%	2.0%	2.0%	2.0%	2.0%	2.0%	2.0%
売上高比	13.2%	13.6%	13.9%	13.8%	12.2%	13.4%	12.5%	13.0%	13.5%	13.5%	13.5%
税率	22.7%	22.2%	18.7%	13.2%	55.3%	26.4%	25.0%	25.0%	25.0%	25.0%	25.0%
売上高比	3.0%	3.0%	2.6%	1.8%	6.8%	3.4%	3.1%	3.3%	3.4%	3.4%	3.4%
売上高比	10.2%	10.6%	11.3%	12.0%	5.5%	9.9%	9.4%	9.8%	10.1%	10.1%	10.1%
照合	0.0%	0.0%	0.0%	0.0%	0.0%	0.0%	0.0%	0.0%	0.0%	0.0%	0.0%

| | | | | | | **予測ドライバー** | | | | | |
	2014	2015	2016	2017	2018	平均	2019	2020	2021	2022	2023
売上高比	**18.5%**	**19.4%**	**16.9%**	**18.0%**	**14.4%**	**17.4%**	**13.5%**	**12.6%**	**11.8%**	**10.9%**	**10.0%**
売上高比	12.4%	11.0%	10.0%	10.7%	9.6%	10.7%	10.0%	10.0%	10.0%	10.0%	10.0%
売上高比	14.2%	14.2%	14.9%	14.7%	14.5%	14.5%	14.4%	14.3%	14.2%	14.1%	14.0%
売上高比	4.2%	7.7%	4.6%	3.3%	3.1%	4.6%	4.0%	4.0%	4.0%	4.0%	4.0%
売上高比	18.1%	20.3%	16.4%	15.9%	16.6%	17.5%	16.6%	16.6%	16.6%	16.6%	16.6%
売上高比	**12.7%**	**12.5%**	**13.1%**	**12.9%**	**10.6%**	**12.4%**	**11.8%**	**11.7%**	**11.6%**	**11.5%**	**11.4%**
売上高比	10.2%	9.8%	10.9%	11.6%	12.2%	11.0%	12.0%	12.0%	12.0%	12.0%	12.0%
売上高比	7.4%	8.5%	8.8%	9.3%	8.1%	8.4%	8.2%	8.3%	8.4%	8.5%	8.5%
売上高比	5.6%	4.8%	5.5%	5.6%	8.8%	6.0%	8.5%	8.3%	8.1%	8.0%	8.0%
売上高比	**12.1%**	**13.5%**	**14.2%**	**15.4%**	**11.5%**	**13.3%**	**11.7%**	**12.0%**	**12.3%**	**12.5%**	**12.5%**
売上高比	**43.3%**	**45.4%**	**44.2%**	**46.2%**	**36.5%**	**43.1%**	**37.0%**	**36.3%**	**35.7%**	**34.9%**	**33.9%**

Forecast FCF and EVA

The future FCF is predicted based on the forecasts of NOPAT and capital. When WACC is brought in, the future EVA will be predicted simultaneously. EVA spread, ROC, NOPAT margin, and capital turnover are calculated by modifying the same data. Analyzing those measures can be effective for ensuring consistency between future performance forecasts and the strategy and competitive advantages of a company.

Performance Forecast of Nike ②

Figure 7.2 illustrates a 5-year predicted FCF and EVA of Nike based on the forecasts of NOPAT and capital.

Figure 7.2 | FCF and EVA Forecast of Nike (in million dollars)

Free Cash Flow		Actual					Estimate				
	2014	2015	2016	2017	2018	2019	2020	2021	2022	2023
NOPAT	2,844	3,250	3,662	4,121	1,987	3,634	4,044	4,514	4,876	5,290
+ Depreciation	518	606	649	706	747	775	830	892	963	1,045
− Increase in Cash and Investments		782	-467	722	-934	0	0	0	0	0
− Increase in Accounts Receivable		-76	-117	436	-179	378	271	311	357	409
− Increase in Inventories		390	501	217	206	321	349	400	458	525
− Increase in Other Current Assets		1,184	-868	-339	-20	421	109	124	143	164
+ Increase in Non interest bearing Liab.		1,143	-623	291	1,875	479	598	685	833	1,007
= **Operating Cash Flow**		**2,719**	**4,639**	**4,082**	**5,536**	**3,769**	**4,742**	**5,256**	**5,714**	**6,244**
Invest in Plant, Property, Equipment		783	1,158	1,175	1,212	973	1,155	1,265	1,391	1,536
+ Invest in Other Assets		549	221	375	-261	231	264	303	348	348
= **Investment**		**1,332**	**1,379**	**1,550**	**951**	**1,203**	**1,419**	**1,568**	**1,739**	**1,884**
Free Cash Flow		**1,387**	**3,260**	**2,532**	**4,585**	**2,566**	**3,323**	**3,688**	**3,975**	**4,360**
FCF Growth			135.1%	-22.3%	81.1%	-44.0%	29.5%	11.0%	7.8%	9.7%
Net Investment			1,863	402	1,589	-2,598	1,068	721	826	901	930

EVA		Actual					Estimate				
	2014	2015	2016	2017	2018	2019	2020	2021	2022	2023
NOPAT		3,250	3,662	4,121	1,987	3,634	4,044	4,514	4,876	5,290
Capital (Beg.)		12,030	13,893	14,295	15,884	13,286	14,354	15,075	15,901	16,802
WACC		7.0%	7.0%	7.0%	7.0%	7.0%	7.0%	7.0%	7.0%	7.0%
− Capital Charge		845	976	1,005	1,116	934	1,009	1,059	1,118	1,181
= **EVA**		**2,404**	**2,685**	**3,116**	**870**	**2,700**	**3,035**	**3,455**	**3,758**	**4,109**
ROC =NOPAT/Beg. Cap		27%	26%	29%	13%	27%	28%	30%	31%	31%
− WACC		7.0%	7.0%	7.0%	7.0%	7.0%	7.0%	7.0%	7.0%	7.0%
= EVA Spread		20.0%	19.3%	21.8%	5.5%	20.3%	21.1%	22.9%	23.6%	24.5%
NOPAT Margin = NOPAT/Sales	10.2%	10.6%	11.3%	12.0%	5.5%	9.4%	9.8%	10.1%	10.1%	10.1%
Capital Turnover = Sales/Beg. Cap		2.5	2.3	2.4	2.3	2.9	2.9	3.0	3.0	3.1

142   Chapter 7   Forecasting Future Performance

● FCF，EVA の予測

NOPAT，投下資本の予測数値に基づき，将来の FCF は予測される。また，WACC と組み合わせることにより将来の EVA も同時に予測することができる。さらに，同じ情報を組み替えるだけで EVA スプレッド，ROC，NOPAT マージン，投下資本回転率なども計算されるため，将来の業績予測が企業の戦略や強み・弱みといった競争優位性と整合しているのか確認しておくとよい。

● ナイキの業績予測②

図表 7.2 は NOPAT，投下資本の予測数値に基づいた，今後 5 年間のナイキの FCF と EVA の予測値を示している。

図表7.2 ┃ ナイキの FCF，EVA の予測（百万ドル）

フリー・キャッシュフロー	実績					予測				
	2014	2015	2016	2017	2018	2019	2020	2021	2022	2023
NOPAT	2,844	3,250	3,662	4,121	1,987	3,634	4,044	4,514	4,876	5,290
＋ 減価償却費	518	606	649	706	747	775	830	892	963	1,045
－ 現金及び金融投資の増額		782	-467	722	-934	0	0	0	0	0
－ 売掛債権の増額		-76	-117	436	-179	378	271	311	357	409
－ 棚卸資産の増額		390	501	217	206	321	349	400	458	525
－ その他流動資産の増額		1,184	-868	-339	-20	421	109	124	143	164
＋ 無利子負債の増額		1,143	-623	291	1,875	479	598	685	833	1,007
＝ 営業キャッシュフロー		2,719	4,639	4,082	5,536	3,769	4,742	5,256	5,714	6,244
有形固定資産への投資		783	1,158	1,175	1,212	973	1,155	1,265	1,391	1,536
＋ その他資産への投資		549	221	375	-261	231	264	303	348	348
＝ 投資額		1,332	1,379	1,550	951	1,203	1,419	1,568	1,739	1,884
フリー・キャッシュフロー		1,387	3,260	2,532	4,585	2,566	3,323	3,688	3,975	4,360
FCF 成長率			135.1%	-22.3%	81.1%	-44.0%	29.5%	11.0%	7.8%	9.7%
純投資額		1,863	402	1,589	-2,598	1,068	721	826	901	930

EVA	実績					予測				
	2014	2015	2016	2017	2018	2019	2020	2021	2022	2023
NOPAT		3,250	3,662	4,121	1,987	3,634	4,044	4,514	4,876	5,290
期首投下資本		12,030	13,893	14,295	15,884	13,286	14,354	15,075	15,901	16,802
WACC		7.0%	7.0%	7.0%	7.0%	7.0%	7.0%	7.0%	7.0%	7.0%
－ 資本費用		845	976	1,005	1,116	934	1,009	1,059	1,118	1,181
＝ EVA		2,404	2,685	3,116	870	2,700	3,035	3,455	3,758	4,109
ROC ＝NOPAT ÷期首投下資本		27%	26%	29%	13%	27%	28%	30%	31%	31%
－ WACC		7.0%	7.0%	7.0%	7.0%	7.0%	7.0%	7.0%	7.0%	7.0%
＝ EVA スプレッド		20.0%	19.3%	21.8%	5.5%	20.3%	21.1%	22.9%	23.6%	24.5%
NOPAT マージン ＝ NOPAT ÷売上	10.2%	10.6%	11.3%	12.0%	5.5%	9.4%	9.8%	10.1%	10.1%	10.1%
投下資本回転率＝売上÷期首投下資本		2.5	2.3	2.4	2.3	2.9	2.9	3.0	3.0	3.1

第 7 章　将来業績の予測　143

Chapter

Forecasting Terminal Value

> **Points!**
> ✓ When you attempt to evaluate a long lasting investment, terminal value estimation is unavoidable
> ✓ It is advisable to use a value driver model to estimate terminal value

● Terminal Value

Since the value of a company is the present value of total future FCF, forecasting long term cash flows is absolutely necessary.

You can project cash flows for all periods. It is technically feasible to forecast FCF every year over the life of the project even as far out as 100 years. However, obtaining reasonable forecasts for FCF in each year would be difficult and quite cumbersome. Thus, in practice, FCF over only a fixed period of time (the forecast period) such as 5-10 years is forecasted with attention to detail. FCF beyond the forecast period is estimated by making assumptions. The value of the FCF beyond the forecast period is referred to as the terminal value.

● Calculating Terminal Value

The terminal value is usually estimated in one of two ways.

One is based on the assumption that the company (or project) will dissolve at some point in the future and so the estimated liquidation value represents a terminal value. The liquation-based terminal value tends to be relatively conservative.

The second approach assumes that the company will continue forever and can thus be valued using the perpetuity formula or the perpetuity with growth formula.

第8章 ターミナル・バリューの予測

ポイント！

✔ 長期間にわたる投資の価値を評価する際には，ターミナル・バリューの推定が必要となる

✔ ターミナル・バリューの計算にあたっては価値ドライバーモデルを活用することが望ましい

● ターミナル・バリュー

企業価値は将来のすべての FCF の現在価値であるから，企業価値を評価する際には必然的に長期間にわたるキャッシュフローを予想する必要がある。

もちろんすべての期におけるキャッシュフローを予想してもかまわない。100年間の FCF を年度別に予想することも技術的には可能である。しかし，そのような遠い年度の FCF を精緻に予想することは非常に困難であり，また煩雑である。そのため，たとえば5～10年間などある一定の期間（予想期間）はFCF の予想を詳細に行い，残りの期間（予想期間後）については，何らかの簡単な前提をおき価値を推定することがよく行われる。この，予想期間後の価値のことを「ターミナル・バリュー」と呼ぶ。

● ターミナル・バリューの計算

ターミナル・バリューを算出する際によくおかれる前提が2つある。

1つは，企業（あるいは投資案件）が将来のある時点において解散・終了するという前提である。この場合は清算価値がターミナル・バリューとなる。この清算価値に基づくターミナル・バリューは比較的保守的となる。

もう1つは予想期間後も企業が永遠に継続するという前提であり，永久年金式および定率成長の永久年金式を活用する。

第8章 ターミナル・バリューの予測 145

Figure 8.1 | **Terminal Value and Assumptions**

Liquidation Value	Assuming that the company will end at some point in the future
Perpetuity Value	Assuming that the company will continue in a "steady state" (using the perpetuity formula)
	Assuming that the company will continue at a specified growth rate (using the perpetuity with growth formula)

○ Perpetuity Formula

The perpetuity formula can be applied to assets that generate cash flows indefinitely starting from the next period.

$$PV = \frac{CF}{r}$$

CF: cash flow (starting one period from now)
r : expected return (WACC)

Suppose that an annual FCF of 100 starting in year one is expected to continue forever with the WACC of 5 percent. The present value of this infinite stream of cash flows would be $100 / 5\% = 2,000$.

○ Perpetuity with Growth Formula

When the cash flows continue to grow into the future at a constant rate, "perpetuity with growth formula" with a constant growth rate for the cash flows, g, in the denominator is applied:

$$PV = \frac{CF_1}{r - g}$$

CF_1: cash flow in year 1
r : expected return (WACC)
g : growth rate

The formula requires that $r > g$.

146 | Chapter 8 Forecasting Terminal Value

図表 8.1 | ターミナル・バリューと前提

清算価値	企業が将来のある時点において解散するという仮定に基づく
永続価値	企業の業績が一定という仮定に基づく （永久年金式を活用）
	企業の業績が一定の率で成長していくという仮定に基づく （定率成長の永久年金式を活用）

● 永久年金式

永久年金式は翌期以降毎期同じ金額（キャッシュフロー）が永久に発生する場合の価値を表わす式である。

$$PV = \frac{CF}{r}$$

CF：翌期から発生するキャッシュフロー
r ：期待リターン（WACC）

たとえば，1 年後から 100 という FCF が永久に続く場合の現在価値は，WACC が 5%の場合，$100 \div 5\% = 2,000$ となる。

● 定率成長の永久年金式

キャッシュフローが永久に一定の率で増えていく場合にはその成長率（g）を分母に含んだ以下の「定率成長の永久年金式」を活用する。

$$PV = \frac{CF_1}{r - g}$$

CF_1：1 年後のキャッシュフロー
r ：期待リターン（WACC）
g ：成長率

ただし，この式は $r > g$ となることが必要である。

第 8 章 ターミナル・バリューの予測 147

For example, to obtain the present value of a perpetual stream of FCF where the initial FCF in year one is 100, the constant growth rate is 2 percent forever, and the WACC is 5 percent, the formula looks like;

$$\frac{100}{5\% - 2\%} = 3,333$$

Note that the terminal value as measured at the end of the forecast period must be discounted back to present value when obtaining the present value. For example, if the forecast period is 5 years and the FCF from year 6 is 100, then assuming a 5% WACC, the terminal value is calculated as 100 / 5% = 2,000. This 2,000 is the value discounted back to year 5. The present value of the terminal value is then $2,000/(1.05)^5 = 1,567$.

◉ Common Mistakes in Terminal Value

It is popular to estimate the terminal value using the perpetuity formula, but it has a problem that requires attention. The following examples demonstrate common errors.

Suppose that NOPAT and FCF will grow at 10% for the three year forecast period, and stops growing after three years for the terminal value period. Let us estimate the terminal value (Figure 8.2). NOPAT in year one is 100 and the half of NOPAT will be reinvested every year for the three year forecast period. Therefore, FCF is estimated to be half of NOPAT and both FCF and NOPAT will grow at 10% from year one to year three. How should we forecast NOPAT and FCF to estimate the terminal value?

148 | Chapter 8 Forecasting Terminal Value

たとえば，1年後における最初のFCFが100であり，これがそれ以後2%の成長で永久に続いていく場合の現在価値は，WACCを5%とすると，以下のように計算される。

$$\frac{100}{5\% - 2\%} = 3,333$$

なお，ターミナル・バリューを価値に反映させるためには，ターミナル・バリューを現在価値に割り引く必要がある。たとえば，6年度以降は100というFCFが永久に続くと仮定した場合，WACCが5%だとすると，ターミナル・バリューは100 ÷ 5% = 2,000となる。この2,000という価値は1つ前の期である5年度時点の価値であり，現在価値は，2,000 ÷ (1.05)^5 = 1,567となる。

● ターミナル・バリューの陥りがちな間違い

永続価値に基づくターミナル・バリューの推定は広く行われるが，注意が必要な点がある。以下の例でターミナル・バリューを計算する際に陥りがちな間違いを確認しておこう。

NOPATおよびFCFが予想期間の3年間において10%で成長し，予想期間終了後のターミナル・バリューの推定においては成長率がゼロになるという前提でターミナル・バリューを推定しよう（図表8.2）。初年度のNOPATは100であり，予想期間の3年間においては毎年NOPATの半分が再投資されていくとする。そのためFCFはNOPATの半分となり，NOPATとFCFは3年目まではともに10%で成長していく。では，ターミナル・バリューを予測するためのNOPAT，FCFはどう考えるべきであろうか。

第8章　ターミナル・バリューの予測　　149

Figure 8.2 | **Common Mistakes in Terminal Value(no growth)**

No Growth (Incorrect)	Year1	Year2	Year3	Year4-
NOPAT	100.0	110.0	121.0	121.0
Net Investment	50.0	55.0	60.5	60.5
FCF	50.0	55.0	60.5	60.5

No Growth (Correct)	Year1	Year2	Year3	Year4-
NOPAT	100.0	110.0	121.0	121.0
Net Investment	50.0	55.0	60.5	0.0
FCF	50.0	55.0	60.5	121.0

Since we assume zero growth from year 4, the NOPAT in year 4 will be the same as it is in year 3. But FCF in year 4 is not the same as it is in year 3, though it looks like it would be at a glance. No further investment to increase NOPAT will be demanded from the fourth year because zero growth is assumed.

In order to generate the same NOPAT, you do not need additional (net) investment, meaning that the depreciation expense exactly matches investment, so that NOPAT and FCF are identical in every period. Zero growth condition implies that the level of performance continues without any improvement or deterioration. It assumes constant capacity, productivity, and profitability, therefore requires investments to restore the value depreciated to maintain the same size and shape. Hence, the net investment should be zero, and the identical NOPAT and FCF will be produced from year 4. That is the appropriate estimate.

● Terminal Value in Growth Deceleration

How about the case in which growth rate is slowed down, but does not reach zero? Figure 8.3 provides an example where NOPAT and FCF will grow at 10% for up to year three and the growth rate drops to 1% from year 4.

図表 8.2 ターミナル・バリューの間違い（ゼロ成長）

ゼロ成長（間違い）	1年度	2年度	3年度	4年度-
NOPAT	100.0	110.0	121.0	121.0
純投資額	50.0	55.0	60.5	60.5
FCF	50.0	55.0	60.5	60.5

ゼロ成長（正）	1年度	2年度	3年度	4年度-
NOPAT	100.0	110.0	121.0	121.0
純投資額	50.0	55.0	60.5	0.0
FCF	50.0	55.0	60.5	121.0

4年目以降ゼロ成長となるのであれば，NOPATは3年目と同額になる。しかし，一見正しいように見えるが4年目のFCFは3年目と同額にはならない。4年目以降は成長がゼロであるならば，それ以降にNOPATを増やすための投資は必要がないからである。

同じNOPATを生み出すのにとどまるのであれば追加的な（純）投資額は必要なくなり（減価償却費と投資額が同額となり），毎年のNOPATはFCFと同額になる。ゼロ成長の状態とは，業績が改善も悪化せず，全く同じ業績が続いていくということである。事業の生産能力，生産性，収益性が一定という仮定であるから，事業が全く同じ状態を維持するためには投資資産の価値が摩耗する減価償却分は必ず補修的な投資をしなければならない。そのため（純）投資額が0であり，NOPATとFCFは同額となって4年目以降続くというのが正しい推定となる。

● 成長鈍化の場合のターミナル・バリュー

ゼロ成長ではなく，成長率が鈍化する前提の場合はどうであろうか。図表8.3は3年目までNOPATとFCFが10％成長し，4年目以降は1％に落ち込むとする場合の推定の例を示している。

Figure 8.3 | **Common Mistakes in Terminal Value (slowed growth)**

1% Growth (Incorrect)	Year1	Year2	Year3	Year4-
NOPAT	100.0	110.0	121.0	122.2
Net Investment	50.0	55.0	60.5	61.1
FCF	50.0	55.0	60.5	61.1

1% Growth (Correct)	Year1	Year2	Year3	Year4-
NOPAT	100.0	110.0	121.0	122.2
Net Investment	50.0	55.0	60.5	1.2
FCF	50.0	55.0	60.5	121.0

It is incorrect to estimate that FCF in year 4 will grow at 1% which is the same as NOPAT growth. The decline of NOPAT growth implies less investment required to support it. Therefore, the investment rate from the fourth year has to be lower than before, causing the higher growth rate of the fourth year FCF. If you forecast FCF in year 4 will grow at 1%, the terminal value will be significantly underestimated.

As we have seen, the forecast of an initial FCF for a terminal value is liable to be wrong, accordingly, the terminal value calculated with perpetuity or perpetuity with growth formula applying FCF in the numerator is subject to making mistakes unknowingly. So as to avoid this error, an alternative is taking advantage of the value driver model which we will discuss next.

Value Driver Model

The value driver model is expressed as follows;

$$\text{Value} = \frac{\text{NOPAT}_1 \left(1 - \dfrac{g}{\text{ROC}}\right)}{\text{WACC} - g}$$

based on the perpetuity with growth formula.

図表 8.3 ┃ ターミナル・バリューの間違い（成長鈍化）

1% 成長（間違い）	1 年度	2 年度	3 年度	4 年度 -
NOPAT	100.0	110.0	121.0	122.2
純投資額	50.0	55.0	60.5	61.1
FCF	50.0	55.0	60.5	61.1

1% 成長（正）	1 年度	2 年度	3 年度	4 年度 -
NOPAT	100.0	110.0	121.0	122.2
純投資額	50.0	55.0	60.5	1.2
FCF	50.0	55.0	60.5	121.0

　4 年目の NOPAT は 1% で成長するが，4 年目の FCF も NOPAT と同様に 1%の成長率にとどまると考えると誤りである。NOPAT の成長率が落ちるのであればその成長を支えるための必要な追加的な資本は減少する。そのため 4 年目の再投資率はそれ以前よりも低くなるはずであり，そのため 4 年目の FCF の成長率は高くなる。もし 4 年目の FCF も 1% で成長すると計算をしてしまうと，ターミナル・バリューを大きく過小評価してしまうことになりかねない。

　このようにターミナル・バリューの初年度の FCF の予測は間違いやすく，分子に FCF を用いた永久年金式，あるいは定率成長の永久年金式によりターミナル・バリューを推定しようとすると無意識のうちに計算を間違えてしまう可能性が高い。このような間違いを避けるためには次に紹介する価値ドライバーモデルを活用するのが望ましい。

⬤ 価値ドライバーモデル

　価値ドライバーモデルは以下のように表わされ，

$$価値 = \frac{NOPAT_1 \left(1 - \dfrac{g}{ROC} \right)}{WACC - g}$$

この式は定率成長の永久年金式をもとにしている。

第 8 章　ターミナル・バリューの予測　　153

Perpetuity with Growth Formula: $\dfrac{CF_1}{r-g}$

FCF used in the numerator of the formula is defined with NOPAT and the investment rate (I %) as;

$$
\begin{aligned}
FCF &= NOPAT - Net\ Investment \\
&= NOPAT - (NOPAT \times Investment\ Rate\ (I\%)) \\
&= NOPAT\ (1 - I\%)
\end{aligned}
$$

Since the growth rate is the product of the investment rate and ROC (g= I % × ROC, refer to chapter 4), the investment rate can be shown as follows;

$$
I\% = \dfrac{g}{ROC}
$$

Substituting those variables for FCF in the perpetuity with growth formula, you will get the value driver model.

$$
Value = \dfrac{NOPAT_1 \left(1 - \dfrac{g}{ROC}\right)}{WACC - g}
$$

The value driver model is mathematically identical to the perpetuity with growth formula. The model lets you forecast the components of FCF, but not FCF directly. This helps to calculate an appropriate terminal value.

● Growth Rate for Terminal Value

It is not an easy question to set the growth rate for a terminal value, but here is a guideline for a reasonable estimate.

The growth rate of a company will generally converge with the growth rate of the industry where it operates as time goes by. Therefore, the appropriate growth rate for a terminal value should be considered the nominal growth rate for the consumption of products or services the industry provides, and the rate will settle somewhere between

154   Chapter 8   Forecasting Terminal Value

$$\text{定率成長の永久年金式：} \quad \frac{CF_1}{r - g}$$

式の分子となる FCF は NOPAT と再投資率（I ％）によって以下のように定義される。

$$
\begin{aligned}
\text{FCF} &= \text{NOPAT} - \text{純投資額} \\
&= \text{NOPAT} - (\text{NOPAT} \times \text{再投資率 I \%}) \\
&= \text{NOPAT} (1 - \text{I \%})
\end{aligned}
$$

成長率は再投資率に ROC を掛け合わせたもの（g = I ％ × ROC）であった（第4章参照）から，再投資率は成長率を ROC で割ることで表わされる。

$$\text{I \%} = \frac{g}{\text{ROC}}$$

定率成長の永久年金式の FCF をこれらの変数に置き換えたのが価値ドライバーモデルである。

$$\text{価値} = \frac{\text{NOPAT}_1 \left(1 - \dfrac{g}{\text{ROC}}\right)}{\text{WACC} - g}$$

価値ドライバーモデルは FCF を用いた定率成長の永久年金式と数式的には同一なものであるが，FCF を直接的に推定するのではなく，FCF をその構成要素に分解して推定することにより，適切なターミナル・バリューの推定を可能にする。

● ターミナル・バリューの成長率

ターミナル・バリューを推定する際に使用する成長率をどう設定するのかは簡単な問題ではないが，ここではその考え方のガイドを示しておく。

時を経るにつれて企業の成長率は，通常その企業が属する産業自体の成長率に近づいていく。そのため適切な成長率は，その産業が生み出す製品・サービス消費の長期的な（名目）成長率であると考えられる。そして，それはリスクフリー・レートと長期的な（名目）GDP（国内総生産）の成長率の間のどこか

a risk-free rate and a long term nominal GDP (gross domestic products) growth rate. That is because a GDP growth rate representing the growth of the entire economy must surpass a risk-free rate due to the risk premium in the long run, while the industry growth rate will approach a risk-free rate as the industry matures. The growth rate of an individual industry will dip below a GDP growth at some stage, and a subsequent industry will overtake an old industry and lead the economy with an outstanding growth rate. However, it is natural to assume that the growth rate of a subsequent industry also gets closer to GDP growth and then to a risk-free rate at some point in the future.

● Supplementary Note for Value Driver Model

The value driver model reveals how a profit growth influences the value of a company.

Suppose a company expected to generate NOPAT of 200 in the next year, and a WACC of 10%. If NOPAT will not change going forward, the value of the company is simply measured with the perpetuity formula as $200/10\% = 2,000$.

If the NOPAT of the company is expected to grow at the constant rate of 3% assuming 15% ROC, the value of the company is estimated, with the value driver model as;

$$\frac{200\left(1 - \dfrac{3\%}{15\%}\right)}{10\% - 3\%} = 2,285.7$$

If the NOPAT grows at 3% going forward and its ROC is assumed to be 7.5% sinking below WACC, the estimated value of the company is;

$$\frac{200\left(1 - \dfrac{3\%}{7.5\%}\right)}{10\% - 3\%} = 1,714.3$$

which is lower than the value with no growth condition of 2,000.

Figure 8.4 summarizes the estimated value when ROC and the growth rate of NOPAT change in the same manner.

に収斂していくと考えられる。なぜなら，長期的には経済全体の成長率である GDP の成長率はリスクフリー・レートよりもリスク・プレミアムの分だけ高くなるはずであり，一方で産業の成長率は，いずれその産業が成熟していくに従ってリスクフリー・レートに近づいていくと考えられるからである。特定の産業の成長率は，いずれ GDP よりも低くなっていくが，新しく生まれたビジネスが古い産業を追い抜き，高い成長率で経済をけん引していく。しかしそのような新しい産業の成長率もいずれは経済全体の伸び率に落ち着き，さらに時がたてばリスクフリー・レートに近づいていくと考えるのが自然である。

● 価値ドライバーモデルの補足

価値ドライバーモデルは利益成長が企業価値にどのように影響を与えるのかを示してくれる。

次年度の NOPAT が 200 だと予想される企業を想定する。WACC は 10% であるとする。もし NOPAT がゼロ成長であるとすると，単純に永久年金式を活用することにより，企業の価値は 200 ÷ 10% = 2,000 と算出できる。

では，この企業の ROC は 15% であるとし，NOPAT は以後 3% の成長が見込まれるとする。その場合の企業価値は価値ドライバーモデルにより以下のように計算される。

$$\frac{200 \left(1 - \dfrac{3\%}{15\%}\right)}{10\% - 3\%} = 2,285.7$$

次に，NOPAT は以後 3% で成長するが，ROC は 7.5% と WACC を下回っているとする。すると企業価値は

$$\frac{200 \left(1 - \dfrac{3\%}{7.5\%}\right)}{10\% - 3\%} = 1,714.3$$

とゼロ成長の場合の価値 2,000 を下回る。

同様の条件で，ROC と NOPAT 成長率を変化させたときに価値がどのように変化するのか試算した結果を図表 8.4 にまとめている。

第 8 章　ターミナル・バリューの予測　　157

Figure 8.4 | **Value Given First Year NOPAT of 200 and 10% WACC**

		ROC					
		5%	7.5%	10%	12.5%	15%	20%
NOPAT Growth	0%	2,000.0	2,000.0	2,000.0	2,000.0	2,000.0	2,000.0
	3%	1,142.9	1,714.3	2,000.0	2,171.4	2,285.7	2,428.6
	5%	—	1,333.3	2,000.0	2,400.0	2,666.7	3,000.0

As seen in the figure, the high NOPAT growth contributes increasing value only if ROC exceeds WACC. The profit growth when ROC is equal to WACC does not affect anything, and the profit growth where ROC falls below WACC hurts the value of a company.

This relation accommodates the definition of EVA formulated as (ROC−WACC) × Capital. Namely, value is created when ROC surpasses WACC, and value is destroyed when ROC falls short of WACC.

Note that the additional investment whose ROC is lower than WACC will be illustrated as the lower rightward movement in Figure 6.2.

158 | Chapter 8   Forecasting Terminal Value

図表 8.4 ┃ 初年度 NOPAT200，WACC10% の場合の価値

		ROC					
		5%	7.5%	10%	12.5%	15%	20%
NOPAT 成長率	0%	2,000.0	2,000.0	2,000.0	2,000.0	2,000.0	2,000.0
	3%	1,142.9	1,714.3	2,000.0	2,171.4	2,285.7	2,428.6
	5%	—	1,333.3	2,000.0	2,400.0	2,666.7	3,000.0

　このように ROC が WACC を上回る場合にのみ，高い NOPAT の成長率は高い価値を実現する。ROC が WACC を上回らない場合には利益の成長は意味がなく，ROC が WACC を下回る状態での利益の増大は価値を毀損してしまうのである。

　この関係は（ROC － WACC）×投下資本と表された EVA とも整合する。つまり，ROC が WACC を上回っていれば価値創造であり，ROC が WACC を下回っていれば価値破壊だということである。

　なお，ROC が WACC を下回る状態での追加的な投資は図表 6.2 における右下へのシフトにあたる。

第 8 章　ターミナル・バリューの予測　　159

Part 4
Value Estimate

- While future forecasts explored in the previous part are one of the most important factors in valuation, there are other issues that remain to be worked out. Chapter 9 describes the process to lead a share price.

- Next, in chapter 10, we take a look at the alternative valuation approach based on share price data of comparable companies in addition to the discounting approach discussed so far.

Chapter 9   Valuing Company, Equity and Shares

Chapter 10   Valuing with Multiples

第 4 部

価値の推定

★★★★

● 第 3 部で紹介した将来の業績予測は企業価値評価の最重要な要素だが，企業全体の価値や株価を推定する際には，さらに考慮しなければならない点がある。第 4 部の前半ではこの株価を推定するまでの手順を紹介する。

● 後半の第 10 章では，これまで議論してきた将来の業績を割り引くというアプローチではなく，競合事業の株価データを活用した別の価値評価アプローチを紹介する。

第 9 章　企業価値，株主価値，および株価

第10章　価値倍率法

Chapter 9 Valuing Company, Equity and Shares

Points!

- ✓ The value of non-operating assets constitutes the value of a company
- ✓ The estimated share price is calculated as the value of equity divided by the number of shares outstanding
- ✓ The results of valuation based on EVA and FCF are identical

○ Value of Operation

Forecasted future FCF and a terminal value will be discounted to the present value (PV). The value of a business operation is then obtained by taking the sum of the PV of the forecast period FCF and the PV of the terminal value.

Value of an Operation = PV of FCF of the Forecast Period + PV of Terminal Value

$$= \frac{FCF_1}{(1+r)^1} + \frac{FCF_2}{(1+r)^2} + \frac{FCF_3}{(1+r)^3} + \cdots + \frac{FCF_H}{(1+r)^H} + \frac{TV_H}{(1+r)^H}$$

FCF_t: free cash flow at time t
TV : terminal value
r : expected return (WACC)
H: forecast horizon, final period of forecast period

○ Sensitivity Analysis and Scenario Analysis

It is useful to deal with estimation errors or volatility in the future because forecasting future performance with high accuracy is often immensely difficult. A sensitivity analysis figures out the impacts due to the changes in the crucial forecasted variables on value.

A scenario analysis that provides multiple results of valuation based on multiple scenarios is also beneficial. Figure 9.1 demonstrates the outcome of a scenario analysis estimating the value based on optimistic and pessimistic forecasts in addition

第**9**章　企業価値，株主価値，および株価

ポイント！

✔　企業の価値を評価するためには非事業資産の価値を加味する必要がある

✔　推定株価は株主資本の価値を流通株式数で割ることにより算出される

✔　EVA を用いた価値評価は，FCF による価値評価の結果と同一となる

● 事業の価値

　生み出される FCF とターミナル・バリューが予想されたら，それらは現在価値に割り引かれる。予想期間における毎年の FCF の現在価値と，ターミナル・バリューの現在価値の合計がその事業の価値である。

事業の価値＝予想期間の FCF の現在価値＋ターミナル・バリューの現在価値

$$= \frac{FCF_1}{(1+r)^1} + \frac{FCF_2}{(1+r)^2} + \frac{FCF_3}{(1+r)^3} + \cdots \frac{FCF_H}{(1+r)^H} + \frac{TV_H}{(1+r)^H}$$

FCF_t：t 時点のフリー・キャッシュフロー　　　r：期待リターン（WACC）

TV　：ターミナル・バリュー　　　　　　　　　H：予想期間の終了時点

● 感応度分析とシナリオ分析

　将来業績を正確に予測することはしばしば非常に困難なので，予測の不確実性に対処しておくのも有効である。感応度分析は，業績予測にあたって重要な変数がある一定程度変化した時に，価値にどれだけの影響を及ぼすのかを把握するものである。

　また，将来の複数のシナリオに基づいて価値を複数算出することも有効である（シナリオ分析）。図表9.1では，ベースとなる基本シナリオに基づいた価値に加えて，楽観的な予想に基づいた価値と悲観的な予想に基づいた価値を算

第 9 章　企業価値，株主価値，および株価　　163

to the basic forecast. If you set probabilities to each scenario, the weighted average value can be measured.

Figure 9.1 | Scenario Analysis

	Value	Probability
Basic Scenario	2,250	50%
Optimistic Scenario	2,800	30%
Pessimistic Scenario	2,000	20%
Weighted Average	2,365	

● Evaluating Non-operating Assets

The total present value of FCF generated by operation corresponds to the value of the business operated in a company. Yet, a company sometimes has assets which are unrelated to the operation. Excess cash is one of them. A company could also hold artwork, real estate, and other companies' stocks for the sake of different from operating activities. The value of these non-operating assets constitutes the value of a company and are added for valuation.

However, it is quite difficult to distinguish non-operating assets from operating assets. Stocks of other companies are usually defined as a non-operating asset if it is simply for the purpose of financial investment. However, they can be categorized as operating capital if it facilitates a smooth commercial transaction with the company. Also, it is difficult to judge how much excess cash is actually excess, and how much cash should be kept to secure consistent business operations.

The current value of a non-operating asset might become detached from the book value in the balance sheet. You should take into consideration the difference for valuation if you can identify the market value of it. Realistically speaking however, it is difficult to find information relating to that.

At any rate, the total value of a company is estimated as the value of non-operating assets added to the value of operation.

出する例を表わしている。過去の経験や同種のプロジェクトの実績などからそれぞれのシナリオの発生確率が推定できれば，加重平均の価値も算出できる。

図表9.1 ┃ シナリオ分析

	価値	発生確率
基本シナリオ	2,250	50%
楽観シナリオ	2,800	30%
悲観シナリオ	2,000	20%
加重平均値	2,365	

◉ 非事業資産の加味

　企業が事業から生み出す FCF の現在価値の合計は，その企業が営む事業に関する価値である。ただし企業は事業活動とは関係のない資産を保有していることもある。余剰資金はその一例である。企業によっては美術品や不動産，他社の株式などを事業活動とは異なる目的で保有していることがある。これらの非事業資産の価値も企業価値の一部を構成していると考えられることから，企業価値評価の際には加算しなければならない。

　しかし，事業資産と非事業資産を区別することはなかなか難しい問題である。仮に他社の株式を保有しているとしても，それが単純な金融投資であるならば非事業資産であるが，その株式を保有することによってその企業との取引が円滑になるのであれば，この株式は事業活動のための投下資本と考えられる。余剰資金についても，どこまでが事業活動を行うために保有しておかなければならない現金であり，どこからが余剰資金であるのかを判断するのは難しい。

　非事業資産の実際の価値はバランスシート上の価値と乖離していることはしばしばある。もしそれらの市場価値がわかればその価値を企業価値の計算の際には考慮すべきであるが，実際にどのくらいの価値をもっているのかを把握するのは難しいのが現実である。

　いずれにしても，企業全体の価値は，事業の価値と非事業資産の価値を合計することで推定される。

第9章　企業価値，株主価値，および株価　165

● Value of Equity

The value of equity is measured as subtracting debt and non-controlling (minority) interests from the value of a company. Figure 9.2 illustrates the process so far graphically.

Figure 9.2 | Process to Measure Value of Equity

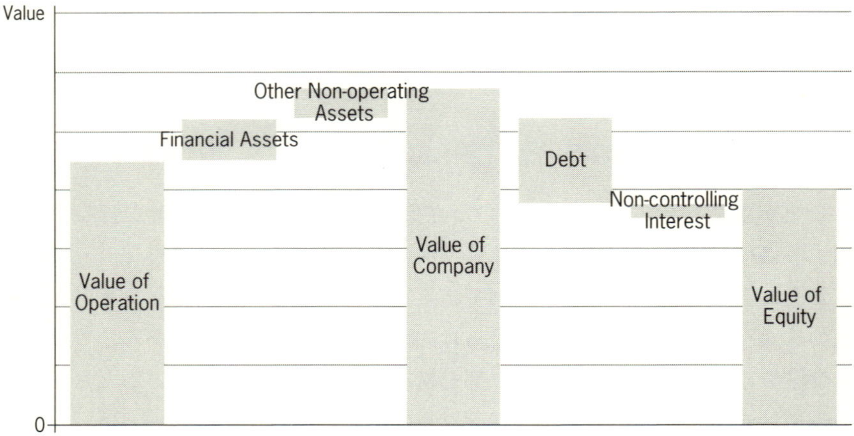

Valuation analysis in practice sometimes requires detailed projection for some more items including lease obligations, pension obligations, and non-controlling interests.

Note that, as we have discussed to define capital, reserves deducted as expenses to calculate NOPAT are considered outflowed from a company and do not constitute a debt capital to be paid in the future, unless they are adjusted to calculate FCF, (they are added back to FCF).

166 │ Chapter 9   Valuing Company, Equity and Shares

● 株主価値の推定

株主資本の価値を算出するためには，企業価値から負債の価値および非支配株主持ち分を差し引く。図表9.2はここまでのプロセスを示している。

図表9.2 ┃ 株主資本の価値の算出プロセス

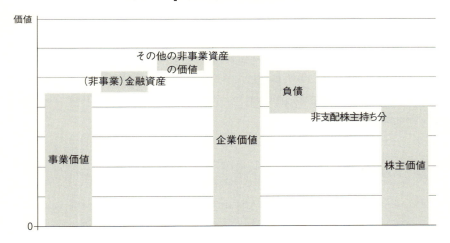

実際の企業価値分析の際には，リース負債や年金債務引当金，非支配株主持ち分などの見積もりをより厳密に行う必要がある場合も多い。

なお，投下資本の計算でも触れたように，利益の計算上費用として計上した引当金はそれをFCFの計算の際に調整しない限り，つまりFCFの計算の際に足し戻さない限り，すでに企業から流出してしまった費用であるから，今後支払いが必要な負債と認識する必要はない。つまり負債には含めない。

Price per Share

A share price is calculated as the value of equity divided by the number of shares.

The total possible number of shares that a company can issue is confirmed in a shareholders' meeting, and a large portion are usually issued. Issued shares are outstanding except for the treasury shares which have been repurchased by the company. Therefore, outstanding shares are shares issued by the company and held by investors. The number of outstanding shares are used to calculate dividends per share and earnings per share.

The number of outstanding shares, or issued shares minus treasury shares are also used to measure the price per share. The treasury shares are repurchased by the company. The purchase price paid out to the investors no longer constitute the value of a company.

EVA and Valuation

We are concerned here how EVA is linked with value. What is the value of a company raising 1,000 capital invested and expected to generate 250 in NOPAT every year going forward in perpetuity? Suppose there is no non-operating assets affecting the value of the company. Generating level profits forever implies a no-growth condition where the amount of capital reinvested is equal to depreciation, and accordingly, profits are the same as the FCF each year. WACC is assumed to be 10%.

We can apply the perpetuity formula because the FCF of 250 continues forever. The value of the company will be calculated as 250 / 10% = 2,500.

Figure 9.3 | **Valuation Based on FCF**

	Year 0	Year 1	Year 2	···
FCF		250	250	···
Company Value	2,500	↓	↓	↓

● 株価の推定

株主資本の価値を株式数で割ると株価が算出される。

企業の発行可能株式総数は株主総会において決定され，そのうちの大部分は発行される。発行済みの株式は，企業が自社株買いを行い金庫株とならない限り流通している。したがって，企業によって発行され投資家に保有されている株式が流通株式である。1株あたり配当，1株あたり利益を計算する際にはこの流通株式数が使用される。

株価を算出する際に使用するのも発行済み株式数から自社株買いにより取得した株式数を差し引いた流通株式数である。自社株買いした株式は企業によって再取得されており，その取得価額は投資家に支払われているためすでに企業価値を構成していないからである。

● EVA と価値評価

ここでは EVA が価値と関連していることを確認しよう。1,000 資金を調達して投資し，毎年 250 の利益（NOPAT）を永久に生み出すと期待される企業の価値はいくらになるだろうか。なお，非事業資産は価値に影響しないとする。永久に同じ利益が生み出されるということは，減価償却費と同額の投資額が行われるゼロ成長を意味するので，毎年の NOPAT は FCF と同額になる。WACC は 10% とする。

250 の FCF が永久に続いていくので，永久年金式により，企業価値は 250 ÷ 10% = 2,500 と計算される。

図表 9.3 ┃ FCF による価値評価

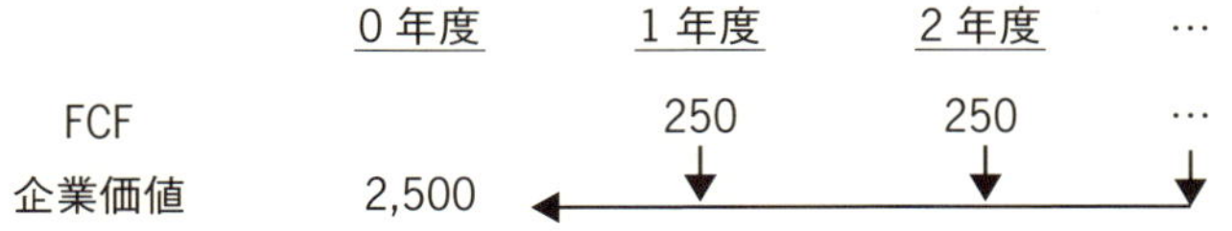

	0 年度	1 年度	2 年度	…
FCF		250	250	…
企業価値	2,500			

第 9 章　企業価値，株主価値，および株価

Next, we estimate the value using EVA (see Figure 9.4). The NOPAT each year is 250. The initial capital is 1,000, and capital in the future would remain constant at 1,000 due to the no-growth assumption. As a result, the capital charge in every year would be $1,000 \times 10\% = 100$. Subtracting the capital charge from NOPAT, EVA in each year would be 150. Since this EVA of 150 continues forever, again applying the perpetuity formula, the PV of all future EVA will be calculated at $150 / 10\% = 1,500$. This 1,500 is the economic value created utilizing an original capital of 1,000, and both are added to make the total value of the company, 2,500. The results of valuation based on EVA and FCF are identical.

Figure 9.4 | **Valuation Based on EVA**

	Year 0	Year 1	Year 2	⋯
NOPAT (=FCF)		250	250	⋯
Investment	1,000			
Capital		1,000	1,000	⋯
× WACC		10%	10%	⋯
Capital Charge		100	100	⋯
EVA		150	150	⋯
PV of EVA	1,500			
+ Capital	1,000			
Company Value	2,500			

In short, the value of a company is the PV of all future FCF, and the sum of the PV of all future EVA and its capital. This numerical equality must hold when the same financial data and assumptions are used.

次に EVA で価値を求めてみよう（図表 9.4）。毎年の利益は 250 であった。投資時点の投下資本は 1,000 であり，ゼロ成長の仮定から，投下資本は将来的にも 1,000 のままである。そのため，毎年の資本費用も 1,000 × 10% = 100 となる。NOPAT から資本費用を引いた毎年の EVA は 150 である。この EVA は永久に継続するので，やはり永久年金式により，将来の EVA 現在価値合計は 150 ÷ 10% = 1,500 となる。これは 1,000 という資本を活用して追加的に生み出された経済的な価値であるから，これにもともとの投資額 1,000 を加えた 2,500 が企業価値となる。この額は FCF による価値評価の結果と同じである。

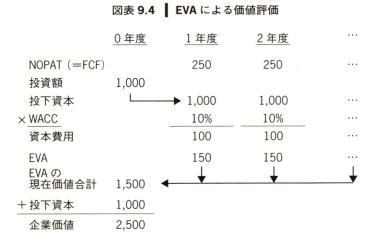

図表 9.4 ┃ EVA による価値評価

つまり，企業の価値は将来の FCF の現在価値の合計であるとともに，将来の EVA の現在価値の合計に投下資本を加えたものでもあるのである。この等価性は同じ前提で同じ財務情報を使用する限り，必ず成立する。

● MVA Connecting EVA to Value

The results of Figure 9.3 and 9.4 are exhibited in Figure 9.5.

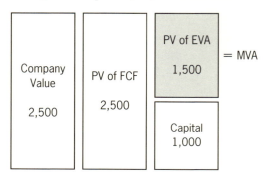

Figure 9.5 | Company Value and MVA

The value of a company is determined by the PV of FCF. If a company raises capital and does nothing with it, the market value of the company will be unchanged from the original value. However, the market value will change when a company makes investments that are expected to change FCF in the future. The value of a company becomes greater than the value funded when a company successfully creates value. On the other hand, the value of a company declines lower than its capital if the company's financial performance falls below investors' expectations.

There is usually a gap between the market value of a company and capital. Capital is the historical value of investment recorded on a company's books. The difference between the market value and the book value of a company is produced by future EVA expectation and is called Market Value Added, or MVA because it represents the value added in the market.

● EVAと企業価値を結びつけるMVA

図表9.3, 9.4の結果を図示したのが図表9.5である。

図表9.5 ｜ 企業価値とMVA

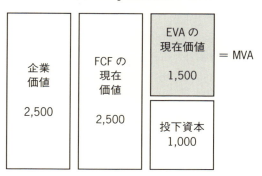

企業の価値はFCFの現在価値によって決まる。企業が資金調達をしたままで何もしなければ、市場価値は調達額である投下資本のままである。しかし、企業が事業投資を行って将来のFCFに対する期待が変わると市場価値は変化する。価値の創造に成功すれば、企業の価値は調達した金額以上となる。一方で、企業の業績が投資家の期待に届かなければ、企業価値は調達した金額以下になってしまうということである。

通常、上場企業の市場価値と企業が調達し活用している投下資本には乖離が生じている。投下資本は帳簿上に記録されている価値なので、簿価である。市場価値と簿価である投下資本の差は将来の期待EVAによるものであり、この差は市場において付加された価値であることから、MVA（市場付加価値）とも呼ばれる。

● Estimated Share Price of Nike

Figure 9.6 shows the result of a share price valuation of Nike. The terminal value has been estimated with the value driver model introduced in chapter 8 with the growth rate of 3.5% which is slightly higher than the risk-free rate, to be 137.6 billion dollars. Please refer to the downloadable "Financial Analysis and Valuation File" introduced in the appendix for details regarding calculation.

The value of operation is the sum of the present values of FCF for five years and the present value of the terminal value, totaling 112.4 billion dollars. Adding financial assets, the value of the company is estimated to be 117.7 billion dollars. The estimated value of equity is calculated by subtracting debt from it to be 114.2 billion dollars.

According to the annual report, Nike issues two types of stock; Class B stock is listed on the New York Stock Exchange and traded, and Class A stock is not publicly traded. And as of July 2018, the total number of shares outstanding was 1.6 billion. The share price of Nike is estimated as the estimated value of equity, 114.2 billion dollars, divided by the number of shares outstanding, 1.6 billion, which is around 71 dollars.

The bottom of Figure 9.6 shows the result of EVA valuation. You can confirm that the estimated share price based on EVA and FCF are equivalent.

174　　Chapter 9　Valuing Company, Equity and Shares

ナイキの株価の推定

　図表9.6はナイキの株価を推定した結果を示している。ターミナル・バリューは，成長率をリスクフリー・レートを若干上回る 3.5% とし，第 8 章で紹介した価値ドライバー・モデルによって 1,376 億ドルと計算された（詳細について興味のある方は巻末に紹介する「財務分析・企業価値評価ファイル」をダウンロードして確認いただきたい）。

　5 年間の FCF の現在価値の合計とターミナル・バリューの現在価値の合計額 1,124 億ドルが事業価値であり，金融資産を加えた企業価値は 1,177 億ドルと推定された。ここから有利子負債 35 億ドルを差し引いた 1,142 億ドルが推定株主価値である。

　アニュアルレポートによるとナイキはニューヨーク証券取引所に上場されているクラス B 株式と，一般には取引されていないクラス A 株式の 2 種類の株式を発行しており，2018 年 7 月時点で合計で 16 億株が株主に保有されている。推定株主価値 1,142 億ドルを流通株式 16 億株で割ると，ナイキの株価は約 71 ドルと推定される。

　図表9.6の下段には EVA による推定結果も示している。EVA を用いた推定株価も FCF による推定結果と同額であることが確認できる。

Figure 9.6 | Estimated Share Price of Nike (in millions except for share price)

Valuation Based on DCF		Estimate					
	2018	2019	2020	2021	2022	2023	
NOPAT	1,987	3,634	4,044	4,514	4,876	5,290	
Operating Cash Flow	5,536	3,769	4,742	5,256	5,714	6,244	
− Investment	951	1,203	1,419	1,568	1,739	1,884	
= FCF	**4,585**	**2,566**	**3,323**	**3,688**	**3,975**	**4,360**	
Investment Rate = I/NOPAT	-130.8%	29.4%	17.8%	18.3%	18.5%	17.6%	
WACC	**7.03%**						
PV of FCF		2,397	2,901	3,008	3,029	3,104	
Growth Rate for Terminal Value	3.5%						
Terminal Value	**137,595**						
Sum of PV of FCF for 5 years	14,440						
+ PV of Terminal Value	97,974						
= **Value of Operation**	**112,415**						
Cash and Equivalent	4,249						
Short-term Investments	996						
Long-term Investments	0						
+ **Financial Assets (BV at valuation)**	**5,245**						
+ **Other Non-operating Assets (MV)**							
= **Value of Company**	**117,660**						
Short-term Debt	6						
Long-term Debt	3,468						
− **Debt**	**3,474**						
− **Non-controlling Interest**	**0**						
= **Value of Equity**	**114,186**						
/ Number of Shares Outstanding	1,601						
= Share Price	71.34						

Valuation Based on EVA		Estimate					
	2018	2019	2020	2021	2022	2023	
NOPAT	1,987	3,634	4,044	4,514	4,876	5,290	
Capital (Beg.)	15,884	13,286	14,354	15,075	15,901	16,802	
Capital Charge	1,116	934	1,009	1,059	1,118	1,181	
EVA	870	2,700	3,035	3,455	3,758	4,109	
ROC = NOPAT/Beg. Cap	12.5%	27.4%	28.2%	29.9%	30.7%	31.5%	
PV of EVA		2,523	2,650	2,818	2,864	2,926	
Terminal Value	**119,863**						
Sum of PV of EVA for 5 years	13,780						
+ Capital	13,286						
+ PV of Terminal Value	85,348						
= **Value of Operation**	**112,415**						
Cash and Equivalent	4,249						
Short-term Investments	996						
Long-term Investments	0						
+ **Financial Assets (BV at valuation)**	**5,245**						
+ **Other Non-operating Assets (MV)**	**0**						
= **Value of Company**	**117,660**						
Short-term Debt	6						
Long-term Debt	3,468						
− **Debt**	**3,474**						
− **Non-controlling Interest**	**0**						
= **Value of Equity**	**114,186**						
/ Number of Shares Outstanding	1,601						
= Share Price	71.34						

図表 9.6 ┃ ナイキの株価の推定（株価以外は百万）

DCF に基づく企業価値評価

	2018	予測 2019	2020	2021	2022	2023
NOPAT	1,987	3,634	4,044	4,514	4,876	5,290
営業キャッシュフロー	5,536	3,769	4,742	5,256	5,714	6,244
− 投資額	951	1,203	1,419	1,568	1,739	1,884
= FCF	4,585	2,566	3,323	3,688	3,975	4,360
再投資率 ＝純投資額÷ NOPAT	-130.8%	29.4%	17.8%	18.3%	18.5%	17.6%
WACC	7.03%					
FCF の現在価値		2,397	2,901	3,008	3,029	3,104
ターミナル・バリュー成長率	3.5%					
ターミナル・バリュー	137,595					
5 年間の FCF の現在価値計	14,440					
＋ ターミナル・バリューの現在価値	97,974					
= 事業価値	112,415					
現金及び同等物	4,249					
有価証券	996					
投資有価証券	0					
＋ 金融資産（簿価）	5,245					
＋ その他の非事業資産（時価）	0					
= 推定企業価値	117,660					
短期有利子負債	6					
長期有利子負債	3,468					
− 有利子負債	3,474					
− 非支配株主持ち分	0					
= 推定株主価値	114,186					
÷ 流通株式数	1,601					
= 推定株価	71.34					

EVA に基づく企業価値評価

	2018	予測 2019	2020	2021	2022	2023
NOPAT	1,987	3,634	4,044	4,514	4,876	5,290
期首投下資本	15,884	13,286	14,354	15,075	15,901	16,802
資本費用	1,116	934	1,009	1,059	1,118	1,181
EVA	870	2,700	3,035	3,455	3,758	4,109
ROC ＝ NOPAT ÷ 期首投下資本	12.5%	27.4%	28.2%	29.9%	30.7%	31.5%
EVA の現在価値		2,523	2,650	2,818	2,864	2,926
ターミナル・バリュー	119,863					
5 年間の EVA の現在価値計	13,780					
＋ 投下資本	13,286					
＋ ターミナル・バリューの現在価値	85,348					
= 事業価値	112,415					
現金及び同等物	4,249					
有価証券	996					
投資有価証券	0					
＋ 金融資産（簿価）	5,245					
＋ その他の非事業資産（時価）	0					
= 推定企業価値	117,660					
短期有利子負債	6					
長期有利子負債	3,468					
− 有利子負債	3,474					
− 非支配株主持ち分	0					
= 推定株主価値	114,186					
÷ 流通株式数	1,601					
= 推定株価	71.34					

第 9 章　企業価値，株主価値，および株価

Chapter

10 Valuing with Multiples

> **Points !**
> ✓ A multiple approach estimates a market value based on the multiplier of various financial figures
> ✓ Both discounting approach and multiple approach have advantages and disadvantages and are commonly applied in combination

● Basic of Multiples

The primary method for a valuation analysis requires forecasting and discounting future FCF or EVA back to the present values. This "discounting" approach theoretically incorporates essential factors of economics and finance such as a cost of capital, and provides flexibility to estimate value, and is therefore applied extensively. On the other hand, there is another approach to estimate the value of a company called "multiples", based on the data in security markets (also referred to as the comparable valuation), to be introduced in this chapter.

A multiples approach relies on the idea that similar assets basically have similar prices. The market value of a company is estimated as seeing the ratio of the market value of a comparable company relative to a certain financial metric of it, and the ratio or the multiplier is applied to the same financial metric of the company to be estimated.

$$MV_T = \frac{MV_C}{I_C} \times I_T$$

MV_T: market value of a company to be estimated $\quad$ MV_C: market value of a comparable company
I_T: financial metric of a company to be estimated $\quad$ I_C: financial metric of a comparable company
MV_C/I_C: multiple

The part where the market value of a comparable company divided by a financial metric of it represents a multiple.

第10章 価値倍率法

ポイント！

✔ 価値倍率法は，市場価値を特定の財務数値の倍数として推定する手法であり，使用される数値にはさまざまなものがある

✔ 割引現在価値法，価値倍率法ともにメリット・デメリットがあるため，実務においては併用されることが多い

● 価値倍率法の基本

企業価値評価のためには，将来の FCF や EVA を予想し，現在価値に割り引くというアプローチ（割引現在価値法）がメインとなる。これらの手法は資本コストといった経済・ファイナンスの理論的に不可欠な要素を組み込んでおり，また柔軟な価値評価が可能なことから広く使用されている。一方で，企業の価値を推定する際には，株式市場のデータに基づく価値倍率法（比較評価アプローチ）と呼ばれる全く異なるアプローチもあり，本章ではそれらを紹介する。

価値倍率法は基本的に同じような資産は同じような価格になるはずだという考え方に基づいている。比較すべき類似の企業の市場価値がその企業の何らかの財務指標の何倍になっているのかを捉え，その倍数を評価対象企業の同じ財務指標に掛け合わせることによって，評価対象企業の市場価値を推定するのが価値倍率法のプロセスである。数式で示すと以下のようになる。

$$MV_T = \frac{MV_C}{I_C} \times I_T$$

MV_T ：評価対象企業の市場価値 　　MV_C：比較類似企業の市場価値
I_T 　：評価対象企業の財務指標 　　I_C 　：比較類似企業の財務指標
MV_C / I_C：価値倍率

この式の比較類似企業の市場価値をその企業の財務指標で割った部分が価値倍率である。

第10章 価値倍率法 179

A lot of figures are used to measure multiples. In addition to financial figures such as net income, cash flow, sales, gross profit, total assets, shareholders' equity, and EBITDA, there can be another relevant multiples unique to each industry. For example, the number of registered members or subscribers (a cable TV or internet service), the area of a shop floor (retail), the population in the area covered by facilities (hospital or healthcare), or the number of patents and scientists (technology oriented) may all be effective measures.

When you calculate multiples, you should use a normal number without occasional outliers and a future prospect rather than past data if available. The multiple based on future forecasts is consistent with the principle of valuation that the value of a company is determined by future FCF, and eliminating discontinued occasional factors accommodates the valuation approach to estimate a value based on long-term FCF projection.

● Selection of Comparable Companies

It is crucial to select relevant companies to compare (peer companies) so that you can get the appropriate estimates with a multiple valuation. In practice, the average multiple of a peer group consisting of several comparable companies are used. Peer companies are not necessarily in the same industry, and rather often include companies with similar profitability, risk, or growth stage. The size of the company, client attributes, and technologies implemented can be criteria for peer selection.

● PER and PBR

The popular multiples among many are PER and PBR. They are available and continually updated on websites such as Yahoo!Finance and are access-friendly.

倍率を計算する指標にはさまざまなものがある。当期純利益，キャッシュフロー，売上高，粗利益，総資産，株主資本，EBITDA，といった財務指標の他にも，産業固有の倍率を考えることができる。たとえば，ケーブルテレビやインターネットサービス業であれば登録会員数や有料会員数などの倍率が考えられる。小売業であれば売り場面積なども考えられるであろうし，病院やヘルスケアビジネスにおいてはその施設がカバーする地域の人口なども対象となり得る。技術力が重要な業界であれば特許の数や科学者の数の倍率なども考えてもよいであろう。

倍率を計算する際に使用する数値は，一時的に発生した例外の影響を排除した標準的な値であり，かつできれば過去の平均値などよりも将来の見通しを使うほうが望ましい。将来の数値を活用した価値倍率であれば，企業の市場価値は将来の FCF によって決まるという企業価値評価の原則とも整合する。また，継続しない短期的な影響を排除することは，長期的な FCF を予測して価値を評価することとも整合する。

◉ 比較類似企業の選定

価値倍率法による企業価値評価を適切なものとするためには，比較対象として適切な企業（比較類似企業）を選択することが非常に重要となる。実務的には複数の比較類似企業を設定し，それらの倍率の平均値を使用することが多い。比較類似企業は必ずしも同じ産業の企業である必要はなく，収益性やリスク，企業の成長ステージなどの特徴が似ている企業が含まれる。企業規模，顧客の属性，活用する技術などによって選別することも可能である。

◉ PER と PBR

価値倍率の中でも頻繁に使われるのが PER と PBR である。これらの指標は Yahoo! ファイナンスなどのホームページにおいても随時数値が更新されており容易に入手が可能である。

第 10 章　価値倍率法　181

The PER (Price Earnings Ratio) shows how much investors are prepared to pay for a share of stock per unit of earnings.

$$PER = \frac{Share\ Price}{Earnings\ per\ Share}$$

Earnings per Share (EPS) is equal to net income divided by the number of shares outstanding. Earnings are measured per share to be consistent with a share price that is usually quoted on a per share basis. If we refer to total value as opposed to per share value, then PER is equal to:

$$PER = \frac{Market\ Capitalization}{Net\ Income}$$

A high PER implies that investors expect the company to maintain its current level of profits and to improve on its performance in the future.

PBR (Price to book value ratio) shows how much investors are prepared to pay for a share of stock per unit of shareholders' equity.

$$PBR = \frac{Share\ Price}{Equity\ per\ Share}$$

Equity per share is calculated by total shareholders' equity divided by the number of shares outstanding. Recall that shareholders' equity is the book value of equity on the balance sheet. Therefore, PBR is the ratio of the market value or share price to the book value of the firm.

PBR is 1 when the share price is equal to the book value per share. A PBR of less than 1 indicates that the market price is less than the book value per share. A share with PBR less than 1 is often perceived as undervalued. Note, however, that shareholders' equity is simply a book value on the balance sheet and does not ensure that actual cash is distributed to the investors if the company liquidates.

● Mathematical Breakdown of PER and PBR

The value driver model introduced with the discussion about a terminal value indicates that ROC and a growth rate settles multiples such as PER and PBR.

PER（株価収益率）は1株あたり利益（EPS）に対し，株価が何倍になっているのかを表わす。

$$PER = \frac{株価}{1株あたり利益}$$

ここで，EPS は当期純利益を流通株式数で割った数値である。株価は1株あたりの株主価値なので，PER は，1株あたりの利益に対してどれだけの価値がつけられているのかを表わす。もし，1株あたりではなく，価値全体を考えれば PER は以下のようにも定義できる。

$$PER = \frac{株式時価総額}{当期純利益}$$

PER が高いということは，現在の利益が将来にわたって持続していき，さらに高い利益成長が期待されていると考えることができる。

PBR（株価純資産倍率）は1株あたり純資産に対し，株価が何倍になっているのかを表わす。

$$PBR = \frac{株価}{1株あたり純資産}$$

1株あたり純資産は，純資産を流通株式数で割った数値である。純資産は貸借対照表上の株主資本の帳簿上の価値（簿価）である。したがって，PBR は時価である株価と1株あたりの簿価を比較した指標ということになる。

もし，1株あたりの簿価と株価が一致している場合には PBR はちょうど1倍になる。そして，1株あたりの簿価よりも株価が低い場合には PBR は1倍以下となり，株価は割安であるとの判断がなされる。ただし，純資産はあくまで帳簿上の価値なので，実際に企業が解散・清算されるときに分配される額を保証するものではないことには注意が必要である。

● PER，PBR の数式展開

ターミナル・バリューの際に紹介した価値ドライバーモデルは，ROC と成長率が PER や PBR といった価値倍率を決定することも示してくれる。価値ド

第 10 章　価値倍率法　　183

Dividing both sides of the value driver model by NOPAT, the formula can be rearranged as;

$$\text{Value} = \frac{\text{NOPAT}_1 \left(1 - \dfrac{g}{\text{ROC}}\right)}{\text{WACC} - g}$$

$$\frac{\text{Value}}{\text{NOPAT}_1} = \frac{\left(1 - \dfrac{g}{\text{ROC}}\right)}{\text{WACC} - g}$$

The left side of the formula which divides the value by profit has the same connotation as PER. It shows PER is derived by a growth rate, ROC and WACC.

PBR also can be explained by the value driver model. Since NOPAT is calculated as capital×ROC, that can replace NOPAT, and the formula is rearranged as;

$$\text{Value} = \frac{\text{Capital} \times \text{ROC} \times \left(1 - \dfrac{g}{\text{ROC}}\right)}{\text{WACC} - g}$$

Dividing both sides by capital, value/capital emerges in the left side, which corresponds to PBR.

$$\frac{\text{Value}}{\text{Capital}} = \frac{\text{ROC} \times \left(1 - \dfrac{g}{\text{ROC}}\right)}{\text{WACC} - g}$$

These rearrangements justify the fundamental idea that the multiple methods accommodate discounting approaches.

● EBITDA Multiple

EBITDA is also applied as a multiple for valuation. The EBITDA multiple shows how many times greater the total value of a company is than its EBITDA.

$$\text{EBITDA Multiple} = \frac{\text{Company Value}}{\text{EBITDA}}$$

ライバーモデルの両辺を NOPAT で割ることにより以下の式が得られる。

$$価値 = \frac{NOPAT_1 \left(1 - \frac{g}{ROC}\right)}{WACC - g}$$

$$\frac{価値}{NOPAT_1} = \frac{\left(1 - \frac{g}{ROC}\right)}{WACC - g}$$

　価値を利益で割った左辺は PER と同じ意味合いである。PER は企業の期待成長率と ROC，および WACC によって導かれていることがわかる。

　また PBR も価値ドライバーモデルを展開することによって説明できる。NOPAT は投下資本×ROC であるからこれを式に代入すると以下のようになる。

$$価値 = \frac{投下資本 \times ROC \times \left(1 - \frac{g}{ROC}\right)}{WACC - g}$$

　両辺を投下資本で割ることにより，価値÷投下資本が左辺に表われるが，これは PBR にあたる。

$$\frac{価値}{投下資本} = \frac{ROC \times \left(1 - \frac{g}{ROC}\right)}{WACC - g}$$

　このように価値倍率の根源的な考え方は割引現在価値法の価値評価方法と実は整合しているのである。

● EBITDA 倍率

　EBITDA も価値倍率の1つとして使用される。EBITDA 倍率は EBITDA に対して企業の市場価値が何倍になっているのかを表わす。

$$EBITDA\ 倍率 = \frac{企業価値}{EBITDA}$$

第 10 章　価値倍率法　185

EBITDA eliminates the effects of interest rates, tax rates and the treatment of depreciation expenses which vary by country. Therefore, EBITDA multiple is often preferred to PER which relies on accounting net income when companies in different regions are compared.

● Company Valuation for Conglomerate

Many companies run more than one business or operate in a number of different markets. The more relevant multiple might vary by each business unit, therefore, adding up all estimated values of each business based on different multiples is a procedure to value such a conglomerate company.

Let us estimate the value of Asahi Kasei Corporation having several businesses applying PER. The Asahi Kasei Group operates business in the three segments of "Material", including fibers & textiles, chemical and electronics operations, "Homes" and "Health Care". Sales and operating income of each operation are available in the annual report and on the website. Segment operating incomes are disclosed on a before-tax basis and must be adjusted to be on an after-tax basis. For this study, net (after tax) income for each business is approximated by multiplying the operating income by $(1 - \text{tax rate})$.

PER applied for each business is referred to data provided by Japan Exchange Group (JPX). The average (simple and weighted average) PER and PBR by sizes and types of Industry at the end of each month are posted in the website of JPX.

https://www.jpx.co.jp/english/markets/statistics-equities/misc/04.html

The simple average PER at the end of October 2018 is used for the analysis here.

Since PER is the multiple for net income, the equity value of each business can be estimated as after-tax income of a business multiplied by the corresponding industry average PER. (Note that the average PER based on net income is subject to profits/losses associated with non-operating and unusual items, but those factors are assumed to be negligible when averaging.)

186　　Chapter 10　Valuing with Multiples

EBITDA は国ごとに異なる金利水準や税率，減価償却費の会計上の取扱いの影響を取り除いている。そのため，異なる地域の企業を比較評価する際には，当期純利益を使用した倍率である PER ではなく EBITDA 倍率がしばしば好まれる。

❍ 多事業展開をする企業の評価

多くの企業は複数の事業を展開したり，異なる市場においてビジネスを展開している。それらの事業単位にはそれぞれ異なる価値倍率が当てはまると考えられ，このような多事業展開する企業の価値を価値倍率により評価するためには，各事業の価値倍率による評価額を合計するのが 1 つの方法である。

ここでは多くの事業を展開する旭化成を例にとって，PER による企業価値評価をしてみよう。旭化成は繊維事業，ケミカル事業，エレクトロニクス事業からなるマテリアルセグメント，住宅セグメント，そしてヘルスケアセグメントを有している。それぞれの事業の売上高と営業利益はホームページやアニュアルレポートなどで開示されており入手可能である。ただし開示されている営業利益は税引前の利益であるため，税引後の利益を算出する必要がある。今回は概算となるが営業利益に（1 −税率）を掛けた値をそれぞれの事業の当期純利益の近似値と考える。

業界別の PER に関しては日本取引所グループのデータを活用する。日本取引所グループはホームページにおいて毎月末時点での規模別・業種別の PER と PBR（単純平均および加重平均）を掲載している。

https://www.jpx.co.jp/markets/statistics-equities/misc/04.html

今回は 2018 年 10 月末時点の単純平均 PER 値を使用する。

PER は当期純利益に対する株式時価総額の倍率なので，各事業の税引後利益にそれぞれの業種別平均 PER を掛け合わせることによって各事業の株主価値が推定できる。なお，当期純利益に基づいて算出される各社の PER の平均値である業種別 PER はそれぞれの会社の営業外損益や特別損益の影響を含んでいるが，平均されていることでそれらの影響は無視できるものと想定する。

第 10 章　価値倍率法　187

Figure 10.1 | Valuation of Asahi Kasei with PER

	Operating Income (billion yen)	After Tax Income (billion yen)	Types of Industry	Average PER	Equity Value (billion yen)
fibers & textiles operations	12.1	8.5	Textiles & Apparels	16.0	135.5
chemical operations	100.1	70.1	Chemicals	15.8	1,107.1
electronics operations	9.7	6.8	Metal Products	12.3	83.5
Material	121.9				
Homes	64.4	45.1	Construction	10.5	473.3
HealthCare	39.5	27.7	Pharmaceutical	24.7	683.0
Others	-27.2	-19.0	Large	17.9	-340.8
Total	198.5				2,141.6
Number of Shares Outstanding (in billion)					1.396
Estimated Share Price (yen)					1,534.0
Actual Share Price as at the end of Oct. 2018					1,357.0

Segment profits based on fiscal year ending March 2018, PER as at the end of October 2018

Fibers & textiles, chemical, and electronics operations in the Material segment are applied to JPX's industry PER of Textiles & Apparels, Chemicals, and Metal Products respectively. For example, the after tax income of the chemical operation was 70.1 billion yen, multiplied by the Chemicals industry PER of 15.8, which results in the estimate of the equity value to be 1.1 trillion yen. In a similar manner, the industry PER of Construction for Homes segment, the industry PER of Pharmaceutical for Health Care segment and average PER of Large companies for "Others" category, including corporate level expenses, is used to estimate the equity value of each unit. The total of equity values is measured to be 2.1416 trillion yen. The estimated share price is 1,534 yen, calculated by dividing total equity value by the number of shares outstanding.

For comparison, the actual share price of Asahi Kasei as of the end of October 2018 was 1,357 yen.

図表10.1 ┃ PER による旭化成の価値評価例

	営業利益 (10億円)	税引後利益 (10億円)	適用業種	平均PER	株主価値 (10億円)
繊維	12.1	8.5	繊維製品	16.0	135.5
ケミカル	100.1	70.1	化学	15.8	1,107.1
エレクトロニクス	9.7	6.8	金属製品	12.3	83.5
マテリアル	121.9				
住宅	64.4	45.1	建設業	10.5	473.3
ヘルスケア	39.5	27.7	医薬品	24.7	683.0
その他	-27.2	-19.0	大型株	17.9	-340.8
合計	198.5				2,141.6
流通株式数 (10億株)					1.396
推定株価 (円)					1,534.0
2018年10月末時点株価					1,357.0

2018年3月期のセグメント別業績を使用，PERは2018年10月末時点

　まずマテリアルセグメントからだが，マテリアルセグメントには繊維事業，ケミカル事業，エレクトロニクス事業があった。繊維事業には繊維業種のPERを適用し，ケミカル事業には化学業種のPERを，そしてエレクトロニクス事業にはその他金属業種のPERを適用する。たとえば，ケミカル事業の税引後利益は701億円であり，そこに化学業種のPER15.8を掛け合わせると株主価値は1.1兆円と推定される。同様にして住宅セグメントに関しては建設業のPER，ヘルスケアセグメントについては医薬品のPER，全社共通費用を含むその他に関しては大型株の平均PERを適用して各事業の株主価値を計算する。株主価値の合計は2兆1,416億円と推定された。これを流通株式数で割ると株価は1,534円となる。

　なお，2018年10月末時点での旭化成の株価は1,357円であった。

第10章　価値倍率法　189

Pros and Cons of Discounting Approach

Both the discounting and multiple approach have advantages and disadvantages. A strong point of a discounting method is that various factors and figures are taken into consideration with great discretion. The detailed consideration enables one to identify the key factors affecting the value and to simulate the value based on more than one scenario or with different inputs.

On the other hand, an inherent limitation is that it encompasses a subjective view of the person who conducts analysis. A person who is emotionally attached to the business might fabricate favorable numbers. Also in the discounting approach, the considerable portion of total value is often attributed to the terminal value. The significance can be reduced if you lengthen the forecast period of financial performance, yet the terminal value will not be diminished. The large terminal value itself will not undermine the accuracy of a valuation. However, it might be harder to accept that the measurable part of the value is explained by the value after forecast periods.

Pros and Cons of Multiple Approach

Objectivity is a prime advantage of the multiple method. Most numbers used in multiples such as actual results and share price information are observable and do not allow arbitrary manipulations. Multiples based on share prices are also meant to encompass various investors' views about the value of a company. If you focus on a particular industry, you might be obsessed with a stereotype and might overlook an important element to consider. Information implied in the share price can help you to include hidden value recognized by investors in the market. Moreover, it can be said that the simplicity contributes to the popularity of multiples such as PER and PBR. The multiples approach is quickly understandable and calculates the value instantly.

On the other hand, there exists a fair number of drawbacks of the multiple method. Despite the advantage, the simple calculation does not incorporate the detailed

190 | Chapter 10   Valuing with Multiples

● 割引現在価値法のメリット・デメリット

　割引現在価値法，価値倍率法ともに，長所・短所がある。まず，割引現在価値法のメリットとしては，さまざまな要因を考慮し，数値を精緻に積み上げて推定するという点があげられる。このような詳細な検討は，価値に大きな影響を与える要因の特定を可能にし，そのため，シナリオ分析や感応度分析なども可能となる。

　一方で，デメリットとしては，数値を積み上げる際に分析者の主観が入ってしまうということがあげられる。特に，事業に思い入れがある場合には，恣意的に望ましい数値を「作る」ことが行われるかもしれない。また，割引現在価値法では，しばしば価値の大部分がターミナル・バリューによって説明される。予想期間を長くすることによってある程度この影響は小さくできるが，やはり価値全体に占める影響は大きいままの場合が少なくない。大きなターミナル・バリュー自体が価値評価の正確性を損なうというわけではないが，予想期間以降の価値であるターミナル・バリューが価値の少なくない部分を説明するというのは，心理的に受け入れがたい場合もある。

● 価値倍率法のメリット・デメリット

　価値倍率法のメリットとしては，客観性があげられる。価値倍率法で使用される数値は，その多くが実績データと他社の株価という客観的なものである。そのため，恣意性が入る余地が少ない。また，株価データに基づく倍率は，さまざまな投資家の価値に関する意見を価値評価に織り込んでいる。1つの業界ばかりを見ていると固定観念にとらわれてしまい，本来考慮すべき要素を見過ごしてしまうかもしれない。しかし，株価データを活用することにより，投資家が認識している潜在的な価値をも価値評価に組み入れることが可能になると考えられる。さらに，PER，PBR などの価値倍率法の魅力は価値算出が容易だということである。価値倍率法はわかりやすく，そして計算も即座にできる。

　しかしながら，価値倍率法にも多くの問題点は存在する。1つはメリットとも関連するが，価値倍率法はあまりにも簡便的に計算を行っており，企業の状

第 10 章　価値倍率法　　191

condition of a company, and the information about key value drivers will not be provided because it only deals with some main variables such as profit or sales.

Additionally, there is the unavoidable question of choosing the right peer group. Many companies run a number of businesses and try to differentiate themselves in the market. Amid such circumstances, you can at best find the company whose business is similar to the company of interest on some level.

Furthermore, the multiple approach which relies on share price data is subject to the overall climate of the stock market. Multiples rise as a whole in favorable market conditions, and decline in unfavorable conditions. Note that multiples may vary widely depending on the date and change every day.

Figure10.2 | Comparing Two Valuation Approaches

Discounting		Multiple
✓ Incorporate detailed information ✓ Identify key value driver	**Pros**	✓ Objective based on peers' prices ✓ Reflect hidden value ✓ Easy
✓ Subjective(arbitrary) ✓ Large terminal value	**Cons**	✓ Insufficient information ✓ Lack of peers ✓ Affected by stock market condition

● Combination Use in Practice

Since either approach has advantages and disadvantages, in practice both approaches are applied in combination. It is frequently observed that the value is estimated with a discounting approach which is theoretically superior and a multiple approach is used to check the reasonability of the outcome derived by discounting. For example, suppose the estimated value with a discounting approach is 10 billion yen, and a multiple denotes that the acceptable range of a valuation result is between 9 billion and 12 billion. The outcome of 10 billion will then be justified as a reasonable result.

192 | Chapter 10 Valuing with Multiples

況を正確に捉えているとは言えない。また，売上や利益といった主要な数値しか取り扱っていないため，価値に影響を与える変数に関する情報もない。

さらに，比較する企業をどのように選択するのかという問題も現実的には存在する。企業の多くは複数のビジネスを手がけており，また市場の中で差別化を図っている。このような状況の中では，ある程度ビジネスが似ている企業を見つけることはできても，事業が全く同じ企業を選ぶことは困難である。

加えて，株価データに基づく価値倍率法では，株式市場全体の動きの影響を大きく受ける。株式市場環境が良好なときの価値倍率指標は全体として大きくなり，株式市場が低迷するときには小さくなる。価値倍率は日々変動するものであり，使用する時点において大きく変動することにも注意が必要である。

図表 10.2 ┃ 2つのアプローチの比較

割引現在価値法		価値倍率法
✓ 詳細に情報を活用 ✓ 価値に影響を与える要因が特定可能	メリット	✓ 他社株価データに基づいて客観的 ✓ 潜在的な価値も包含 ✓ 算出が容易
✓ 主観的（恣意的） ✓ ターミナル・バリューの影響大	デメリット	✓ 事業の状況把握が不十分 ✓ 比較する企業選定が困難 ✓ 株式市場環境の影響大

◉ 実務においては併用

このように，それぞれメリット・デメリットがあるため，実務的には2つのアプローチは併用されることが多い。特に多く見られるのは，理論的に優れた割引現在価値法により算出した価値を，価値倍率法で妥当かどうかチェックするといったやり方である。たとえばFCFに基づいた価値評価結果が100億円だったとする。そして，価値倍率に基づいた価値の推定額が90億円〜120億円というレンジであれば，100億円という評価額は妥当であるという判断がなされる。

Part 5

Valuation in Management

- Thus far, we have discussed how to evaluate the value of a company. Investors will choose to buy or sell the stock of a company based on the valuation results. However, for companies, valuation is not the end goal. Company managers have to run the business according to the valuation results.

- In these last two chapters, we will think how a company or company managers use the outcome of valuation in the context of management.

Chapter 11   Merger and Acquisition

Chapter 12   Fulfilling Value

第5部
企業価値評価に基づく経営

★★★★★

- これまで本書は企業の価値をどのように評価するのかについて議論してきた。投資家は価値評価の結果を受けて，株式を売る・買うといった投資行動を行うことになるが，経営者はこの結果に基づいて経営を行っていく必要がある。価値評価は企業経営にとっての到達点ではない。

- 第5部では，企業（経営者）がどのように価値評価の結果を経営において活用していくのかについて議論する。

第11章　合併と買収

第12章　価値の具現化

Chapter
11 Merger and Acquisition

Points!

✔ A merger and acquisition is feasible when additional value is produced via the M&A

✔ If the M&A is conducted with share exchanges, the risk and return attached to the performance volatility after M&A will be shared between shareholders of an acquiring company and an acquired company

○ Valuation for Management

Although the result of valuation is used by investors buying and selling stocks, the valuation is not only for their information. A valuation affects the management of a company and is an indispensable process to execute strategic initiatives.

One of the most major strategic decisions a company may face is with regards to M&A, or merger and acquisition. The appropriate valuation is crucial information to contemplate M&A.

○ Conditions for a Successful M&A

A successful M&A for both an acquiring company and an acquired company must satisfy the following conditions;

● An acquiring company must view the company to be acquired at a higher value than the acquired company views themselves.

● The purchase price is settled somewhere in the difference between the values recognized by the two companies.

The former is the condition that makes a transaction itself happen. The

第11章 合併と買収

ポイント!

✓ 企業の合併・買収は，合併・買収が新たな価値を生み出すと期待される ことで成立する
✓ 合併・買収が株式交換によって行われる場合，合併・買収後の業績変動 のリスクおよびリターンは買い手企業，売り手企業双方の株主で共有さ れる

経営に不可欠な企業価値評価

企業価値評価の結果に基づき，投資家は株式を売買するが，企業価値評価は 投資家のためだけのものではない。企業価値評価は企業経営に大きな影響を与 えたり，また戦略実行の際にも必要不可欠なプロセスとなりうる。

企業にとって大きな意思決定の1つが他社を買収したり，他社との合併であ る M&A（企業の合併・買収）の場面である。適切な企業価値評価は M&A を 検討する際に非常に重要な情報となる。

成功する M&A の条件

M&A が買い手企業，売り手企業双方にとって成功となるためには，以下の 条件が成立していなければならない。

● 買い手企業の認識する売り手企業の価値が，売り手企業が認識している 価値よりも高い。
● 買収金額が買い手・売り手双方の認識する売り手企業の価値の間のどこ かに決まる。

前者は売買が成立する条件である。もし買い手企業の認識する売り手企業の

第11章　合併と買収　197

shareholders of an acquired company will not relinquish the ownership if the value considered by an acquiring company falls below the value they think their company has. Meanwhile, the latter is the condition that allows M&A to create value for both parties.

The value that M&A produces for an acquired company is associated with the amount by which the purchase price exceeds the value viewed by the acquired company. The owner of an acquired company will obtain a greater value with the deal. On the other hand, the value produced for an acquiring company is denoted as the estimated value of an acquired company minus the purchase price.

The exceeding price put on the market value of a company based on the current share price called, an acquisition premium, is often as high as 30-50%. That means an M&A deal likely names a price 30-50% higher for a company. However, the transaction will destroy value for an acquiring company if it pays a generous premium that results in a price higher than the estimated value.

Figure 11.1 | **Condition for Successful M&A**

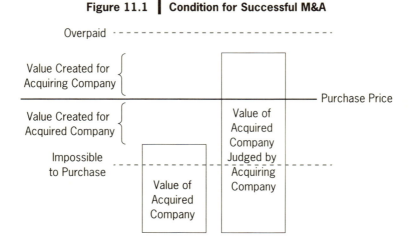

価値が売り手のものよりも低ければ，売り手企業の株主は所有権を手放すはずがないからである。後者は売り手企業，買い手企業双方が M&A により価値を創造する条件といえる。

M&A が売り手企業にもたらす価値創造額は，売り手企業が認識する価値を買収金額が上回った額である。売り手企業の所有者は売買によって，より大きな価値を手に入れることができる。一方で，買い手企業にとっては，買い手が認識する企業価値から買収金額を引いたものが価値創造額となる。

なお，市場において取引されていた株価に基づく企業価値を，買収時に支払われる金額が上回る分を買収プレミアムと呼び，これは通常 30 〜 50％といわれている。M&A においては 3 〜 5 割増しの価値がつけられるということである。しかし，高い買収プレミアムを払いすぎて買収金額が買い手企業が見込む価値以上になってしまっては，M&A は買い手企業にとっては価値を損なう企業行動となってしまうことには注意が必要である。

図表 11.1 ┃ 成功する M&A の条件

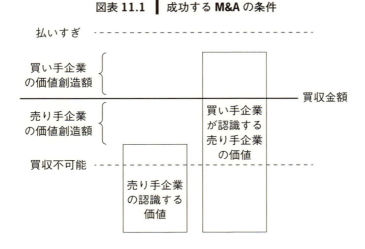

The Reason for Value Difference

There can be various elusive reasons for the difference in perceived values. Among them, it is usually thought to be the synergy effect which is defined as the extra value created due to the integration of two firms in addition to the sum of the two stand alone companies. Streamlining distribution channels and manufacturing processes along with speeding up new product development contributes to the synergy. The possibilities of withdrawal from unprofitable business and the disposal of underused assets can also be ascribed as the cause of the discrepancy in the value. The management shakeup might enhance the value of the company too.

These can be legitimate reasons for acquisitions of a company or a business. Yet, it is more difficult to fulfill the expected benefit from acquisition in reality than on paper.

Classification and Formation of M&A

M&A is classified into three categories; horizontal integration, which refers to the merger or the acquisition of the company running a similar business, vertical integration, which is meant to expand the value chain with the merger or the acquisition of a supplier or a customer, and conglomerate integration, which is M&A for a business unrelated to the existing business.

A merger refers to combining two companies into one. An acquiring company will take over the assets and liabilities of an acquired company, and the organization, employees, stocks, and other capitals are integrated fully. On the other hand, an acquisition allows an acquired company to continue to be a separate entity after its equity is purchased in cash or with stocks, but will be owned and dominated by the acquiring company.

価値の差の理由

価値に差異が存在する理由にはさまざまな把握されにくい要素が考えられる。一般的に期待されるのは，それぞれの会社が単独だった場合の価値の合計以上に統合後によって作り出される追加的な価値として定義されるシナジー効果である。シナジー効果には販売・流通チャネルや製造プロセス面での効率化や新商品開発のスピードアップなどが含まれる。また，不採算事業からの撤退や有効活用されていない資産の売却の可能性も認識差異の要因となる。さらに，不適切な経営陣を刷新することによる企業価値の向上が見込まれている場合もある。

このような理由は企業が企業や事業を買収する正当な目的となりうる。ただし，買収時に想定されていた効果を実現することは実際には難しいことも多い。

M&A の分類と形式

M&A はその性質により水平的統合，垂直的統合，およびコングロマリット型統合に分類される。似通った事業の会社との合併・買収は水平的統合と呼ばれる。供給業者や顧客企業を合併・買収しバリューチェーンの一部が統合されるのが垂直的統合である。コングロマリット型統合は既存事業と関係のないビジネスを行う企業・事業との合併・買収のことをいう。

2 つの会社が 1 つになるのが合併である。買い手企業は売り手企業の資産および負債を引き継ぎ，組織・人材・株式・資金等はすべて統合される。買い手企業が売り手企業の株式を，現金や株式またはその他の証券により取得し，支配するのが買収である。売り手企業は別会社として存続するが，買い手企業によって所有されており，買い手企業の子会社となる。

第 11 章　合併と買収　201

● Distribution of Value Created by M&A

M&A can be executed not only in cash but also with stocks of an acquiring company. It is simple to understand how the value of a merger is distributed to shareholders when cash is used for the deal, yet complicated when stocks are used instead. Let us consider it with the figures as follows, assuming no debt, no tax, and no commission associated with the transaction of merger.

Figure 11.2 illustrates the case in which the surviving company (acquiring company) records a net income of $80 million, and its market value is $1,200 million. The number of shares is 4 million, therefore the share price is $300. EPS is calculated to be $20, and PER is 15.

The net income of the target company (acquired company) is $25 million, and its market value is $800 million. The number of shares is 3 million, therefore the share price is $267. EPS is calculated to be $8.33, and PER is 32.

The cost of capital for both companies are a supposed 7%. The synergy effect due to the merger is expected to boost the net income by $20 million, hence the net income of the combined company will increase to $125 million (=net income of surviving 80+net income of target 25+synergy of 20). Assuming the synergy will be consistently sustainable, the perpetuity formula is applied as $20 million divided by a 7% cost of capital, deriving the economic value created by the merger as $286 million (=$20/7%).

◉ 合併・買収の価値の分配

合併・買収は現金だけではなく，買い手企業の株式でも可能（株式交換）である。現金支払いの場合は，合併の価値がどのように株主に分配されるのかわかりやすいが，株式交換によって行われる場合は複雑になる。以下の数値例でその違いを見ていこう。負債はないものとし，法人税や合併の際に発生する手数料もないものとする。

図表 11.2 にあるように存続企業（買い手企業）の利益は 80 百万ドルであり，市場価値は 1,200 百万ドルであるとする。株数は 4 百万であり，したがって株価は 300 ドルである。1 株あたり利益は 20 ドルなので，PER は 15 と計算できる。

一方で対象企業（売り手企業）の利益は 25 百万ドルであり，市場価値は 800 百万ドルである。株数は 3 百万であるため株価は 267 ドルである。1 株あたり利益は 8.33 ドルであり，PER は 32 と計算できる。

双方とも資本コストは 7% であるとする。この 2 社が合併すると，シナジー効果により利益は合計で 20 百万ドル増加するとし，合併後の存続企業の利益は，もともとの存続企業の利益 80 百万ドル＋対象企業の利益 25 百万ドル＋シナジー 20 百万ドル＝125 百万ドルになる。このシナジー効果はこの後も存続すると考えると，永久年金式を使用し 20 百万ドルを資本コスト 7% で割ることにより，合併により生み出される経済的な価値は 286（＝ 20 ÷ 7%）百万ドルと計算できる。

第 11 章　合併と買収　203

Figure 11.2 | Merger in Cash

	Surviving Company	Target Company	Synergy Effect	Cash Paid	Combined Company	Surviving Company Shareholders' Gain	Target Company Shareholders' Gain
Net Income (million$)	80	25	20		125		
Market Value (million$)	1,200	800	286	960	1,326	125.7	160.0
Number of Shares (million)	4.0	3.0		3.0	4.0	= Value after merger	= Cash received − value of
Share Price	300	267		320	331.4	− value before merger	target company before merger
Acquisition Premium				20.0%		= 1,326 − 1,200	= 960 − 800
EPS	20.00	8.33			31.25		
PER	15.00	32.00			10.61		

Cost of capital: 7%

● Merger in Cash

If the merger is conducted in cash, the top management and shareholders of the target company will agree only on a purchase price higher than $800 million, or $267 per share. Suppose that the surviving company will purchase all of the target company's outstanding stock for $320 per share, paying a 20% acquisition premium. Given that the target has 3 million shares, the surviving company is to pay $960 million (=320×3). Since the market value of the target is $800 million, $160 million out of the value created by the merger of $286 million will be distributed to the shareholders of the target company. The remaining value of $125.7 million is retained as part of the value of the combined company.

The value of the combined company will increase to $1,326 million measured by adding value created by the merger of $286 million to the original values of both companies ($1,200+800 million) and subtracting the cash paid to the target company's shareholders. The number of shares of the surviving company is unchanged at 4 million, therefore the share price is $331.4 (=1,326/4). The gain

図表 11.2 現金支払いによる合併

	存続企業	対象企業	シナジー効果	現金支払額	合併後企業	存続企業の株主の取り分	対象企業の株主の取り分
利益 (百万ドル)	80	25	20		125		
市場価値 (百万ドル)	1,200	800	286	960	1,326	125.7	160.0
株数 (百万)	4.0	3.0		3.0	4.0	=合併後企業価値	=現金受取額
株価	300	267		320	331.4	−合併前企業価値	−買収前の対象
買収 プレミアム				20.0%		= 1,326 − 1,200	企業価値 = 960 − 800
EPS	20.00	8.33			31.25		
PER	15.00	32.00			10.61		

資本コスト：7%

● 現金支払いによる合併

　合併が現金によって行われる場合，対象企業の経営陣または株主は少なくとも買収金額が 800 百万ドル以上，株価 267 ドル以上でなければ合併に合意しないだろう。存続企業は 20% のプレミアムを加えた対象企業の株式のすべてを 320 ドルで購入するとする。対象企業の株式数は 3 百万であるから，存続企業は合計で 960 (= 320 × 3) 百万ドルを支払うということになる。もともと対象企業の市場価値は 800 百万ドルであったから，プレミアムは 20% であり，このことは合併によって生み出される価値 286 百万ドルのうち，160 百万ドル分が対象企業の株主に分配されることを意味する。残りの 125.7 百万ドル分は存続企業の価値の一部となる。

　存続会社の合併後の合計の価値は 1,326 百万ドルとなり，これはもともとのそれぞれの会社の価値の合計 (1,200+800) から合併によって生み出された価値 286 百万ドルを加え，そこから対象企業の株主に支払われた現金を差し引いた額である。存続会社の株数は 4 百万と変わらないから，株価は 1,326÷4 = 331.4 ドルとなる。存続会社の株主にもたらされる価値は合併後の価値と合併

to the surviving company's shareholders is $125.7 million which is the difference between the values before and after the merger.

By the way, the net income of the combined company is $125 million, and the number of shares will not increase in the case of a cash purchase, thus the earnings per share rises to $31.25. But the share price will be $331.4, letting PER drop to 10.61.

● Merger with Stock

The merger with stock requires more complex discussion (Figure 11.3). Considering that the current share price of the surviving and the target are $300 and $267, respectively, it is natural to give the target company shareholders 0.89 shares (267/300) of the surviving company in exchange for 1 share of the target. The acquisition with stocks is not associated with cash outflows, so the value of the combined company is simply measured by adding value created by the merger of $286 million to the original values of both companies ($1,200+800 million).

On the other hand, the surviving company instead issues new shares to give to the target company's shareholders. Since one share of the target company is exchanged with 0.89 share of the surviving company, it needs to issue 2.67 million shares (0.89×3 million shares). The number of shares of the combined company will increase to 6.67 million, adding additional shares of 2.67 million to the original 4 million, and the share price becomes $342.9 (=2,286/6.67).

The shareholders of the target company will receive the value of $914.3 million (=2.67 million shares×$342.9) in total, an increase of $114.3 million from the original market value of $800 million.

206 | Chapter 11   Merger and Acquisition

前の価値の差であるから，125.7 百万ドルとなる。

　なお，合併後の利益は 125 百万ドルとなり，現金で買収する場合には株数は増えないため，存続企業の 1 株あたり利益は増大し，31.25 ドルとなる。しかし，株価は 331.4 ドルとなるため，PER が 10.61 と低下する。

● 株式による合併

　株式による合併の場合は説明がやや複雑になる（図表 11.3）。現在の株価は，存続企業が 300 ドル，対象企業が 267 ドルであるから，対象企業の株式 1 株を存続企業の株式 0.89 株（267 ÷ 300）と交換すれば自然である。株式交換の場合は，対象企業の株式に対する現金の支払いがないため合併後の企業価値はもともとの双方の会社の価値合計（1,200 百万ドル + 800 百万ドル）と合併によって生み出される価値（286 百万ドル）を加えた 2,286 百万ドルである。

　しかし，対象企業の株主に対して存続企業の株式を差し出すことになるため存続企業は株式を新規に発行する。対象企業の 1 株に対して存続企業の 0.89 株を割り当てることになるため，存続企業は 2.67 百万株が必要となる（0.89 × 3 百万株）。存続企業の合併後の株数はもともとの 4 百万から 2.67 百万増加した 6.67 百万になる。株価は 2,286 ÷ 6.67 ＝ 342.9 ドルとなる。

　対象企業の株主は合計で 2.67 百万株 × 342.9 ドル =914.3 百万ドルを手にすることになり，これはもともとの市場価値 800 百万ドルから 114.3 百万ドル増加している。

第 11 章　合併と買収　　207

Figure 11.3 | Merger with Stock

	Surviving Company	Target Company	Synergy Effect	Share Issued	Combined Company	Surviving Company Shareholders' Gain	Target Company Shareholders' Gain
Net Income (million$)	80	25	20		125		
Market Value (million$)	1,200	800	286		2,286	171.4	114.3
Number of Shares (million)	4.0	3.0		2.67	6.67	= Share price after merger × original number of shares	= Share price after merger × additional number of shares −
Share Price	300	267			342.9	− value before merger	value of target company before merger
EPS	20.00	8.33			18.75		
PER	15.00	32.00			18.29		

Cost of capital: 7%

The shareholders of the surviving company will receive total value of $1,371.4 million (=4 million shares×$342.9), which is greater than the original market value of $171.4 million. The total gain from the merger is constant, $286 million regardless of whether it is in cash or with stocks. However, the gain to either companies' shareholders depends on the merger ratio deciding how many shares of the surviving company will be exchanged for the shares of the target company.

The number of shares will increase to 6.67 million, resulting in the earnings per share of the combined company being $18.75, and PER being 18.29.

The cash payment by the surviving company to the target company's shareholders is fixed at the acquisition if cash is offered, while the shareholders of the target company will hold the shares of the combined company if stock is offered. Therefore, the shareholders of the target company and surviving company will share the value resulting from the future performance of the combined company.

図表 11.3 ┃ 株式による合併

	存続企業	対象企業	シナジー効果	発行株式	合併後企業	存続企業の株主の取り分	対象企業の株主の取り分
利益 （百万ドル）	80	25	20		125		
市場価値 （百万ドル）	1,200	800	286		2,286	171.4	114.3
株数 （百万）	4.0	3.0		2.67	6.67	＝合併後株価×合併前株式数－合併前企業価値	＝合併後株価×新規発行株式数－買収前の対象企業価値
株価	300	267			342.9		
EPS	20.00	8.33			18.75		
PER	15.00	32.00			18.29		

資本コスト：7%

　存続企業の株主は合計で株数 4 百万 × 342.9 ドル =1,371.4 百万ドルを手にすることになり，もともとの価値から 171.4 百万ドル増加している。現金であろうとも株式交換であろうとも合併により増大する価値は 286 百万ドルと同一である。しかし，対象企業の株に対して存続企業の株数をどれだけ割り当てるのかという合併比率によって，それぞれの会社の株主が受け取る価値は異なる。

　合併後の 1 株あたり利益は，株数が 6.67 百万と増えるため，18.75 ドルとなる。PER は 18.29 となる。

　現金による合併の場合は，買収時点において存続企業が対象企業の株主に支払う金額は確定するのに対し，株式での合併の場合は対象企業の株主は合併企業の株式を持ち続けることになる。そのため，合併後の企業業績の影響は存続企業の株主と対象企業の株主とで分かち合われることになる。

第 11 章　合併と買収　　209

A stock merger can mitigate the risk of over or under estimation of either company.

⊙ Leveraged Buyout and Management Buyout

This chapter closes with the introduction of the acquisition having peculiar characteristics. A leveraged buyout (or LBO) is known as acquisitions of a company by a limited number of investors using substantial debt financing.

The shares of LBO are no longer traded in the market, and are held by a small group of investors such as investment funds called private equity. LBO with huge debt has to generate cash to service it sustainably. Therefore, managers are expected to be more serious about earning money, and a drastic initiative such as steep cost reduction will be more likely executed.

When the acquirers of a company are the company's current or former management, the acquisition is called a management buyout (or MBO). Sometimes, it a small business or division away from the mainstream business lies neglected. It will be a candidate to be spun off in the form of MBO. MBO business or company is also unlisted, insulated from various legal requirements. Moreover, they say that the managers of MBO can focus on longer term strategic initiatives without short term oriented pressure from investors.

210　　Chapter 11　Merger and Acquisition

株式による合併は対象企業を過大評価，過小評価するリスクを低減させることができるのである。

● レバレッジ・バイアウトとマネジメント・バイアウト

本章の最後に，買収の特殊な形式を紹介しよう。レバレッジ・バイアウト（LBO）は少数の投資家が多くの資金を負債により調達して企業を買収する手法をいう。

LBO された企業の株式は市場で取引されることはなくなり，プライベート・エクイティーと呼ばれる投資ファンドなど少人数の投資家によって所有される。LBO 企業は多くの負債を抱えており，それを返済をするためには安定的に現金を生み出す必要がある。そのため，経営者はより緊張感をもって経営を行うことが期待されており，たとえば大幅なコスト削減といった思い切った施策が実行されやすい。

また，企業の買収者が現在あるいは以前の経営者である場合はマネジメント・バイアウト（MBO）と呼ばれる。大企業において主たるビジネスとみなされない小さな事業や部署は，社内の関心を集めないことがしばしばある。そのような事業は MBO としてスピンオフされる対象となりやすい。MBO された事業はやはり非上場企業となるため，上場維持に必要なさまざまな法規制から逃れることができるようになる。また，短期的なリターンを求める投資家からのプレッシャーがなくなるため，より中長期的な視点に立った経営ができるメリットがあるとされている。

第 11 章　合併と買収　211

Chapter

12 Fulfilling Value

Points !

✔ If the gap between the estimated value based on valuation analysis and the actual market value of a company is significant, the reason should be investigated

✔ The appropriate delegation of authority and compensation design can encourage each organization in a company to create value

● Absorbing the Value of Company

The share of a listed company is traded in a stock market, and the share price reflects investors' expectation about the future performance of the company. While a company informs investors of its condition and prospects via IR (investors relations) activity, investors signal their expectation in the market. Managers should absorb investors' expectation, and then formulate and execute a strategic plan to achieve the performance required in the stock market. Incorporating the investors' expectation into the performance goal encourages management that focuses on the shareholders' value creation.

Appropriate valuation gives managers confidence and calmness, and prevents them from swinging emotionally between hope and despair by occasional stock price fluctuations.

● Analyzing Expectation Gap

It is advisable that managers analyze the reasons for the difference between the estimated value based on their valuation and the actual market value based on the current stock price. A significant gap implies that there is a big difference with respect to future prospects and assumptions for valuations between managers and

第12章 価値の具現化

> **ポイント！**
>
> ✓ 企業価値評価の結果と，市場における価値が異なる場合はその理由を把握すべきである
>
> ✓ 企業内の各組織に企業価値の創造を促すためには，適切な権限委譲と報酬制度の設計が重要となる

● 企業価値の理解

　上場している企業であれば，株式は日々市場において取引されており，そこでつけられた株価には，投資家がどのように企業の将来を評価しているのかが表われる。企業が IR と呼ばれる活動によって企業の状態や見通しを投資家に知らせるように，投資家もまた企業への期待を市場において伝達するのである。経営陣は，投資家の期待を把握し，株式市場で求められている業績を達成するためにどのような戦略を立て，実行していくのかを考えるべきである。これにより，市場の期待を業績目標に取り入れた，投資家の価値を増大させる経営が実現できる。

　また，企業価値評価によって自社の価値を冷静に判断できていれば，一時的に株価が高騰したり，またその後に修正される段階においても一喜一憂せず，落ち着いて受け止めることができる。

● 期待のギャップ分析

　経営陣が行った企業価値評価の結果に基づく推定価値と，現在の株価に基づく実際の市場価値に乖離が生じているのであれば，その違いの理由を検討することが望ましい。もし乖離が大きい場合は，価値算定の前提や将来業績に対する見方が経営陣と投資家とで大きく異なっているということであり，投資家と

investors, and accordingly demands more communication.

If the result of valuation exceeds the current market value, the assumptions for the valuation might be too optimistic, and managers have to review specific initiatives and conditions to make the assumptions feasible. On the other hand, if the result of valuation is lower than the current market value, the assumptions might be too pessimistic, and managers should study what the investors evaluate highly.

Figure 12.1 | Analyzing Expectation Gap

- Are assumptions for valuation too optimistic?
- Are there sufficient initiatives to achieve the valuation result?

- What is necessary to improve performance further?
- What do investors evaluate highly?

Company Value Based on Valuation

Company Value Based on Current Share Price

Company Value Based on Valuation

Company Value Based on Current Share Price

○ Integrating into Mid-term Plan

If the result of their valuation is close to the current market value, the main agenda for mid-term planning is embodying strategic initiatives to realize the scenario which the projected performance is based on. However, if the estimated value does not achieve the current market value, additional initiatives to enhance future performance are required. Otherwise, a company will not able to meet investors' expectation and end up with a fall in share price sooner or later.

The recommended mid-term plan;

● Accommodates a company's vision (how an organization is managed or what it would like to accomplish) and mission (an organization's role in the society)

214   Chapter 12   Fulfilling Value

のコミュニケーションの必要があるということである。

　企業価値評価の結果のほうが実際の市場価値よりも高い場合は，企業価値評価の前提が楽観的過ぎるかもしれず，その前提を可能にする具体策や条件が実現可能かどうかを確認する必要がある。逆に，企業価値評価の結果のほうが実際の市場価値よりも低い場合は，企業価値評価の前提が悲観的過ぎるかもしれない。投資家はどのような要素を評価しているのかを探る必要があるだろう。

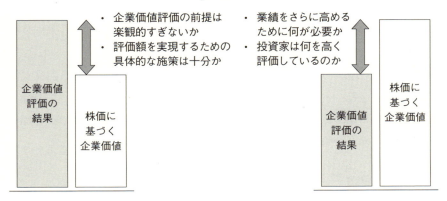

図表12.1　期待のギャップ分析

中期計画への統合

　経営陣による企業価値評価の結果が現在の株価水準と近いのであれば，予測した業績を実現するために何をするのかを具体的に明らかにしていくのが中期計画策定の中心課題となる。しかし，企業価値評価の結果が現在の株価水準に届いていない場合は，価値評価を行った際の業績予測の前提以上の戦略施策を検討しなければ，投資家の期待に応えることができず，将来的に株価の下落に直面することになる。

　優れた中期計画は，
- 企業経営のあり方や将来的に成し遂げたい状況（ビジョン）や，企業の社会における役割（ミッション）と合致しており，

第12章　価値の具現化　　215

- Declares a financial goal
- Specifies strategic policy and detailed action plans to achieve the financial goal
- Defines operational and financial activities and their corresponding drivers (financial as well as non-financial variable measures) to be monitored and revised

Please note that the important performance driver showing the progress of strategic activities is referred to as KPI (Key Performance Indicator).

● Delegation of Authority to Activate Plan

In order to accomplish the planned financial goal, each organization in a company carries out activities toward value creation autonomously. "Information", "authority" and "evaluation" are three requirements to be deployed in organizations.

Figure 12.2 | Requirements for Autonomous Organization

Information
(Measure)
Performance is
measures and
provided

Authority
Decision making
authority is
delegated

Evaluation
Outcome of
decision is
evaluated

The minimum requirement to facilitate an organization to create value is the availability and accessibility of a performance measure. The appropriate performance measure is specified and its information should be provided to the organization.

Chapter 12   Fulfilling Value

- 財務的なゴールが示され，
- それを実現するための戦略方針と詳細なアクションプランが明確であり，
- 活動の進捗状況をモニタリングし，必要に応じて軌道修正をするための営業活動や財務政策の重要な財務・非財務の変数（ドライバー）が定められている。

業績に関連する重要な指標であり，戦略が順調に進捗しているのかを表わすドライバーは KPI（重要業績評価指標）とも呼ばれる。

◉ 権限移譲による計画の実行

計画された業績を達成するためには，社内の各組織が自律的に価値創造に向けた行動を実行しなければならない。そのためには「情報」，「権限」，「評価」という 3 つの要件を各組織に整える必要がある。

図表 12.2 ┃ 自律的なマネジメント組織の要件

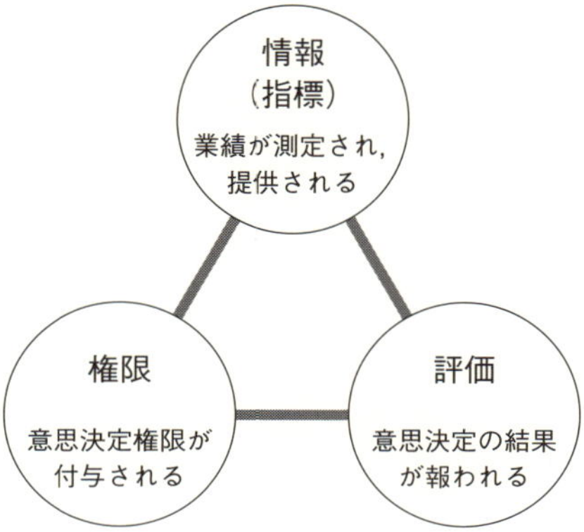

情報
（指標）

業績が測定され，
提供される

権限

意思決定権限が
付与される

評価

意思決定の結果
が報われる

各組織に価値創造に向けた行動を促すためには，注目すべき指標・数値が明確になっており，かつ測定・把握できることが最低限の条件となる。適切な業績指標に関する情報は各組織に提供され，入手可能でなければならない。

第 12 章　価値の具現化　　217

In addition to information provided, an organization should have the freedom and authority to improve the performance measure based on the information.

Then, an organization is accountable for the measure and is evaluated based on it. The evaluation is usually linked with a financial compensation such as a bonus.

Even if the actions and performance measures are clarified, you can do nothing without any authority to take action. It is not fair if you are evaluated based on the actions and performance measures without any authority. Furthermore, you cannot be delegated the authority or evaluated without information. Hence, these three factors are in one set for a self-directive organization.

● Incentive Compensation for Value Creation

Many executive compensation packages consist of a fixed salary and a variable payment based on profits or other financial performances. The compensation linked with the value of a company motivates managers to increase the company's value. If the compensation is designed to connect a company's value, managers earn a generous bonus when they increase a company's value and satisfy shareholders, and accept a small, or no bonus at all, when they cannot satisfy shareholders. The incentive compensation based on a company value aligns the interest of managers with the shareholders. Seen in that light, non-cash, equity compensation including stock options are also beneficial.

Figure 12.3 summarizes the characteristics of three incentive compensation schemes.

業績指標が提供されることに加え，組織にはその数値を改善するための自由
度と権限が与えられている必要がある。

さらに，組織はその業績指標に責任を持ち，その数値に応じて評価されるべ
きだ。評価は通常，賞与などの金銭的報酬に結びつけられる。

取組みや指標が明らかになっていたとしても，そこにアクションを起こせる
だけの権限が与えられなければ行動は起こせない。また，権限が与えられない
取組みや指標の責任を問われ評価されるのはおかしい。一方で，情報がなけれ
ば権限は与えられないし，また評価されることもない。したがって，自律的な
組織には，この3つの要件がセットで備わっていなければならないのである。

● 企業価値を高めるインセンティブ報酬設計

企業経営者の報酬の多くは，固定的な報酬と，利益やそれに準じた財務業績
に基づいた変動部分（ボーナス）とからなる。企業価値の向上を経営者に促す
ためには，企業価値と連動した報酬制度を設計することが望ましい。報酬が企
業価値にリンクしているのであれば，経営者は企業価値を高めて投資家を満足
させた場合に多くの報酬を得ることができ，投資家を満足させられなかった場
合には報酬が小額になることになる。企業価値に基づく報酬制度により，経営
者と株主との利害の一致を図ることができる。そのためには，現金ではなく株
式による報酬やストックオプションの付与が有効な手段となる。

図表12.3は各種のインセンティブ報酬の特徴をまとめている。

Figure 12.3 | Characteristics of Incentive Compensation

	Equity Compensation	Profit-based Compensation	Driver(KPI)-based Compensation
Pros	• Aligns managers' interest with the shareholders • Reflects expected future value • Objective based on figures in the market	• Accommodate a mid-term plan • Independent of the temporal market fluctuation	• Encourage actions accommodating to strategy • Flexible to design
Cons	• Relies on share price fluctuating with various reasons • Weakly relates daily activities of the average employee	• Might encourage short-term oriented actions	• Artificial • Relies on the hypothetical relationship between drivers and value

○ Equity Compensation

Equity compensation is payment a company offers its managers and employees in the form of stocks. Due to the restriction on transfer usually attached, it cannot be sold immediately. Equity compensation allows the managers and employees to earn more wealth if the share price appreciates, and vice versa.

A company can offer stock options which is the right to purchase shares of the companies' stocks at a predetermined price, called exercise price. A stock options holder can make money if the stock price increases above the exercise price but gain nothing otherwise. Therefore, stock options strongly motivate the managers and employees to raise the share price.

The most beneficial feature of equity compensation lies in the capability to align shareholders' interests with the managers and employees. Also, since a share price reflects long term forecasts, equity compensation is presumed to be linked with the activities leading to future performance as well. Another advantage of equity compensation is that it eliminates artificiality because a share price is set in the

220 | Chapter 12 Fulfilling Value

図表 12.3 ┃ 各種インセンティブ報酬の特徴

	株式報酬	利益連動報酬	ドライバー（KPI）連動報酬
長所	・投資家と経営者との利害が一致する ・将来の期待価値も反映される ・株式市場に存在する数値に基づくため客観的である	・中期計画と整合している ・短期的な株価の変動の影響を排除できる	・戦略推進に合致した行動を促進する ・設計の際の自由度が高い
短所	・株価はさまざまな要因で変動する ・平均的な社員の日々の取組みとの関連が薄い	・短期的な指向を助長する可能性がある	・恣意性が混入 ・KPIと企業価値との関係性は仮説

● 株式報酬

　株式報酬はその名の通り，現金の代わりに自社の株式を経営者や従業員に対する報酬とするものである。通常受け取った株式はすぐに売却することができない譲渡制限付きである。経営者・従業員は企業の株価が上昇すれば多くの富を得ることができ，株価が下落すれば報酬金額は目減りすることになる。

　また，ストックオプションは経営者あるいは従業員に自社の株をある一定の価格で購入する権利を与えるものである。ストックオプションの保有者は，株価が権利行使価格より高くなればメリットを得られるが，そうでなければストックオプションは何の利益も生み出さない。そのため，ストックオプションは経営者・従業員に株価を上げる非常に強いインセンティブを与えることになる。

　株式報酬の一番の長所は，経営者・従業員と株主の利益を一致させる点にある。また，株価は長期的な業績予測も反映するものなので，株式報酬は，将来の業績につながる取組みの巧拙にもリンクしているともいえる。株価は市場において決まる値段であり，客観的な数値なので，株式報酬には恣意性が入らないということも長所の1つである。

第12章　価値の具現化　　221

market.

It is well known that equity compensation dominates a large portion of executive compensation packages in U.S. companies (heavy usage of it is less often seen in Japanese companies).

In the meantime, a share price may fluctuate greatly depending on factors unrelated to the fundamental value of a company. So, it might not be a good idea to rely excessively on equity compensation. A share price is subject to company-wide future prospects and is far from the operations that an average employee faces. Therefore, equity compensation is not appropriate to apply for lower level managers and employees.

● Profit-based Compensation

Cash bonuses based on earnings are a standard form of compensation. If the mid-term plan is consistent with value creation, performance-based pay depending on the planned profits function to align the shareholders' interest with the managers and employees indirectly. The payment related to the profit has an advantage to be free from share price fluctuations.

However, it must be noted that a strict bond between the periodic earnings and compensation might facilitate myopic behaviors of the managers and employees such as prioritizing immediate profits over long term value creation.

● Driver-based Compensation

It may be more preferable for managers and employees on the front line to design a payment scheme relating to the progress of strategic activities. A possible arrangement includes driver (KPI)-based compensation.

It is to be noted that while financial measures based on accounting are ordinarily objective, non-financial measures are inherently artificial to some degree. Selecting and defining drivers appropriately, setting the target level, and weighing them

米国企業においては，経営者の報酬のうち大部分が株式連動報酬であること
はよく知られている（日本企業の経営者報酬に株式報酬が占める割合は高くな
い）。

一方で，残念ながら株価は短期的には企業の本質的な価値とは関係のない別
の要素で変動することもある。そのため株式報酬に過度に頼ることは望ましく
ない場合も多い。また，株価は企業全体の将来見通しに左右されるものなので，
平均的な従業員が携わる業務からは距離があり，したがって組織の下層レベル
の社員にまで展開することが難しい。

● 利益連動報酬

インセンティブ報酬としてより一般的なのは，利益などに連動した現金ボー
ナスであろう。企業価値を上げるような中期計画が策定できていれば，その計
画上の利益の達成度合いを報酬の基準とすれば，間接的に経営者・従業員と株
主の利害を一致させることができる。利益に基づく報酬は，大きく変動しうる
株価の値動きの影響から解放されるという利点がある。

ただし，利益のような一定期間の業績指標と報酬とを強固に結びつけること
は，長期的な価値創造よりも短期的な利益を優先させるといった近視眼的な行
動を経営者・従業員に促してしまう危険性もある。

● ドライバー連動報酬

より現場に近い管理職や従業員には，戦略の推進状況に連動した取組みを直
接的に報酬に反映するほうが望ましいであろう。その際には，ドライバー（KPI）
の進捗状況を報酬に連動させることが解決策の１つになる。

注意しなければならないことは，会計指標に基づく財務数値が通常客観的に
算出されるのに対し，非財務的な指標には恣意性が必然的に入ってしまうとい
うことである。指標自体の選定・定義，その目標水準の決定，複数ある指標の

第 12 章　価値の具現化　　223

necessitate deliberate decisions. Moreover, although the increases in drivers or KPIs are considered to increase the value of a company, they are just hypothetical relationships used in planning, therefore driver-based pay is subject to later revision.

Designing an incentive adequately is surprisingly difficult, and there is no versatile or optimum solution. You should try to compose the most appropriate possible package bearing in mind the features of each scheme.

● Separation of Ownership and Management

A business run by one-person or family has no managerial conflict of interests because they are both owners and managers. They receive a deserving reward of hardworking and wise decisions, and suffer the consequences of laziness and wasteful decisions. The personal wealth of managers and the value of the business coincide.

Meanwhile, the owners of most large companies are outside investors, so the managers might be inclined to pursue their own benefits, instead of increasing the company or equity value. The value destroying behavior due to a separation of ownership and management causes so-called agency problems. A wrongdoing of top executives (such as using a corporate jet for their personal travel) arises because they are not the owners of the company but agents of the owners (shareholders).

Mechanisms to control this problem are collectively referred to as corporate governance.

● Elements of Corporate Governance

There are various elements constituting corporate governance.

● Laws and regulations require managers of a company to engage in activities

224   Chapter 12 Fulfilling Value

ウエイト付け等,意思をもって決定すべき事項が多くある。さらに,ドライバー,KPI が企業の価値の増大に結びついているのかは計画策定段階では単に仮説であるため,報酬デザインは後に見直される可能性があることも考慮するべきである

適切にインセンティブを設計することは思いのほか難しく,どのようなときにも万能な最適解は存在しない。報酬制度を設計する際には,それぞれのスキームの特徴を踏まえたうえで,より適切なものを作りあげるしかない。

● 所有と経営の分離

個人や家族でビジネスを行う場合には通常は経営上の利害の衝突は生じない。彼らは所有者であり経営者でもあるため,懸命に働き正しい意思決定をすればその報酬を受け取ることになるし,不真面目であったり良くない意思決定を行えば損失を被る。経営者の個人的な財産は事業の価値と一体である。

一方で大企業の多くにおいては企業の所有者は外部の投資家であり,そのため経営者は企業・株主価値の増大よりも,むしろ自らの利益のために行動を起こす可能性がある。このような,所有と経営の分離によって発生する価値を毀損する行動がエージェンシー問題である。企業の経営者が,企業が所有するジェット機を個人の旅行で使用するといった好ましくない行動は,経営者が企業の所有者ではなく,所有者(株主)の代理人(エージェント)であるために生じるのである。

このような問題をコントロールするためのメカニズムを総称してコーポレート・ガバナンスと呼ぶ。

● コーポレート・ガバナンスの要素

コーポレート・ガバナンスを構成する要素にはさまざまなものがある。
- 法律や規則により,企業の経営陣は公正にかつ責任をもって株主の利益

第 12 章 価値の具現化 225

in the best interest of shareholders with fairness and responsibility. They will be charged with criminal liability if they conduct improper activities including accounting fraud or pocketing money and are subject to an action for damages filed by the shareholders or the company itself.

● The board of directors elected by the shareholders has the authority to appoint the top executive of the company, therefore is an important element of good corporate governance.

● Institutional investors fulfill the great role to monitor a company, express opinions, and request changes when needed.

● If the share price remains stagnant, other companies are tempted to purchase the company. Stock markets provide the place and the opportunity to make takeovers happen, which incites discipline in a company.

● Accounting and other information disclosed according to rules permits security analysts, credit rating agencies, banks and other creditors to diagnose the company.

● Debt, one mean of financing also functions as a form of corporate governance. Managers in a company deep in debt, therefore needing money for service payments, are expected to be more serious about slashing wasteful spending and defeating the competitors.

● Governance from Inside Stem from Valuation

As described above, many elements of corporate governance are attempts to check and discipline management from outside of the company. Meanwhile, management focusing on the value of the company and aiming to maximize it means establishing a corporate governance structure inside of the company.

It is obviously important to deploy the internal control system and procedures to ensure appropriate decision making (for example, double-checking before payment and concluding contracts). In addition to that, using valuation to absorb the value of the company, encompass it in the mid-term plan, and design incentive compensation

226 Chapter 12 Fulfilling Value

のために行動することが求められる。粉飾決算や私的な利益誘導などの不正行為を働いた企業の経営者は刑事責任を追及されるほか，株主や会社自体から損害賠償を求める訴訟を起こされる可能性がある。

- 株主によって選任される取締役も，企業の経営陣を指名するという権限をもつことにより，望ましいコーポレート・ガバナンスのためには大きな役割を担う。
- 経営を監視し，企業経営に意見し，時に経営陣に変化を要求する機関投資家も重要な役割を担う。
- 株価が低迷している企業は，他社にとって買収しやすくなる。このような企業買収が可能となる機会を提供する株式市場は企業に規律を与えている。
- 情報開示ルールによる会計情報その他の開示情報は証券アナリストや債券の格付機関，および銀行やその他の債権者による企業の分析を可能にする。
- 企業の資金調達の方法の1つである負債の活用もコーポレート・ガバナンスの1つの仕組みとなる。負債の返済や定期的な利息支払いに直面して，そのための資金が必要となる経営者は，無駄な経費削減や競合他社との競争に勝つことに，より真剣になると期待される。

● 企業価値評価による内からのガバナンス

以上のように，コーポレート・ガバナンスの要素の多くは外部から経営をチェックし，規律付けをしようという試みである。しかし，企業価値を意識しその最大化を目指す経営を行うことは「内からのガバナンス」体制の整備を意味している。

適切な意思決定プロセスを確実にする内部統制の仕組みの整備（支払いや契約締結の際には複数名がチェックする仕組みなど）はもちろん重要である。加えて，企業価値を適切にとらえてそれを中期計画に組み込み，企業価値の最大化に向けて経営者・従業員が努力するように投資家と利害を一致させる報酬

第12章　価値の具現化　227

to motivate managers and employees contributes to good corporate governance. Thus valuation is key to strengthening corporate governance.

Figure 12.4 | Governance from Inside

Classic Governance

- Legal requirements
- Appointment and audit by board of directors
- Pressure from institutional investor
- Threat of takeover
- Information disclosure
- Debt usage

Governance from Inside

- Internal control system
- Management focusing on company value
- Planning and execution to meet investor's expectation
- Compensation toward value maximization aligning interest with investors

体制を構築することはガバナンスの強化にもつながる。企業価値評価はコーポレート・ガバナンスの力を高めるのである。

図表 12.4 ┃ 内からのガバナンス

典型的なガバナンス

- 法律・規則の要請
- 取締役による経営陣の指名・監視
- 機関投資家によるプレッシャー
- 敵対的買収の脅威
- 情報開示ルール
- 負債の活用

内からのガバナンス

- 内部統制
- 企業価値を意識した経営
- 投資家の期待する価値と整合した中期計画の策定と実行
- 投資家と利害を一致させた，価値の最大化を促す報酬制度

Appendix: Financial Analysis and Valuation File

All financial analysis and valuation exhibited in the text has been demonstrated on the Excel-based spreadsheet introduced here in the appendix. The excel file is downloadable online. (Please note that I expressly disclaim any and all liability relating or resulting from the use of all or any part of the file or any of the information contained therein.)

(https://www.biz-book.jp/isbn/978-4-502-31671-5)

Financial Analysis and Valuation File consist of worksheets shown in Figure A.1.

Figure A.1 ▎ Contents of Financial Analysis and Valuation File

· Historical Data Input
  — Input basic data and historical financial data

· Drivers & Forecast
  — Calculates NOPAT, Capital, FCF, and EVA
  — Input forecast drivers for valuation

· Figures
  — Shows various financial ratios and measures graphically

· WACC
  — Calculates weighted average cost of capital

· DCF
  — Estimates the value of company based on your input with DCF approach and EVA approach

· DCF Figure
  — Shows each elements of company value as waterfall chart

· Multiples
  — Estimates the value of company based on multiples

· Summary
  — Summarizes valuation results and compare with the actual share price

付録：財務分析・企業価値評価ファイルの紹介

　これまで紹介した財務分析，企業価値評価の分析例は，ここで紹介するエクセルベースでのファイルに基づいて行われている。興味のある方は以下のホームページにアクセスして入手可能である（ただし，本ファイルおよびファイル内のデータを使用して投資を行った結果の責任を著者は一切負わないことをご了承いただきたい）。

（https://www.biz-book.jp/isbn/978-4-502-31671-5）

　このファイルは図表 A.1 に示すシートによって構成されている。

図表 A.1 ▎ 財務分析・企業価値評価ファイルの構成

・Historical Data Input
　　 ─企業の基礎情報と過去の財務データを入力する

・Drivers & Forecast
　　 ─ NOPAT，投下資本，FCF，EVA が計算される
　　 ─企業価値評価のためにドライバーを予測する

・Figures
　　 ─さまざまな財務指標をグラフで表わす

・WACC
　　 ─加重平均資本コストを推定する

・DCF
　　 ─入力された情報に基づき割引キャッシュフロー法と割引 EVA 法により企業
　　　 価値，株価を推定する

・DCF Figure
　　 ─企業価値の構成要素を滝グラフによって示す

・Multiples
　　 ─株価を価値倍率法により推定する

・Summary
　　 ─価値評価結果のまとめて示し，実際の株価と比較する

付　録　231

⬤ Historical Data Input

The first worksheet asks you to enter the basic information such as a company name, a currency unit, and the most recent year when financial data is available, as well as financial performances in the past. The cells requesting your input are colored gray throughout the file, and other cells are entered or calculated by the spreadsheet. For example, once the most recent fiscal year is entered, prior years appear automatically.

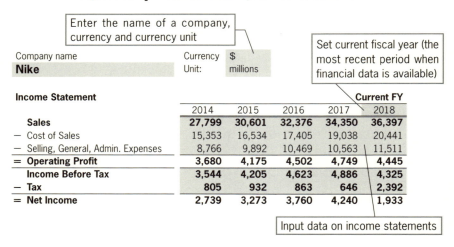

Figure A.2 | Historical Data Input: Income Statement

Input cells for the income statement and the balance sheet are prepared for the past five year periods.

● Historical Data Input

　最初のシートには，企業名や通貨単位，分析時点で財務情報が入手可能な最も新しい実績年度などの基礎的な情報と，過去の財務業績を入力する。ファイル全体を通じて入力が必要なセルはすべてグレーに色つけされており，その他の数値は自動的に計算，入力される。たとえば，分析時点の年度を入力すると，過去の年度には自動的に数値が入る。

図表 A.2 ┃ Historical Data Input：損益計算書

企業名，通貨，単位を入力する

分析時点で財務情報が入手可能な最も新しい実績年度を入力する

企業名		通貨	ドル			
ナイキ		単位	百万			

損益計算書					直近年度
	2014	2015	2016	2017	2018
売上高	27,799	30,601	32,376	34,350	36,397
－ 原価	15,353	16,534	17,405	19,038	20,441
－ 販管費	8,766	9,892	10,469	10,563	11,511
＝ 営業利益	3,680	4,175	4,502	4,749	4,445
税引前利益	3,544	4,205	4,623	4,886	4,325
－ 税金	805	932	863	646	2,392
＝ 当期純利益	2,739	3,273	3,760	4,240	1,933

損益計算書のデータを入力する

　損益計算書と貸借対照表といった過去の実績財務データは5年間分入力できるようになっている。

付　録 ｜ 233

The credit side of the balance sheet is designed to distinguish between debt and non-interest bearing liabilities.

0 or close to 0 appears in the row of validation if the data is entered without errors. It is possible to see a slight difference because financial data is likely to be rounded off.

Note: some totals and subtotals require your input so that the spreadsheet can automatically calculate miscellaneous figures.

Figure A.3 | Historical Data Input: Balance Sheet

Balance Sheet

	2014	2015	2016	2017	2018
Current Assets					
Cash and Equivalent	2,220	3,852	3,138	3,808	4,249
Short-term Investments	2,922	2,072	2,319	2,371	996
Notes, Accounts Receivable	3,434	3,358	3,241	3,677	3,498
Inventories	3,947	4,337	4,838	5,055	5,261
Other Current Assets	1,173	2,357	1,489	1,150	1,130
Total Current Assets	13,696	15,976	15,025	16,061	15,134
Property, Plant, Equipment	2,834	3,011	3,520	3,989	4,454
Long-term Investments					
Other Assets	2,064	2,613	2,834	3,209	2,948
Total Assets	18,594	21,600	21,379	23,259	22,536
Current Liabilities					
Short-term Debt	7	107	44	6	6
Others(Non interest bearing liab.)	5,020	6,227	5,314	5,468	6,034
Total Current Liabilities	5,027	6,334	5,358	5,474	6,040
Long-term Liabilities					
Long-term Debt	1,199	1,079	1,993	3,471	3,468
Others(Non interest bearing liab.)	1,544	1,480	1,770	1,907	3,216
Total Long-term Liabilities	2,743	2,559	3,763	5,378	6,684
Non-controlling Interest					
Shareholders' Equity					
Common Stock, Surplus Retained Earnings	10,739	11,461	11,940	12,620	9,904
Treasury Stock					
Others	85	1,246	318	-213	-92
Shareholders' Equity	10,824	12,707	12,258	12,407	9,812
Total Liabilities and Equity	18,594	21,600	21,379	23,259	22,536
Validation	0	0	0	0	0

Input data on balance sheet

Cells for the credit side is designed to distinguish between debt and non interest bearing liabilities

0 or close to 0 when you enter data correctly

"Long term investments" corresponds to financial assets such as securities that will not be disposed of in the near future.

234 | Appendix

貸借対照表の負債・純資産サイドは無利子の負債を明確に区別している。

　貸借対照表のデータが正しく入力されているのかどうかは，「照合」の欄が0あるいはほぼ0になっていることで確認できる。企業が公表する財務データは表示通貨単位以下の数値を切り捨てることが多いため，若干の誤差が生じる可能性がある。

　なお，いくつかの小計も入力セルとすることで，その他の項目が自動的に計算されるようになっている。

図表 A.3 ┃ Historical Data Input：貸借対照表

貸借対照表

	2014	2015	2016	2017	2018
流動資産					
現金及び同等物	2,220	3,852	3,138	3,808	4,249
有価証券	2,922	2,072	2,319	2,371	996
売掛債権	3,434	3,358	3,241	3,677	3,498
棚卸資産	3,947	4,337	4,838	5,055	5,261
その他流動資産	1,173	2,357	1,489	1,150	1,130
流動資産	13,696	15,976	15,025	16,061	15,134
有形固定資産	2,834	3,011	3,520	3,989	4,454
投資有価証券					
その他固定資産	2,064	2,613	2,834	3,209	2,948
総資産	18,594	21,600	21,379	23,259	22,536
流動負債					
短期有利子負債	7	107	44	6	6
その他流動負債（無利子流動負債）	5,020	6,227	5,314	5,468	6,034
流動負債	5,027	6,334	5,358	5,474	6,040
固定負債					
長期有利子負債	1,199	1,079	1,993	3,471	3,468
その他固定負債（無利子固定負債）	1,544	1,480	1,770	1,907	3,216
固定負債	2,743	2,559	3,763	5,378	6,684
非支配株主持ち分					
株主資本					
資本金，準備金，剰余金	10,739	11,461	11,940	12,620	9,904
自己株式					
その他	85	1,246	318	-213	-92
株主資本	10,824	12,707	12,258	12,407	9,812
負債純資産計	18,594	21,600	21,379	23,259	22,536
照合	0	0	0	0	0

貸借対照表のデータを入力する

負債・純資産サイドは無利子の負債を明確に区別している

データが正しく入力されていれば0あるいはほぼ0となる

付録　235

Data for the cash flow statement will be inputted next. The actual cash flow statement represents a lot of items, but this file combines and narrows them down to only relevant items for analysis.

Following that, the number of shares outstanding, a credit rate, and the actual share price as at the date of analysis are to be entered. At the bottom of the sheet, the basic profitability ratios based on accounting data such as ROA and ROE, and total liabilities to total assets ratio indicating financial health of a company are shown. ROA and ROE are calculated based on ending balance in this file.

Figure A.4 | Historical Data Input: Cash Flow Statements and Others

Cash Flow Statements

	2014	2015	2016	2017	2018	
Net Income	2,739	3,273	3,760	4,240	1,933	Input data on cash flow statements
+ Depreciation	518	606	649	706	747	
+ Others	-244	801	-1,010	-1,100	2,275	
= **Cash Flow From Operating Activities**	3,013	4,680	3,399	3,846	4,955	
Capital Expenditures	-877	-960	-1,133	-1,092	-1,025	
+ Financial Investments	-328	785	93	118	1,326	
+ Others	-2	0	6	-34	-25	
= **Cash Flows From Investing Activities**	-1,207	-175	-1,034	-1,008	276	
Dividends Paid	-799	-899	-1,022	-1,133	-1,243	
+ Share Repurchase	-2,628	-2,534	-3,238	-3,223	-4,254	
+ Net Borrowing	15	-70	808	1,765	7	
+ Others	498	713	478	443	655	
= **Cash Flows From Financing Activities**	-2,914	-2,790	-2,974	-2,148	-4,835	

Enter current credit rating

Others

Enter number of shares outstanding

Number of Share Outstanding	1,601
Credit Rating	AA-

Enter actual share price and date

Current Share Price at	10/31/2018	74.82

Basic Accounting Ratios

ROA =Opr Profit/Ending TA	19.8%	19.3%	21.1%	20.4%	19.7%	Basic ratios calculated and shown
ROE =NI/Ending Equity	25.3%	25.8%	30.7%	34.2%	19.7%	
Total Liabilities / Total Assets	41.8%	41.2%	42.7%	46.7%	56.5%	

236 | Appendix

次にキャッシュフロー計算書のデータを入力する。実際のキャッシュフロー計算書は多くの項目によって構成されているが，このファイルでは項目をまとめ，分析に必要なもののみとしている。

その下には，流通株式数，格付データ，および分析時点の実際の株価を入力する。このシートの一番下には会計データに基づく基本的な利益率指標ROA，ROEと，企業の財務健全性を示す負債総資産比率が計算される。なお，このファイルにおいては，簡便的に期末の貸借対照表の数値を用いてROA，ROEを計算している。

図表A.4 | **Historical Data Input**：キャッシュフロー計算書とその他

キャッシュフロー計算書

	2014	2015	2016	2017	2018
当期純利益	2,739	3,273	3,760	4,240	1,933
＋ 減価償却費	518	606	649	706	747
＋ その他	-244	801	-1,010	-1,100	2,275
＝ 営業活動からのキャッシュフロー	3,013	4,680	3,399	3,846	4,955
設備投資	-877	-960	-1,133	-1,092	-1,025
＋ 金融投資	-328	785	93	118	1,326
＋ その他	-2	0	6	-34	-25
＝ 投資活動からのキャッシュフロー	-1,207	-175	-1,034	-1,008	276
配当支払い	-799	-899	-1,022	-1,133	-1,243
＋ 自己株式取得	-2,628	-2,534	-3,238	-3,223	-4,254
＋ 借入金の増額（純額）	15	-70	808	1,765	7
＋ その他	498	713	478	443	655
＝ 財務活動からのキャッシュフロー	-2,914	-2,790	-2,974	-2,148	-4,835

過去5年のキャッシュフロー計算書のデータを入力する

流通株式数を入力する　　信用格付を入力する

その他

流通株式数		1,601
信用格付		AA-
現時点株価	2018/10/31	74.82

分析時点の実際の株価を入力する

基本的な会計指標

	2014	2015	2016	2017	2018
ROA＝営業利益÷期末総資産	19.8%	19.3%	21.1%	20.4%	19.7%
ROE＝当期純利益÷期末株主資本	25.3%	25.8%	30.7%	34.2%	19.7%
負債総資産比率	41.8%	41.2%	42.7%	46.7%	56.5%

基本的な財務指標が計算される

⬤ Drivers & Forecast

The second worksheet named "Drivers & Forecast" calculates historical NOPAT, capital, FCF, and EVA based on your input in "Historical Data Input".

Items in NOPAT and capital are also expressed as a percentage of sales as forecast drivers for future performance.

Figure A.5 | Drivers & Forecast: NOPAT

NOPAT — Actual — | Historical NOPAT | — Forecast Drivers

NOPAT	2014	2015	2016	2017	2018		2014	2015	2016	2017	2018	Avg
Sales	**27,799**	**30,601**	**32,376**	**34,350**	**36,397**	Growth%		10.1%	5.8%	6.1%	6.0%	7.0%
— Cost of Sales	15,353	16,534	17,405	19,038	20,441	% of Sales	55.2%	54.0%	53.8%	55.4%	56.2%	54.9%
— Selling, General, Admin. Expenses	8,766	9,892	10,469	10,563	11,511	% of Sales	31.5%	32.3%	32.3%	30.8%	31.6%	31.7%
Depreciation	518	606	649	706	747	% of Sales	1.9%	2.0%	2.0%	2.1%	2.1%	2.0%
= **Operating Profit**	**3,680**	**4,175**	**4,502**	**4,749**	**4,445**	% of Sales	13.2%	13.6%	13.9%	13.8%	12.2%	13.4%
						Tax Rate	22.7%	22.2%	18.7%	13.2%	55.3%	26.4%
— Operating Tax	836	925	840	628	2,458	% of Sales	3.0%	3.0%	2.6%	1.8%	6.8%	3.4%
= **NOPAT**	**2,844**	**3,250**	**3,662**	**4,121**	**1,987**	% of Sales	10.2%	10.6%	11.3%	12.0%	5.5%	9.9%
NOPAT Growth		14.3%	12.7%	12.5%	-51.8%	Validation	0.0%	0.0%	0.0%	0.0%	0.0%	

NOPAT shown as drivers for forecasting

238 | Appendix

Drivers & Forecast

2番目のシートである「Drivers & Forecast」では，「Historical Data Input」に入力されたデータに基づき，NOPAT，投下資本，FCF，EVA の実績値が計算される。

NOPAT，投下資本の項目は絶対額だけではなく，将来予測のためのドライバーとして売上高の比率としても表わされる。

図表 A.5 | Drivers & Forecast：NOPAT

NOPAT の過去実績

NOPAT	実績 2014	2015	2016	2017	2018	予測ドライバー	2014	2015	2016	2017	2018	平均
売上高	27,799	30,601	32,376	34,350	36,397	売上成長率		10.1%	5.8%	6.1%	6.0%	7.0%
－ 原価	15,353	16,534	17,405	19,038	20,441	売上高比	55.2%	54.0%	53.8%	55.4%	56.2%	54.9%
－ 販管費	8,766	9,892	10,469	10,563	11,511	売上高比	31.5%	32.3%	32.3%	30.8%	31.6%	31.7%
減価償却費	518	606	649	706	747	売上高比	1.9%	2.0%	2.0%	2.1%	2.1%	2.0%
＝ 営業利益	3,680	4,175	4,502	4,749	4,445	売上高比	13.2%	13.6%	13.9%	13.8%	12.2%	13.4%
						税率	22.7%	22.2%	18.7%	13.2%	55.3%	26.4%
－ 税金	836	925	840	628	2,458	売上高比	3.0%	3.0%	2.6%	1.8%	6.8%	3.4%
＝ NOPAT	2,844	3,250	3,662	4,121	1,987	売上高比	10.2%	10.6%	11.3%	12.0%	5.5%	9.9%
NOPAT 成長率		14.3%	12.7%	12.5%	-51.8%	照合	0.0%	0.0%	0.0%	0.0%	0.0%	

将来予測のためドライバーとして売上高の比率でも表示

付　録　239

Capital is calculated in two ways; from the side of operating assets and the side of financing.

This file subtracts long-term (financial) investments from debt to calculate net debt.

Figure A.6 | Drivers & Forecast: Capital

Capital in the past calculated with two approaches

Capital	Actual						Forecast Drivers					
	2014	2015	2016	2017	2018		2014	2015	2016	2017	2018	Avg
Cash and Equivalent	2,220	3,852	3,138	3,808	4,249							
Short-term Investments	2,922	2,072	2,319	2,371	996							
Long-term Investments	0	0	0	0	0							
= Cash and Investments	5,142	5,924	5,457	6,179	5,245	% of Sales	18.5%	19.4%	16.9%	18.0%	14.4%	17.4%
Notes, Accounts Receivable	3,434	3,358	3,241	3,677	3,498	% of Sales	12.4%	11.0%	10.0%	10.7%	9.6%	10.7%
Inventories	3,947	4,337	4,838	5,055	5,261	% of Sales	14.2%	14.2%	14.9%	14.7%	14.5%	14.5%
Other Current Assets	1,173	2,357	1,489	1,150	1,130	% of Sales	4.2%	7.7%	4.6%	3.3%	3.1%	4.6%
− Others (Non interest bearing liab.)	5,020	6,227	5,314	5,468	6,034	% of Sales	18.1%	20.3%	16.4%	15.9%	16.6%	17.5%
= Net Working Capital	3,534	3,825	4,254	4,414	3,855	% of Sales	12.7%	12.5%	13.1%	12.9%	10.6%	12.4%
Property, Plant, Equipment	2,834	3,011	3,520	3,989	4,454	% of Sales	10.2%	9.8%	10.9%	11.6%	12.2%	11.0%
Other Assets	2,064	2,613	2,834	3,209	2,948	% of Sales	7.4%	8.5%	8.8%	9.3%	8.1%	8.4%
− Others (Non interest bearing liab.)	1,544	1,480	1,770	1,907	3,216	% of Sales	5.6%	4.8%	5.5%	5.6%	8.8%	6.0%
= Fixed Operating Capital	3,354	4,144	4,584	5,291	4,186	% of Sales	12.1%	13.5%	14.2%	15.4%	11.5%	13.3%
Capital (Operating Apporach)	12,030	13,893	14,295	15,884	13,286	% of Sales	43.3%	45.4%	44.2%	46.2%	36.5%	43.1%
Short-term Debt	7	107	44	6	6							
Long-term Debt	1,199	1,079	1,993	3,471	3,468							
= Debt	1,206	1,186	2,037	3,477	3,474							
Non-controlling Interest	0	0	0	0	0							
Shareholders' Equity	10,824	12,707	12,258	12,407	9,812							
Capital (Financing Apporach)	12,030	13,893	14,295	15,884	13,286							
Net Debt	−3,936	−4,738	−3,420	−2,702	−1,771							

Capital shown as drivers for forecasting

FCF and net investment which is the difference between NOPAT and FCF, appears below.

240 | Appendix

投下資本は資産サイドからのアプローチと調達サイドからのアプローチの2通りの計算方法で算出される。

このファイルでは長期の金融資産も純有利子負債額の計算では控除している。

図表 A.6 ┃ Drivers & Forecast：投下資本

投下資本の過去実績は2つの方法によって計算される

投下資本	実績						予測ドライバー					
	2014	2015	2016	2017	2018		2014	2015	2016	2017	2018	平均
現金及び同等物	2,220	3,852	3,138	3,808	4,249							
有価証券	2,922	2,072	2,319	2,371	996							
投資有価証券	0	0	0	0	0							
＝ 現金及び金融投資	5,142	5,924	5,457	6,179	5,245	売上高比	18.5%	19.4%	16.9%	18.0%	14.4%	17.4%
売掛債権	3,434	3,358	3,241	3,677	3,498	売上高比	12.4%	11.0%	10.0%	10.7%	9.6%	10.7%
棚卸資産	3,947	4,337	4,838	5,055	5,261	売上高比	14.2%	14.2%	14.9%	14.7%	14.5%	14.5%
その他流動資産	1,173	2,357	1,489	1,150	1,130	売上高比	4.2%	7.7%	4.6%	3.3%	3.1%	4.6%
－ その他流動負債（無利子流動負債）	5,020	6,227	5,314	5,468	6,034	売上高比	18.1%	20.3%	16.4%	15.9%	16.6%	17.5%
＝ 正味運転資本	3,534	3,825	4,254	4,414	3,855	売上高比	12.7%	12.5%	13.1%	12.9%	10.6%	12.4%
有形固定資産	2,834	3,011	3,520	3,989	4,454	売上高比	10.2%	9.8%	10.9%	11.6%	12.2%	11.0%
その他固定資産	2,064	2,613	2,834	3,209	2,948	売上高比	7.4%	8.5%	8.8%	9.3%	8.1%	8.4%
－ その他固定負債（無利子固定負債）	1,544	1,480	1,770	1,907	3,216	売上高比	5.6%	4.8%	5.5%	5.6%	8.8%	6.0%
＝ 固定資本	3,354	4,144	4,584	5,291	4,186	売上高比	12.1%	13.5%	14.2%	15.4%	11.5%	13.3%
投下資本	12,030	13,893	14,295	15,884	13,286	売上高比	43.3%	45.4%	44.2%	46.2%	36.5%	43.1%
短期有利子負債	7	107	44	6	6							
長期有利子負債	1,199	1,079	1,993	3,471	3,468							
＝ 有利子負債	1,206	1,186	2,037	3,477	3,474							
非支配株主持分												
株主資本	10,824	12,707	12,258	12,407	9,812							
投下資本	12,030	13,893	14,295	15,884	13,286							
純有利子負債	−3,936	−4,738	−3,420	−2,702	−1,771							

将来予測のためドライバーとして売上高の比率でも表示

その下には FCF と，NOPAT と FCF の差である純投資額が計算される。

付　録　　241

Figure A.7 | Drivers & Forecast: FCF

Free Cash Flow		Actual			
	2014	2015	2016	2017	2018
NOPAT	2,844	3,250	3,662	4,121	1,987
+ Depreciation	518	606	649	706	747
− Increase in Cash and Investments		782	-467	722	-934
− Increase in Accounts Receivable		-76	-117	436	-179
− Increase in Inventories		390	501	217	206
− Increase in Other Current Assets		1,184	-868	-339	-20
+ Increase in Non interest bearing Liab.		1,143	-623	291	1,875
= **Operating Cash Flow**		**2,719**	**4,639**	**4,082**	**5,536**
Invest in Plant, Property, Equipment		783	1,158	1,175	1,212
+ Invest in Other Assets		549	221	375	-261
= **Investment**		**1,332**	**1,379**	**1,550**	**951**
Free Cash Flow		**1,387**	**3,260**	**2,532**	**4,585**
FCF Growth			135.1%	-22.3%	81.1%
Net Investment		1,863	402	1,589	-2,598

Net investment is difference between NOPAT and FCF

EVA is calculated in two ways: NOPAT − capital charge, and EVA spread×capital. The primary financial measures such as NOPAT margin and capital turnover are calculated as well.

WACC in this sheet is linked with another worksheet where WACC is estimated.

Figure A.8 | Drivers & Forecast: EVA

EVA		Actual			
	2014	2015	2016	2017	2018
NOPAT		3,250	3,662	4,121	1,987
Capital (Beg.)		12,030	13,893	14,295	15,884
WACC		7.0%	7.0%	7.0%	7.0%
− Capital Charge		845	976	1,005	1,116
= **EVA**		**2,404**	**2,685**	**3,116**	**870**
ROC =NOPAT/Beg. Cap		27%	26%	29%	13%
− WACC		7.0%	7.0%	7.0%	7.0%
= EVA Spread		20.0%	19.3%	21.8%	5.5%
× Capital (Beg.)		12,030	13,893	14,295	15,884
= **EVA**		**2,404**	**2,685**	**3,116**	**870**
NOPAT Margin =NOPAT/Sales	10.2%	10.6%	11.3%	12.0%	5.5%
Capital Turnover =Sales/Beg. Cap		2.5	2.3	2.4	2.3

Historical EVA calculated with two ways

WACC is calculated in another worksheet

Important financial measures are calculated

図表 A.7 ┃ Drivers & Forecast：FCF

フリー・キャッシュフロー		実績			
	2014	2015	2016	2017	2018
NOPAT	2,844	3,250	3,662	4,121	1,987
＋ 減価償却費	518	606	649	706	747
－ 現金及び金融投資の増額		782	-467	722	-934
－ 売掛債権の増額		-76	-117	436	-179
－ 棚卸資産の増額		390	501	217	206
－ その他流動資産の増額		1,184	-868	-339	-20
＋ 無利子負債の増額		1,143	-623	291	1,875
＝ 営業キャッシュフロー		2,719	4,639	4,082	5,536
有形固定資産への投資		783	1,158	1,175	1,212
＋ その他資産への投資		549	221	375	-261
＝ 投資額		1,332	1,379	1,550	951
フリー・キャッシュフロー		1,387	3,260	2,532	4,585
FCF 成長率			135.1%	-22.3%	81.1%
純投資額		1,863	402	1,589	-2,598

> 純投資額は NOPAT と FCF の差として計算される

　EVA は，NOPAT －資本費用，EVA スプレッド×投下資本，という 2 つの方法で計算されている。また，NOPAT マージンと投下資本回転率といった主要な財務指標もあわせて計算される。

　なお，WACC は別のシートにて計算される値とリンクしている。

図表 A.8 ┃ Drivers & Forecast：EVA

EVA		実績			
	2014	2015	2016	2017	2018
NOPAT		3,250	3,662	4,121	1,987
期首投下資本		12,030	13,893	14,295	15,884
WACC		7.0%	7.0%	7.0%	7.0%
－ 資本費用		845	976	1,005	1,116
＝ EVA		2,404	2,685	3,116	870
ROC ＝ NOPAT ÷ 期首投下資本		27%	26%	29%	13%
－ WACC		7.0%	7.0%	7.0%	7.0%
＝ EVA スプレッド		20.0%	19.3%	21.8%	5.5%
× 期首投下資本		12,030	13,893	14,295	15,884
＝ EVA		2,404	2,685	3,116	870
NOPAT マージン ＝ NOPAT ÷売上高	10.2%	10.6%	11.3%	12.0%	5.5%
投下資本回転率 ＝売上高÷期首投下資本		2.5	2.3	2.4	2.3

> EVA の過去実績は 2 つの方法によって計算される

> WACC は別のシートで計算される

> 主要な財務指標が計算される

付録　243

At the bottom of the sheet measures MVA.

Figure A.9 | Drivers & Forecast: MVA

MV, MVA

	Market Value of Equity (Market Capitalization) Based on Share Price	119,753
+	Short-term Debt	6
+	Long-term Debt	3,468
+	Non-controlling Interest	0
=	**Total Market Value**	123,227
−	Capital	13,286
=	**Market Value Added**	109,941

As illustrated above, "Drivers & Forecast" sheet reconstructs historical NOPAT, capital, FCF, and EVA out of accounting information. In addition, it forecasts future performance in the same worksheet based on historical data. Clicking "+" button located on the top of the sheet shows columns prepared for the input of future forecasts for the next five years. Hence, the explicit forecast period in this file is set to five years, and cash flows arising after five years are grasped as the terminal value.

In order to forecast NOPAT and capital, you enter forecast drivers in the cells to the right of historical data, referring to the past drivers. NOPAT and Capital in the future are forecasted using drivers, not entering estimated figures directly.

このシートの一番下では MVA を計算している。

図表 A.9 | Drivers & Forecast：MVA

MV, MVA

株式時価総額(分析時点)	119,753
＋ 短期有利子負債	6
＋ 長期有利子負債	3,468
＋ 非支配株主持ち分	0
＝ 企業価値	123,227
－ 投下資本	13,286
＝ 市場付加価値(MVA)	109,941

　以上のように，「Drivers & Forecast」シートは会計情報を再構成して NOPAT，投下資本，FCF，EVA，MVA を計算しているが，この実績値に基づいて，将来予測の入力もこのシートで行う。シート上部の「＋」ボタンをクリックすると，以後 5 年間にわたる将来予測用のセルが現れる。つまり，このファイルの予想期間は 5 年間であり，それ以降に発生するキャッシュフローはターミナル・バリューとしてとらえられるということである。

　NOPAT と投下資本の実績値の右側に表示されているドライバーに基づき，さらにその右側の入力セルにおいて，将来の NOPAT ドライバー，投下資本ドライバーを入力する。将来の NOPAT および投下資本は，予測されたドライバーに基づいて計算される。

Figure A.10 | Drivers & Forecast: Future Forecast

> NOPAT and Capital in the future forecasted using drivers, not entering estimated figures directly

NOPAT

		Forecast Drivers										
		2014	2015	2016	2017	2018	Avg	2019	2020	2021	2022	2023
Sales	Growth%		10.1%	5.8%	6.1%	6.0%	7.0%	6.5%	7.0%	7.5%	8.0%	8.5%
− Cost of Sales	% of Sales	55.2%	54.0%	53.8%	55.4%	56.2%	54.9%	56.0%	55.5%	55.0%	55.0%	55.0%
− Selling, General, Admin. Expenses	% of Sales	31.5%	32.3%	32.3%	30.8%	31.6%	31.7%	31.5%	31.5%	31.5%	31.5%	31.5%
Depreciation	% of Sales	1.9%	2.0%	2.0%	2.1%	2.1%	2.0%	2.0%	2.0%	2.0%	2.0%	2.0%
= Operating Profit	% of Sales	13.2%	13.6%	13.9%	13.8%	12.2%	13.4%	12.5%	13.0%	13.5%	13.5%	13.5%
	Tax Rate	22.7%	22.2%	18.7%	13.2%	55.3%	26.4%	25.0%	25.0%	25.0%	25.0%	25.0%
− Operating Tax	% of Sales	3.0%	3.0%	2.6%	1.8%	6.8%	3.4%	3.1%	3.3%	3.4%	3.4%	3.4%
= NOPAT	% of Sales	10.2%	10.6%	11.3%	12.0%	5.5%	9.9%	9.4%	9.8%	10.1%	10.1%	10.1%
NOPAT Growth	Validation	0.0%	0.0%	0.0%	0.0%	0.0%		0.0%	0.0%	0.0%	0.0%	0.0%

Capital

		Forecast Drivers										
		2014	2015	2016	2017	2018	Avg	2019	2020	2021	2022	2023
Cash and Equivalent												
Short-term Investments												
Long-term Investments												
= Cash and Investments	% of Sales	18.5%	19.4%	16.9%	18.0%	14.4%	17.4%	13.5%	12.6%	11.8%	10.9%	10.0%
Notes, Accounts Receivable	% of Sales	12.4%	11.0%	10.0%	10.7%	9.6%	10.7%	10.0%	10.0%	10.0%	10.0%	10.0%
Inventories	% of Sales	14.2%	14.2%	14.9%	14.7%	14.5%	14.5%	14.4%	14.3%	14.2%	14.1%	14.0%

Cash and financial investments are estimated to be unchanged unless you have specific reasons. The value of a company is determined by future cash flows generated in the company, but is independent of how cash is accumulated in the company.

Figure A.11 | Drivers & Forecast: Forecast for Financial Assets

> Cash and financial investments are estimated to be unchanged unless you have specific reasons

Capital	Actual					Estimate				
	2014	2015	2016	2017	2018	2019	2020	2021	2022	2023
Cash and Equivalent	2,220	3,852	3,138	3,808	4,249	4,249	4,249	4,249	4,249	4,249
Short-term Investments	2,922	2,072	2,319	2,371	996	996	996	996	996	996
Long-term Investments	0	0	0	0	0	0	0	0	0	0
= Cash and Investments	5,142	5,924	5,457	6,179	5,245	5,245	5,245	5,245	5,245	5,245

図表 A.10 ┃ Drivers & Forecast：将来予測

> NOPAT と投下資本の将来の値は絶対値を直接入力するのではなく，売上高比率というドライバーを用いて予測する

NOPAT

		予測ドライバー						2019	2020	2021	2022	2023
		2014	2015	2016	2017	2018	平均					
売上高	売上成長率		10.1%	5.8%	6.1%	6.0%	7.0%	6.5%	7.0%	7.5%	8.0%	8.5%
− 原価	売上高比	55.2%	54.0%	53.8%	55.4%	56.2%	54.9%	56.0%	55.5%	55.0%	55.0%	55.0%
− 販管費	売上高比	31.5%	32.3%	32.3%	30.8%	31.6%	31.7%	31.5%	31.5%	31.5%	31.5%	31.5%
減価償却費	売上高比	1.9%	2.0%	2.0%	2.1%	2.1%	2.0%	2.0%	2.0%	2.0%	2.0%	2.0%
= 営業利益	売上高比	13.2%	13.6%	13.9%	13.8%	12.2%	13.4%	12.5%	13.0%	13.5%	13.5%	13.5%
	税率	22.7%	22.2%	18.7%	13.2%	55.3%	26.4%	25.0%	25.0%	25.0%	25.0%	25.0%
− 税金	売上高比	3.0%	3.0%	2.6%	1.8%	6.8%	3.4%	3.1%	3.3%	3.4%	3.4%	3.4%
= NOPAT	売上高比	10.2%	10.6%	11.3%	12.0%	5.5%	9.9%	9.4%	9.8%	10.1%	10.1%	10.1%
NOPAT 成長率	照合	0.0%	0.0%	0.0%	0.0%	0.0%		0.0%	0.0%	0.0%	0.0%	0.0%

投下資本

		予測ドライバー						2019	2020	2021	2022	2023
		2014	2015	2016	2017	2018	平均					
現金及び同等物												
有価証券												
投資有価証券												
= 現金及び金融投資	売上高比	18.5%	19.4%	16.9%	18.0%	14.4%	17.4%	13.5%	12.6%	11.8%	10.9%	10.0%
売掛債権	売上高比	12.4%	11.0%	10.0%	10.7%	9.6%	10.7%	10.0%	10.0%	10.0%	10.0%	10.0%
棚卸資産	売上高比	14.2%	14.2%	14.9%	14.7%	14.5%	14.5%	14.4%	14.3%	14.2%	14.1%	14.0%

　ただし，現金および金融投資に関しては，特別な理由がない限り分析時点と同レベルと予測する。企業の価値は企業が生み出す将来のキャッシュフローによって決まるが，それが企業の中でどのように積み上がろうとも企業価値には影響を与えないと考えるべきである。

図表 A.11 ┃ Drivers & Forecast：金融資産の将来予測

> 現金および金融投資に関しては，特別な理由がない限り分析時点と同レベルと予測する

投下資本

	実績					予測				
	2014	2015	2016	2017	2018	2019	2020	2021	2022	2023
現金及び同等物	2,220	3,852	3,138	3,808	4,249	4,249	4,249	4,249	4,249	4,249
有価証券	2,922	2,072	2,319	2,371	996	996	996	996	996	996
投資有価証券	0	0	0	0	0	0	0	0	0	0
= 現金及び金融投資	5,142	5,924	5,457	6,179	5,245	5,245	5,245	5,245	5,245	5,245

付　録　247

Figures

The worksheet "Figures" illustrates the trends of various financial measures graphically. All figures in the worksheet are linked with data in "Drivers & Forecast". Only five year historical results are depicted unless the forecast cells are shown in "Drivers & Forecast", and data for ten years is shown when the forecasted data is entered there.

Figure A.12 | Figures

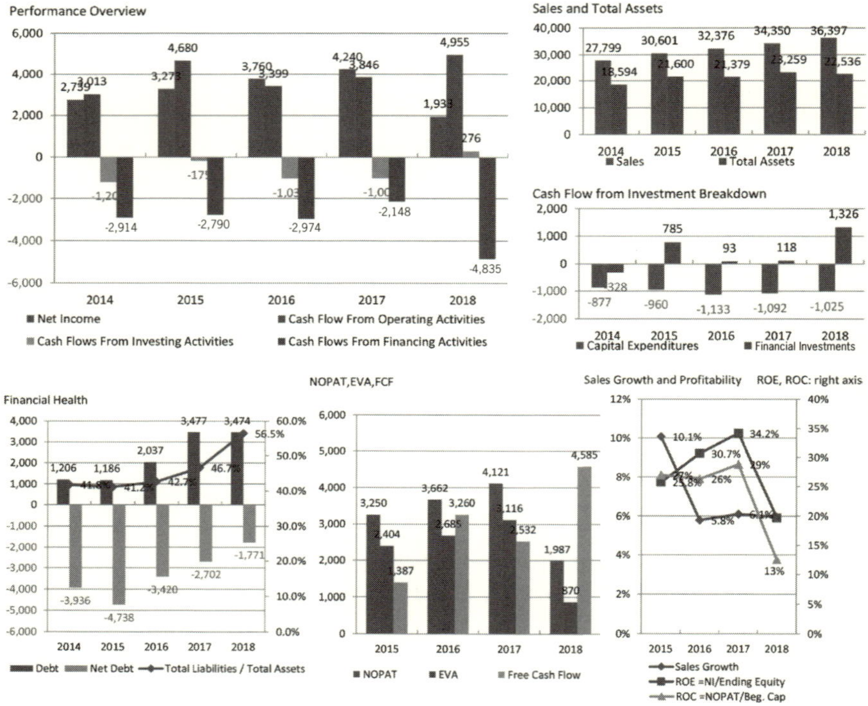

◉ Figures

「Figures」シートは，本書で紹介したさまざまな財務指標の推移をグラフで表わしている。これらのグラフはすべて「Drivers & Forecast」シートとリンクしており，「Drivers & Forecast」シートで「+」ボタンを押さないままであれば5年間の過去実績のみが表示され，予測データを入力すれば10年間のデータが表示される。

図表 A.12 | Figures

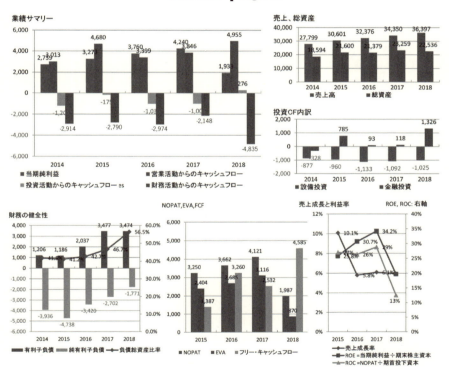

⊙ WACC

"WACC" worksheet estimates a weighted average cost of capital.

A risk-free rate, credit risk premium, tax rate, beta, and market risk premium are required. The websites and the Excel files introduced in chapter 5 can be useful for these inputs.

Capital structure in this file is calculated based on recent market value of equity and debt (in million dollars) .

Figure A.13 ▌ WACC

	Risk-Free Rate	3.15%
	Credit Rating	AA-
+	Credit Risk Premium	0.62%
=	Cost of Debt	3.77%
	Tax Rate (T)	25.00%
	After Tax Cost of Debt	2.83%
	Beta	0.80
×	Market Risk Premium	5.00%
=	Equity Risk Premium	4.00%
+	Risk-Free Rate	3.15%
=	Cost of Equity	7.15%
	Debt	3,474.0
+	Non-controlling Interest	0.0
+	Market Value of Equity	119,753.5
=	Total Market Value	123,227.5
	Debt / (Debt + Equity)	2.82%
	Equity / (Debt + Equity)	97.18%
	WACC	7.03%

Enter risk-free rate, credit risk premium, tax rate, beta, market risk premium

Capital structure is calculated based on recent market value of equity and debt

250 ▌ Appendix

● WACC

「WACC」はその名の通り加重平均資本コストを推定するシートである。

リスクフリー・レート，信用リスク・プレミアム，法人税率，ベータ，市場リスク・プレミアムを入力する。第5章において紹介したホームページやエクセルファイルなどを活用するとよい。

このファイルでは，直近の株式時価総額と直近年度末の負債の額（百万ドル）に基づいて資本構成を計算している。

図表 A.13 ┃ WACC

	リスクフリー・レート	3.15%
	信用格付	AA-
＋	信用リスク・プレミアム	0.62%
＝	負債コスト	3.77%
	税率	25.00%
	税引後負債コスト	2.83%
	ベータ	0.80
×	市場リスク・プレミアム	5.00%
＝	株式リスク・プレミアム	4.00%
＋	リスクフリー・レート	3.15%
＝	株主資本コスト	7.15%
	有利子負債	3,474.0
＋	非支配株主持ち分	0.0
＋	株式時価総額	119,753.5
＝	企業価値	123,227.5
	負債比率	2.82%
	株主資本比率	97.18%
	加重平均資本コスト　WACC	7.03%

> リスクフリー・レート，信用リスクプレミアム，法人税率，ベータ，市場リスクプレミアムを入力する

> 資本構成は直近の株式時価総額と直近年度末の負債の額によって計算される

付録　251

○ DCF

"DCF" estimates the value of a company, shareholders' equity and share price, with discounted FCF and discounted EVA. Some additional inputs are necessary in the sheet.

One input to be entered is the growth rate for a terminal value, referring to the sustainable growth rate or the growth rate in the past. Please note that no company continues to grow faster than the entire economy forever. Also, you should remember that the perpetuity with growth formula cannot hold mathematically when the growth rate is greater than WACC.

If you estimate a terminal value with other assumptions like liquidation value, enter hard numbers in the "Terminal Value" cell directly.

The value of operation is the sum of the present value of FCF for 5 years and the present value of a terminal value. The value of a company is calculated by adding cash, financial investments and unrealized value (loss/gain) of non-operating assets, if there are any, to the value of operation.

The value of equity is measured by subtracting debt and non-controlling interests from the value of a company, and a share price is estimated as the value of equity divided by the number of outstanding shares.

The (identical) result based on EVA is calculated at the bottom of the sheet.

252 | Appendix

● DCF

「DCF」シートは入力された情報に基づき割引キャッシュフロー法と割引EVA法により企業価値から株価までを算出するシートであり，いくつかの追加的入力データが必要となる。

まずサステイナブル成長率や過去の成長率を参考にしながら，ターミナル・バリューの成長率を入力する。どのような企業も経済全体を上回る成長を永久に継続できないことに気をつけるべきである。また，定率成長の永久年金式は，成長率が資本コストを上回ると計算が成り立たないことにも留意が必要である。

また，もし清算価値のように，別の前提でターミナル・バリューを推定する場合はこのターミナル・バリューのセルに直接値を入力する。

5年間の予測キャッシュフローの現在価値とターミナル・バリューの現在価値を加えると事業価値が計算される。これに金融資産の価値を加え，また非事業資産に含み益や含み損がある場合には加味すると企業全体の価値が計算できる。

企業価値から負債と非支配株主持分を差し引くと株主価値が計算され，これを流通株式数で割ると推定株価が算出される。

このシートのさらに下の部分ではEVAに基づく推定株価も同様に計算されている。

付　録　253

Figure A.14 | DCF

Valuation Based on DCF

	2018	Estimate 2019	2020	2021	2022	2023
NOPAT	1,987	3,634	4,044	4,514	4,876	5,290
Operating Cash Flow	5,536	3,769	4,742	5,256	5,714	6,244
− Investment	951	1,203	1,419	1,568	1,739	1,884
= FCF	4,585	2,566	3,323	3,688	3,975	4,360
Investment Rate =I/NOPAT	-130.8%	29.4%	17.8%	18.3%	18.5%	17.6%
WACC	7.03%					
PV of FCF		2,397	2,901	3,008	3,029	3,104

Growth Rate for Terminal Value	3.5%	Enter growth rate for terminal value
Terminal Value	137,595	
Sum of PV of FCF for 5 years	14,440	If you assume liquidation value, enter hard numbers in "Terminal Value" cell directly
+ PV of Terminal Value	97,974	
= Value of Operation	112,415	
Cash and Equivalent	4,249	
Short-term Investments	996	
Long-term Investments	0	
+ Financial Assets (BV at valuation)	5,245	
+ Other Non-operating Assets (MV)		MV of land, financial assets, etc. if any
= Value of Company	117,660	
Short-term Debt	6	Enter unrealized value (loss/gain) of other non-operating assets if there are any
Long-term Debt	3,468	
− Debt	3,474	
− Non-controlling Interest	0	
= Value of Equity	114,186	
/ Number of Shares Outstanding	1,601	Discount EVA derives the identical result
= Share Price	71.34	

254　Appendix

図表 A.14 ┃ DCF

DCF に基づく企業価値評価

	2018	予測				
		2019	2020	2021	2022	2023
NOPAT	1,987	3,634	4,044	4,514	4,876	5,290
営業キャッシュフロー	5,536	3,769	4,742	5,256	5,714	6,244
− 投資額	951	1,203	1,419	1,568	1,739	1,884
＝ FCF	4,585	2,566	3,323	3,688	3,975	4,360
再投資率 ＝ 純投資額÷NOPAT	-130.8%	29.4%	17.8%	18.3%	18.5%	17.6%
WACC	7.03%					
FCF の現在価値		2,397	2,901	3,008	3,029	3,104

ターミナル・バリュー成長率	3.5%
ターミナル・バリュー	137,595
5 年間の FCF の現在価値計	14,440
＋ ターミナル・バリューの現在価値	97,974
＝ 事業の価値	112,415
現金及び同等物	4,249
有価証券	996
投資有価証券	0
＋ 金融資産（簿価）	5,245
＋ その他の非事業資産（時価）	
＝ 推定企業価値	117,660
短期有利子負債	6
長期有利子負債	3,468
− 有利子負債	3,474
− 非支配株主持ち分	0
＝ 推定株主価値	114,186
÷ 流通株式数	1,601
＝ 推定株価	71.34

ターミナルバリューの成長率を入力する

もし清算価値のように，独自にターミナルバリューを推定する場合はこのセルに直接値を入力する

土地や金融資産の時価，もしあれば

非事業資産に含み益や含み損がある場合には入力する

EVA に基づく価値も同一となる

● DCF Figure

A waterfall chart exhibits the components of the estimated value such as the value of operation, the value of the company and the value of equity in "DCF Figure" sheet.

Figure A.15 | DCF Figure

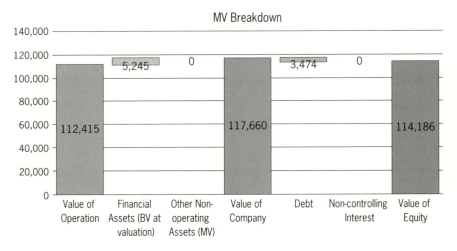

256　　Appendix

◯ DCF Figure

事業価値，企業価値，株主価値といった構成要素は「DCF Figure」において滝グラフによって示される。

図表 A.15 ┃ DCF Figure

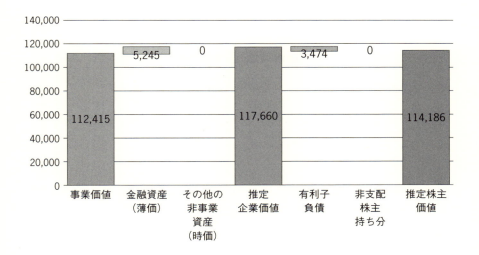

◉ Multiples

"Multiples" sheet estimates the share price of a company with multiples. When you enter the name of comparable companies and their multiples, the share price based on multiples of each comparable company as well as the average, maximum, and minimum estimated share prices will be calculated and shown.

Please note that some data might be unavailable. PER of Under Armour is missing in Figure A.16 because it recorded a loss during that period.

Figure A.16 | Multiples

Valuation Based on Multiples

Enter the name of comparable companies and their multiples

Current FY	2018
Net Income	1,933
Shareholders' Equity	9,812
Sales	36,397

Earnings per Share	1.21
Equity per Share	6.13
Sales per Share	22.74

Market Data as of 10/31/2018

Comparable Companies	Adidas	Under Armour	Asics	Puma		Average	Max	Min
Multiple								
PER	24.60		60.37	37.90		40.96	60.47	24.60
PBR	5.28	3.16	1.71	3.34		3.37	5.28	1.71
Price/Sales	1.61	1.28	0.90	1.31		1.28	1.61	0.90

Estimated Value of Equity						Average	Max	Min
PER	29.71		72.91	45.77		49.46	72.91	29.71
PBR	32.37	19.37	10.48	20.48		20.67	32.37	10.48
Price/Sales	36.61	29.11	20.47	29.79		28.99	36.61	20.47

share prices based on multiples of comparable company, average, maximum, and minimum estimated share prices will be calculated

258 | Appendix

◉ Multiples

　株価を価値倍率法により推定しているのが「Multiples」シートである。比較対象とする企業の企業名とそれぞれの倍率を入力すると各企業の倍率に基づく推定株価と平均値，最大値，最小値が表示される。

　なお，企業によっては倍率のデータがない場合もある。図表 A.16 においてアンダーアーマーの PER のデータが表示されていないのは，この期において損失を計上しているためである。

図表 A.16 ｜ Multiples

価値倍率法による企業価値評価

比較対象とする企業の企業名とそれぞれの倍率を入力する

直近年度	2018
当期純利益	1,933
株主資本	9,812
売上高	36,397

1株あたり利益	1.21
1株あたり株主資本	6.13
1株あたり売上高	22.74

市場データの入手時点　2018/10/31

比較類似会社 価値倍率	Adidas	Under Armour	Asics	Puma		平均	最大値	最小値
PER	24.60		60.37	37.90		40.96	60.47	24.60
PBR	5.28	3.16	1.71	3.34		3.37	5.28	1.71
売上高倍率	1.61	1.28	0.90	1.31		1.28	1.61	0.90

推定株主価値						平均	最大値	最小値
PER	29.71		72.91	45.77		49.46	72.91	29.71
PBR	32.37	19.37	10.48	20.48		20.67	32.37	10.48
売上高倍率	36.61	29.11	20.47	29.79		28.99	36.61	20.47

各企業の倍率に基づく推定株価と平均値，最大値，最小値が表示される

付　録　259

Summary

The last worksheet "Summary" summarizes valuation results based on various approaches and compares them with the actual share price.

Figure A.17 | Summary

Valuation Summary

			Range		
			High		Low
	PER	49.46	72.91	-	29.71
Multiples	PBR	20.67	32.37	-	10.48
	Sales/Price	28.99	36.61	-	20.47
DCF		71.34			
EVA		71.34			

Summarize valuation results based on various approaches

Actual Share Price at

10/31/2018	74.82

Compare your results with the actual share price and enter your recommendation

Your Recommendation

Buy, Sell,...

260 | Appendix

Summary

　最後の「Summary」シートはさまざまなアプローチによる推定株価の結果を
まとめて示し，推定結果と実際の株価を比較するためのものである。

図表 A.17 ┃ Summary

企業価値評価サマリー

				範囲		
				最大		最小
価値倍率	PER	49.46		72.91	-	29.71
	PBR	20.67		32.37	-	10.48
	売上高倍率	28.99		36.61	-	20.47
DCF		71.34				
EVA		71.34				

> さまざまなアプローチによる
> 推定株価が一覧化される

現時点株価

2018/10/31	74.82

> 推定株価と実際の株価を比較する

推奨　　　　　　　　　　　　　　　　売り，買い,…

付　録　　261

Postface and Acknowledgement

Since Temple University Japan Campus (TUJ) where I teach is an "American" university, many of my colleagues are from the U.S., but some are non-native English speakers. (They speak their native tongue and English, plus Japanese with a sufficient fluency to live in Japan without any problems, and I envy them because I have no additional room for a third language.) They speak English as if it is their native lauguage, even if they have not started learning English until they were in junior high-school, as many Japanese do. The trick to making them good English speakers is learning English through learning other subjects such as mathematics, science and social studies. In order to master other subjects, they must learn English as a prerequisite.

I am not an expert on language education, yet I fully understand how effective and how productive it is to learn a language via other subjects. A subject depends on an individual and can be movies, music, or sports. That brings us to one conclusion: finance and valuation can also be an effective topic. I would be more than happy if this book could work as a useful tool to help a lot of people advance their knowledge of valuation (as a main subject) and their language (English or Japanese) skills at the same time.

I take this opportunity to thank all who helped me prepare this book. I want to express the appreciation to my colleagues at TUJ, as well as students who had dealt with and analyzed a sports apparel industry in my valuation course, Jonnathan H. Kwon and Tiana M. Ranjo whose insightful results were referred in the book. I would like to thank Timothy C. Amburn and Adio A. Alexander, TUJ students who have helped to properly convey the contents in English. I am grateful to the dedicated editors at Chuo-Keizai, Ms. Ayumi Sakai and Ms. Yukiko Ichida. Finally, I cannot overstate my gratitude to all who continue to encourage and support me.

Akashi Hongo

あ と が き と 謝 辞

　私が教えているテンプル大学は米国の大学ですので，同僚の多くは米国人ですが，中には母国語が英語ではない外国人もいます（彼らは母国語と英語の他に，日本で暮らすに十分なほどの日本語を操るので，日本語と英語だけでいっぱいいっぱいの私からするとうらやましい限りです）。彼らは流暢な英語を話しますが，決して幼少のころから英語を話す環境にあったわけではなく，多くの日本人と同様に中学生くらいから英語の勉強をスタートしているようです。それでも彼らの英語が堪能なのは，母国語ではない英語を，「英語」という科目で勉強するのではなく，数学や理科や社会という科目を通じて学んでいるからだそうです。英語ができなければ数学も理科もできないわけですので，必然的に英語を学んでしまうのです。

　私は言語教育の専門家ではありませんが，他のサブジェクトを通じて英語を学ぶのが効果的だということはわかります。人によってそれは映画だったり，音楽だったり，あるいはスポーツだったりするのでしょうが，それならファイナンスや企業価値評価といった題材でも有効なはずです。本書がそういうツールとしてうまく機能し，企業価値評価というサブジェクトと英語または日本語という言語力を同時に身につけることに少しでも役立つのであれば大きな喜びです。

　この本の完成を支援していただいた多くの方々に感謝いたします。テンプル大学ジャパンキャンパスの仲間からの意見は大変励みになりましたし，企業価値評価のクラスでスポーツアパレル業界を取り扱った学生のジョナサン クウォン，ティアナ ランジョの分析は本書で参考にしています。英語表現に関しては，同じく学生のティモシー アンバーンとアディオ アレクサンダのアシストを得ました。また，ご担当いただいた中央経済社の阪井あゆみ氏と市田由紀子氏には丁寧に原稿に目を通していただきました。最後に，日頃より応援してくださるすべての皆さんに感謝いたします。

本合暁詩

Index／索引

3C ·· 30, 40
3C 分析 ·································· 31, 41
5 フォース分析 ···················· 31, 37

■ A ～ C ■

Accounting-based Equity Ratio ········· 68
Accounts Payable ···················· 60, 86
Accounts Receivable ··············· 54, 58
Acquisition Premium ···················· 198
adidas ···································· 34
Agency Problem ························· 224
Asahi Kasei Corporation ··············· 186
Asset Turnover ··························· 62
Bank ···································· 226
Beta ································· 96, 98
Board of Director ······················ 226
Boeing ··································· 56
Bottom-up Beta ···················· 100, 106
Bottom-up Beta Calculation File ···· 114, 115
B/S, Balance Sheet ··········· 52, 67, 76, 136
BV, Book Value ········ 54, 88, 182, 254, 256
Capital ······················ 76, 78, 118, 138
Capital Charge ························· 118
Capital Efficiency ······················ 120
Capital Investment ······················ 80
Capital Structure ···················· 86, 108
Capital Turnover ······················· 126
CAPM, Capital Asset Pricing Model ····· 96, 97
Cash Flow ···························· 22, 180
COGS, Cost of Goods Sold ··········· 52, 56
Common-size Balance Sheet ············· 58
Common-size Financial Statement ········· 54
Common-size Income Statement ········· 56
Conglomerate Integration ··············· 200

Corporate Governance ·················· 224
Cost of Debt ························ 86, 88
Cost of Equity ······················ 86, 96
Cost of Sales ···························· 52
Credit ·································· 52
Creditor ···························· 24, 52, 226
Credit Rating ························ 92, 116
Credit Rating Agency ··············· 92, 226
Credit Risk Premium ········· 88, 92, 94, 116
Cross SWOT ····························· 46
Current Ratio ···························· 68

■ D ～ F ■

Debit ···································· 54
Debt ············· 24, 60, 68, 76, 102, 166, 226
Debt Ratio ······························· 86
Debt to Equity ························· 114
Depreciation ····························· 80
Discounting ···························· 190
Discounting Approach ·················· 178
Discount Rate ··························· 86
Dividend ························ 64, 72, 136
Driver ·································· 138
Driver-based Compensation ············· 222
EBITDA, Earnings Before Interest Taxes
　Depreciation and Amortization（利払前・
　税引前・減価償却前・その他償却前
　利益）··················· 84, 85, 180, 181
EBITDA Multiple（EBITDA 倍率）···· 184, 185
Economic Value Added ··············· 118
EDGAR ······························ 50, 51
EDINET ····························· 50, 51
Effective Tax Rate ····················· 76
EPS, Earnings Per Share ······· 168, 182, 202

264

Equity ································ 24, 102	Lease Obligation ······················ 166
Equity Compensation ·················· 220	Leverage ······························· 100
Equity Ratio ·························· 86	Liability ······························· 52
EVA ······· 118, 119, 130, 131, 142, 143, 158, 159, 168, 169	Liquidation Value ····················· 144
EVA Spread（EVA スプレッド）········ 122, 123, 126, 127	■ M〜O ■
Excess Cash ·························· 164	M&A, Merger and Acquisition（企業の合併・買収）····················· 196, 197
Expected Return ······················ 86	Market Beta ····················· 98, 112
FCF, Free Cash Flow ··· 80, 84, 85, 130, 131, 142, 143, 144, 145, 154, 155, 162, 163, 168, 169	Market Beta Calculation File ······· 112, 113
	Market Capitalization ·············· 24, 182
	Market Risk Premium ·············· 96, 116
Financing Cash Flow ················ 64, 72	MV, Market Value ········· 54, 88, 254, 256
Five Force ························ 30, 36	MBO, Management Buyout ·············· 210
Fixed Asset ·························· 54	Mid-term Planning ····················· 214
	Mission ······························· 214
■ G〜I ■	Multiple ·························· 178, 190
GDP, Gross Domestic Products（国内総生産）···························· 155, 156	MVA, Market Value Added（市場付加価値）···························· 172, 173
Government Bond Yields ··········· 88, 116	Net Debt ························· 70, 72
Gross Profit ························· 180	Net Income ··············· 52, 64, 68, 180
Growth rate (g) ··········· 84, 146, 154	Net Investment ························ 78
Horizontal Integration ················ 200	Net Working Capital ··················· 76
Income Statement ············· 50, 72, 136	Net Worth ····························· 52
Increase in Working Capital ············ 80	Nike ····· 34, 44, 72, 110, 130, 138, 142, 174
Industry Beta ························ 116	No-growth ························ 150, 168
Institutional Investor ············· 18, 226	Non-controlling Interest ··············· 166
Intangible Asset ······················ 54	Non-interest Bearing Liability ··········· 60
Interest ······························ 24	Non-operating Assets ·················· 164
Inventory ························ 54, 58	NOPAT Margin（NOPAT マージン）·· 126, 127
Investing Cash Flow ··················· 64	
Investment Rate（I %）············· 82, 154	NOPAT, Net Operating Profit After Tax ·· 76, 77, 78, 79, 84, 85, 118, 119, 130, 131, 138, 139, 154, 155, 156, 157, 168, 169
IR (Investors Relations) ··········· 212, 213	
■ K〜L ■	Number of Shares Outstanding ·········· 182
	OCF, Operating Cash Flow ········ 64, 72, 80
KPI, Key Performance Indicator（重要業績評価指標）················· 216, 217	Operating Profit ················ 52, 56, 68
LBO, Leveraged Buyout ················ 210	Outstanding Share ···················· 168

265

■ P～R ■

PBR, Price to Book Value Ratio（株価純資産倍率）………… 180, 181, 182, 183
Pension Obligation ……………………… 166
PER, Price Earnings Ratio（株価収益率）
…… 180, 181, 182, 183, 186, 187, 202, 203
Perpetuity Formula ……………………… 146
Perpetuity with Growth Formula …… 146, 154
PEST（PEST 分析）………… 30, 31, 32, 33
Pfizer ……………………………………… 56
P/L, Profit and Loss Statement …… 50, 51, 67
PPE, Property, Plant, and Equipment … 58
Porter, Michael E. ………………… 36, 42
Present Value ………………… 22, 86, 162
Principal ………………………………… 24
Profit-based Compensation …………… 222
Quick Ratio ……………………………… 68
Regression ……………………………… 98
Reserve ……………………… 78, 86, 166
Reserve Account ……………………… 78
Retirement Benefit Obligation ………… 78
Risk-free Rate ………… 88, 90, 94, 96, 156
ROA, Return on Asset ……………… 66, 67
ROC, Return on Capital …… 82, 83, 122, 123, 126, 127, 154, 155, 156, 157
ROE, Return on Equity ……… 66, 67, 74, 75
ROIC ……………………………………… 83

■ S～U ■

Sale ……………………………… 64, 180
Sales Growth …………………… 66, 74
Sales Revenue ………………… 52, 138
Scenario Analysis …………………… 162
Security Analyst ……………… 18, 226
Sensitivity Analysis ………………… 162
SG&A, Selling, General and Administrative Expenses …………………… 52, 56

Shareholder ……………………… 24, 52
Shareholders' Equity ………… 52, 76, 180
Share Price ……… 24, 112, 168, 174, 182
Share Repurchase ……………… 52, 64, 72
Stock Market Index ……………… 96, 112
Stock Option …………………… 218, 220
Strategy Framework …………………… 30
Sustainable Growth Rate ……………… 84
SWOT（SWOT 分析）……… 30, 31, 44, 45
Synergy Effect ………………………… 200
Tangible Asset ………………………… 54
Tax Rate ……………………………… 116
Tax Saving …………………………… 102
Tax Savings Effect …………………… 94
Terminal Value ……………… 144, 148, 162
Total Asset ……………… 54, 58, 64, 180
Total Liabilities to Total Assets Ratio …… 68, 72
Treasury Share ……………………… 168
Treasury Stock ………………… 52, 60
Unlevered Beta ………… 100, 106, 114

■ V～Z ■

Value Chain …………………… 30, 42
Value Driver Model …………… 152, 156, 182
Value of Equity ……………………… 166
Vertical Integration ………………… 200
Vision ………………………………… 214
WACC, Weighted Average Cost of Capital
…… 82, 86, 102, 103, 110, 111, 116, 118, 119, 122, 123, 146, 147, 156, 157, 168, 169
Walmart ………………………………… 56
Working Capital ……………………… 76
Zero Growth ………………………… 150

■ あ 行 ■

旭化成 ………………………………… 187

アディダス	35	期待リターン	87, 119
粗利益	181	キャッシュフロー	23, 181
アンレバード・ベータ	101, 107, 115	キャッシュフロー計算書	65
ウォルマート	57	銀行	25, 227
売上成長率	67, 75	金庫株	169
売上高	65, 139, 181	クロス SWOT 分析	47
売掛金	55, 59	経済付加価値	119
運転資本	77	原価	53, 57
運転資本増額	81	減価償却費	81
永久年金式	147	現在価値	23, 87, 163
営業キャッシュフロー（営業 CF）	65, 73, 81	コーポレート・ガバナンス	225
営業利益	53, 57, 69	国債利回り	89, 117
エージェンシー問題	225	固定資産	55
		コングロマリット型統合	201

■か　行■

■さ　行■

買掛金	61, 87	債券格付	93
回帰分析	99	債権者	25, 53, 227
格付	117	在庫	55, 59
格付機関	227	再投資率（I %）	83, 155
加重平均資本コスト（WACC）	83, 87	財務キャッシュフロー（財務 CF）	65, 73
価値ドライバーモデル	153, 157, 183	サステイナブル成長率	85
価値倍率法	179, 191	産業別ベータ	117
株価	25, 113, 169, 175, 183	時価	55, 89, 255, 257
株式交換	203, 207	資金調達	61
株式時価総額	25, 183	自己株式	61
株式市場インデックス	97, 113	自己資本比率	69
株式報酬	221	自社株買い	53, 65, 73, 169
株主	25, 53	市場ベータ	99, 113
株主価値	25, 167	市場ベータ計算ファイル	113
株主資本	25, 53, 77, 103, 181	市場リスク・プレミアム	97, 117
株主資本コスト	87, 97	実効税率	77
株主資本比率	87	シナジー効果	19, 201
株主資本利益率	67	シナリオ分析	163
借方	55	資本構成	87, 109
感応度分析	163	資本効率	121
元本	25	資本費用	119
機関投資家	19, 227		

純資産	53
純投資額	79
純有利子負債	71, 73
証券アナリスト	19, 227
正味運転資本	77
信用リスク・プレミアム	89, 93, 95, 117
垂直的統合	201
水平的統合	201
ストックオプション	219, 221
スピンオフ	211
清算価値	145
成長率（g）	85, 147, 155
節税効果	95, 103
設備投資額	81
ゼロ成長	151, 157, 169
戦略フレームワーク	31
総資産	55, 65, 181
総資産回転率	63
総資産利益率	67
総資本利益率	67
損益計算書（P/L）	51, 73, 137

■た 行■

ターミナル・バリュー	145, 149, 163
貸借対照表（B/S）	53, 77, 137
退職給付債務	79
棚卸資産	55, 59
中期計画	215
定率成長の永久年金式	147, 155
投下資本	77, 79, 119, 139
投下資本回転率	127
投下資本利益率	83, 123
当期純利益	53, 65, 69, 181, 183
当座比率	69
投資 CF	65
ドライバー	139
ドライバー連動報酬	223
取締役	227

■な 行■

ナイキ	35, 45, 73, 111, 131, 139, 143, 175
内部留保	53
年金債務引当金	167

■は 行■

買収プレミアム	199
配当	65, 73, 137
バリューチェーン分析	31, 43
販売費・一般管理費（販管費）	53, 57
引当金	79, 87, 167
非支配株主持ち分	167
非事業資産	165
ビジョン	215
1株あたり純資産	183
1株あたり利益（EPS）	169, 183, 203
標準化財務諸表	55
標準化損益計算書	57
標準化貸借対照表	59
ファイザー	57
負債	25, 103, 167, 227
負債株主資本比率	115
負債コスト	87, 89
負債総資産比率	69, 73
負債比率	87
フリー・キャッシュフロー（FCF）	81
ベータ	97, 99, 113
法人税率	117
ボーイング	57
ポーター, マイケル・E	37, 43
簿価	55, 89, 183, 255, 257
ボトムアップ・ベータ	101, 107
ボトムアップ・ベータ計算ファイル	115

■ま 行■

マネジメント・バイアウト（MBO）	211

ミッション ·················· 215
無形固定資産 ·················· 55
無負債ベータ ·················· 101
無利子負債 ·················· 61

■ や　行 ■

有形固定資産 ··················· 55, 59
有利子負債 ··················· 61, 69, 77
余剰資金 ··················· 165

■ ら　行 ■

リース負債 ··················· 167
利益連動報酬 ··················· 223

リスクフリー・レート ········ 89, 91, 95, 97,
　155
利息 ··················· 25
流通株式 ··················· 169, 183
流動資産 ··················· 55
流動比率 ··················· 69
レバレッジ・バイアウト（LBO）······ 101,
　211

■ わ　行 ■

割引現在価値法 ··················· 179, 191
割引率 ··················· 87

269

About the Author

Akashi Hongo

Dr. Hongo is an associate professor at Temple University, Japan Campus. Prior to joining TUJ, Dr. Hongo was in charge of planning, accounting, human resource, legal, compliance, general affairs, international business development and supply chain management as a corporate officer at Recruit Management Solutions Co., Ltd. Dr. Hongo started his business career at Nippon Steel Co., Ltd. He then led the value-based consulting practice in Japan and served as country representative for Stern Stewart & Co., a global consulting firm focusing on corporate finance and innovating the EVA® framework. Dr. Hongo is the author of many books (in Japanese) on finance and management, including a bi-lingual (J-E) guide to corporate finance. He holds a BA from Keio University, MBA from International University of Japan, and PhD from International Christian University.

Temple University, Japan Campus (TUJ)

TUJ is a branch campus of Temple University in Philadelphia, Pennsylvania, USA. Founded in 1982 in Tokyo, TUJ is the oldest and largest foreign university in Japan. It is also the first educational institution to be officially recognized (in 2005) as a Foreign University, Japan Campus by Japan's Ministry of Education, Culture, Sports, Science and Technology. In addition to its core undergraduate program, TUJ offers graduate programs in law, business and education; an intensive English language program; continuing education courses; and corporate education classes.

著者略歴

本合　暁詩

テンプル大学ジャパンキャンパス　上級准教授

新日本製鐵，スターン スチュワート日本支社長，リクルートマネジメントソリューションズ執行役員等を経て現職。経営指標 EVA® の導入コンサルティング，企業財務分野での企業内研修講師，研究活動に加え，事業会社における経営管理業務全般を経験。
慶應義塾大学法学部卒業，国際大学大学院国際経営学研究科修了（MBA）。国際基督教大学博士（学術）。
著書に『対訳　英語で学ぶコーポレートファイナンス入門〈第 2 版〉』，『組織を動かす経営管理』，『図解　ビジネスファイナンス〈第 2 版〉』（以上中央経済社），『会社のものさし—実学「読む」経営指標入門』（東洋経済新報社）など。

テンプル大学ジャパンキャンパス

米国ペンシルベニア州フィラデルフィアにあるテンプル大学の日本校で，1982 年に東京で開校。外国大学の分校として日本で最も長い歴史と最大の規模を誇り，2005 年には文部科学省から初の外国大学の日本校として指定。米国式カリキュラムに基づき，大学学部課程をはじめとして，大学院課程（教育学修士・博士課程，ロースクール，エグゼクティブ MBA プログラム），アカデミック・イングリッシュ・プログラム，生涯教育プログラム，企業内教育プログラムの 7 つの課程で，世界約 60 の国・地域から約 4,100 人が学ぶ。

対訳
英語で学ぶバリュエーション入門

2019年8月30日　第1版第1刷発行

著　者	本　合　暁　詩	
発行者	山　本　　　継	
発行所	㈱中央経済社	
発売元	㈱中央経済グループ パブリッシング	

〒101-0051　東京都千代田区神田神保町1-31-2
電話 03 (3293) 3371 (編集代表)
03 (3293) 3381 (営業代表)
http://www.chuokeizai.co.jp/

©2019
Printed in Japan

印刷／文唱堂印刷㈱
製本／誠　製　本　㈱

※頁の「欠落」や「順序違い」などがありましたらお取り替えいた
しますので発売元までご送付ください。(送料小社負担)
ISBN 978-4-502-31671-5　C3034

JCOPY 〈出版者著作権管理機構委託出版物〉本書を無断で複写複製 (コピー) することは，著作
権法上の例外を除き，禁じられています。本書をコピーされる場合は事前に出版者著作権管理機構
(JCOPY) の許諾を受けてください。
JCOPY 〈http://www.jcopy.or.jp　eメール：info@jcopy.or.jp〉